A Century of French Fiction

Also from Westphalia Press
westphaliapress.org

A Century of French Fiction

Balzac, Flaubert Stendhal
and More

by Benjamin W. Wells, PhD

WESTPHALIA PRESS
An Imprint of Policy Studies Organization

A Century of French Fiction: Balzac, Flaubert
Stendhal and More

Westphalia Press
An imprint of Policy Studies Organization
1527 New Hampshire Ave., NW
Washington, D.C. 20036
info@ipsonet.org

ISBN-13: 978-1-63391-601-2
ISBN-10: 1-63391-601-4

Cover design by Jeffrey Barnes:
jbarnesbook.design

Daniel Gutierrez-Sandoval, Executive Director
PSO and Westphalia Press

Updated material and comments on this edition
can be found at the Westphalia Press website:
www.westphaliapress.org

A Century of French Fiction

A CENTURY

OF

FRENCH FICTION

BY

BENJAMIN W. WELLS, Ph.D. (Harv.)

PROFESSOR OF MODERN LANGUAGES IN THE
UNIVERSITY OF THE SOUTH

NEW YORK
DODD, MEAD AND COMPANY
1898

University Press:

JOHN WILSON AND SON, CAMBRIDGE, U.S.A.

Preface

THIS book is a study of novels, not of novelists. It seeks to show the development of what has come to be the chief genre in the most artistic of European literatures. The limitations that this purpose involves are obvious. Biography belongs here only in so far as heredity or environment influence those qualities in an author by which he in turn influences the development of fiction. With some novelists, such as George Sand, these are very significant; with others, such as Daudet, they are hardly significant at all. The poems, dramas, or essays of novelists are usually passed in silence, though they may be, as with Sainte-Beuve, the chief title to literary distinction. And in regard to the novels themselves, this book is less concerned with what is done than with how it is done; it seeks, not to retell a story, but to convey an artistic impression, and in the space that it accords to the 115 novelists and 688 novels or short stories that it names it is less influenced by an author's popularity than by the excellence or novelty of his technic, his style, or his ideas of the functions, ethical, social, philosophical, or artistic, of the novel. Many writers are little read who have been studied by those who are read much. The former have more interest to us

than the latter, Stendhal more than Ohnet, the Goncourts than Bourget, while writers who offer only
clever reflections of the innovating ideas of others are
from our point of view of no interest at all. I mention that I may not seem to have forgotten, but, following Dante's counsel, I " look and pass."

If, then, I have given more space to Loti or to
Chateaubriand than to Hugo it is because I think
them as novelists more significant than he, though
their fiction be less read and less entertaining. If
more than a quarter of my book is given to Balzac it
is because I think that is his proportionate due. To
eight others I have accorded separate studies. The
remaining 106 are grouped according to the circumstances of their birth and education, for, as I have
come to see in the course of this study, there is a connection worth noting between the political condition
of France and the gestation of her men of genius, a
certain family resemblance among the sons of the
First Empire, as among those of the Restoration, of
the Bourgeois Monarchy and of the Second Empire.
Of course, as in every large family, there are eccen-
trics that bear no marked likeness to their brothers,
but I trust this arrangement of heterogeneous materials will prove the most helpful and perspicuous.

As my book is intended for English readers I have
translated all titles of novels, and where there seemed
any possibility of misunderstanding I have added the
title in its original French form, under which alone it
appears in the Index. I have read, so far as was necessary to my purpose, every novel mentioned n this

book. I have taken notes of my impressions. I have also read such criticism of these works as was accessible to me, both in French and English, note-book in hand. My ideas have often been clarified or crystallized, my point of view occasionally modified by what I have read, but to acknowledge such debts in detail, were it possible, would be misleading, for, if I seem in any case to echo the opinion of another, it is because I have been led by independent study to share it. What I have taken consciously from others is quoted by name if the citation is exact, indefinitely if the form is altered or the thought modified.

Two years ago I published a book on Modern French Literature, which involved brief mention of the present subject. That phrases of the earlier volume should occasionally recur in this is perhaps inevitable. The two books are, however, distinct in purpose and in method. Chapter VIII. and portions of Chapter I. have appeared in " The Sewanee Review." The origins of fiction in France, and its history till the French Revolution, I hope to treat in another volume, for which all materials are well in hand.

I desire in conclusion to extend my thanks to the officers of the Boston Public Library, whose untiring courtesy has made this book a possibility, while providing for the author the pleasantest and the most profitable of his studious hours.

BENJAMIN W. WELLS.

University of the South,
   Sewanee, Tenn.

Contents

A Century of French Fiction

❧

THE nineteenth century is pre-eminently the age of the
novel. What Voltaire could call the work of one
writing with facility things unworthy to be read by serious
minds has become so predominant in France as almost to
absorb in popular literary consciousness all forms of imaginative writing except the drama. This tendency, manifest
at the outset of the century, has been accentuated by the
spread of superficial culture, the cheapening in the cost of
production of books, and the readier means of diffusion by
post and railway. The French newspapers, too, by their
feuilletons have added greatly to the production of fiction,
though they have tended to lower its literary standard. But
more important perhaps than any of these factors is that
with the first year of our century fiction begins to reflect
popular emotions and states of mind. The novel of the
romantic school was to be lyric in its style, personal
in its appeal. Herein lies the cardinal importance of
Chateaubriand.

The century in fiction opens with the publication of his
Atala in 1801, followed in 1802 by *René*, both short stories

but of far-reaching influence and most characteristic of the mood of the next generation and of this author, who was its most eloquent representative. He was a Breton noble, born at St. Malo, "within hearing of the waves" as he liked to say, on the fourth of September, 1768, the birth-year of Napoleon, to whom he was also wont to take this occasion to compare himself. Neither mother nor father seems to have been a wise or genial parent, and his chief if not his only childish affection was for a sister, Lucile, a frail, nervous invalid, who died young. The relation was certainly morbid, and later in his life Chauteaubriand was pleased to surround it with a sort of incestuous halo that he might explain by this aberration of youth the fascinating indifference that characterised his own relations to women in after years and found their fullest expression in his René, the most strongly marked character, in a sense we may say the only character, of his fiction.

He was himself an intense and somewhat morbid youth. He passed his childhood in an ultra-Catholic environment, listening to the strange legends of the childlike Breton people or nursing meditation by the boundless and mysterious ocean. As a boy he went to various schools, but all within the Breton spell, and then to the gloomy ancestral castle of Combourg; no wonder that his twentieth year found him untaught, timid, eager, and gloomy, above all dissatisfied with all that life gave or promised. He was suffering already from that *maladie du siècle* of which it is impossible not to speak at some length in judging Chateaubriand, but which we shall perhaps treat more profitably if we first trace the course of his life until, with the fall of Napoleon, the man of letters was absorbed in the politician. He tried to go to sea and got actually as far as Brest; he contemplated suicide; then his friends got him a position in the army, and on the eve of the Revolution the young man found himself transported from the solitude of ocean and forest, from the most backward province of France, to Paris, the focus of the intellectual and political world.

The effect, as was natural, was immediate and strong. Its literary significance, however, lies in the strength of the reaction that followed and in the literary stimulus that his associations gave him. He learned to know most of the chief writers of the time, Parny the poet, La Harpe the critic, the two Chéniers, Chamfort the acute philosopher, and most important of all to him, Fontanes, who was the discoverer of his genius, his unswerving friend, and always a shrewd adviser. He began intense though unsystematic studies. Ignorant at twenty, his *Essay on Revolutions* (1797) published at twenty-nine shows a remarkable mass of information, which indeed was never fully assimilated. But acquaintance with the great writings of the century aroused in him, as greatness always did, mingled admiration and envy. Could he not, he seems to have said to himself, catch the imagination of Rousseau and use it to controvert his ideas and so to destroy his ascendency? Could he not eclipse Bernardin de St. Pierre by borrowing his style and making it the bearer of sturdier thought? There remained Voltaire, whose wit he could not borrow. Against him and his ideas he would wage a moral war, and win for himself the mantle of Bossuet. Such seem to have been the literary impulses that he gathered from four intoxicating years. Then in 1791 as the clouds of revolution thickened he set sail for America, where he had a commission to search for the Northwest Passage, obviously a mere pretext. He travelled more or less widely in the United States, met

Washington, and, according to his own account, which is never above suspicion, saw Labrador and the Great Lakes, the prairies of what was then Louisiana, and the semi-tropcal forests of Spanish Florida. Here he might observe the " state of nature " as Rousseau had dreamed and Bernardin described it. Here the morbid imagination of his youth was vivified by contact with a primeval world and untutored man. He was gone but a year and landed again in France in January, 1792, but that year gave him the scene and the direct inspiration for the greater part of his fiction and the indirect inspiration for the rest.

The execution of Louis XVI. made Chateaubriand an *émigré;* he was wounded in the expedition against Thionville, went to England in 1793, and remained there till 1800. It was during this period of exiled poverty that he wrote *The Natchez,* a huge manuscript of 2,383 folio pages, in which he strove to involve his impressions of America and of life. Of this far the greater part was not printed till 1826, but it served as a sort of storehouse from which he drew successively *Atala* (1801), *René* (1802), and considerable parts of the *Genius of Christianity* (1802). This last lies outside our immediate field. Chateaubriand's other contributions to fiction are *The Martyrs* (les Martyrs, 1809), and *The Last Abencerage* (Aventure du dernier Abencérage, 1826), written about the same time. To these last works he brought the added experience of two years of official life at Rome, but he seems to have welcomed the murder of the Duke d'Énghien as an excuse for resuming a haughty opposition to Napoleon, " who," as he somewhat fatuously assures us, " made the world tremble, but me never." Yet these works were not the immediate result of those years, but of what he called a *Journey from*

Paris to Jerusalem (1811), a trip undertaken partly to gather materials for *The Martyrs*, partly at the suggestion of a lady who was not quite ready to yield to his seductive *morgue* and who met him, on his return, in the Alhambra, where for some years their names could be deciphered together. The intermingling of sensuality and religious sentiment is as constant in Chateaubriand as it was in Bernardin and Rousseau.

Thus much of the life of Chateaubriand is necessary to any understanding of the ethical purport of his novels. *Atala* claims to be a story told at the close of the seventeenth century to a melancholy young Frenchman, René, in whom the author intends that we shall see himself. It is narrated by the old Indian Chactas, who has been in France in the *grand siècle*, has talked with Fénelon, listened to Bossuet and to Ninon, seen the tragedies of Racine, and acquired enough of civilization to combine an Homeric simplicity of picturesque imagery with the dainty refinements of the Hôtel Rambouillet. All of which is ridiculous enough, but it serves Chateaubriand's purpose, which is to bring civilization and the "state of nature" into more effective contrast than Rousseau or Bernardin had done. For Chactas, knowing the best that culture has to offer, deliberately prefers the wilderness, as does René himself, and, as Chateaubriand gives us to understand, he would do also were it not that a weary condescending charity forbids him to deprive society of his presence. Both Chactas and René have had experiences somewhat similar to that of Chateaubriand and Lucile. René loves his sister, Chactas a young Indian girl who has sworn perpetual virginity. He is a captive among her nation. She saves him, and to save herself they are forced to fly together. The solitary journey of the young lovers, for she returns his affection though guarding her vow, is described with a lingering dalliance that some take for sentimental purity and others for lurking lubricity. As Joubert said, the passions here are "covered with long white veils." However, the pair come at last to the mission station of Father Aubry, the counterpart of Rousseau's Savoyard Vicar and Bernardin's Solitary Walker. There Atala, who "had extreme sensitiveness joined to profound melancholy," presently died of the disease that poets call unrequited love, martyr to a romantic and therefore false conception of duty. But while this might detract now from the interest of the story, it added greatly to its charm in 1800, in a generation already predisposed to that *maladie du siècle* of which Chateaubriand was in part the first talented exponent and in part the cause.

This is even more clearly the central point of the interest of *René*, a second fragment detached from the *Genius of Christianity* in 1807, probably because its author felt that it would appeal to many who did not fancy the religious dilettantism of the latter work, and would offend perhaps some that the other attracted. The hero of this tale, as the name implies, is the person to whom *Atala* had been related, namely Chateaubriand himself, as he aspired to be or to be thought at twenty-three. He is a young Werther, full of discouraged world-pain, such as was forced on many men of genius, first by the revolt against the dry rot of eighteenth-century philosophy, then by the lie direct given to the utopian dreams of the reformers by the bloody saturnalia of the Revolution. Where men a decade before had felt full of hope and strength, they felt now, at least those of more delicate organization, for it is they alone who had literary genius at this time, helpless and hopeless. From this resulted an anxious introspection and an eager utterance of egoism that had begun with Rousseau and culminated in Chateaubriand and in Byron. Chateaubriand and all the victims of the *maladie du siècle* are prisoned in themselves. All their invention consists of creating a new environment for their individuality. Hence the growing predominance in fiction of local colour. As Brunetière says, "wherever the poet may set up the scenery of his work he is and remains its centre."

Doubtless other agencies contributed to evoke this state of mind in Chateaubriand and in those who read *René* with eager enthusiasm. Among these it is probably safe to reckon the new cosmopolitanism that had inoculated the literature of France with a virus from the North contrary to its nature and so for the moment toxic. The interest in foreign literatures, the knowledge of English and German masterpieces through translations, which grew more frequent in this generation, troubled as it were the equilibrium of the French genius. Speaking of a period a little later, and of the novel *Obermann*, George Sand says: "Ambitions took on a character of feverish intensity, minds overwrought by immense labours were suddenly tried by great fatigues and piercing agonies. All the springs of personal interest, all the forces of egoism, extremely developed under great tension, gave birth to unknown ills for which psychology had as yet assigned no place in its annals." Of this malady all sensitively organized natures seem to have felt more or less since the days of Werther and Saint-Preux. Goethe threw off the disease and attained an Olympian calm, Rousseau became mentally deranged, Bernardin was saved from it by his fatuity, Chateaubriand wrapped himself in egoistic indifference, and in *René, or the Effect of the*

Passions he has given us the most noted French exposition of this state of soul.   It is this that made him the father of romanticism.

The moral influence of *René* was almost wholly evil and obviously so, yet it was so great and the little tale so sums and characterises the morbid virus of romanticism that it is well to let René tell his story, as far as may be in his own words as he sits by the banks of the Mississippi, regarding the world with indifference and his wife and child near by with a weary ennui of which we may read particulars in *The Natchez* quite worthy to rank with the rankest "flowers of evil" of Baudelaire.

René is a character for whom it is hard to feel respect or patience, a man of brilliant genius who becomes the spendthrift of his talent through a complete lack of even a rudimentary sense of social duty or self-control.   He has an utter lack of will, being indeed a monstrosity of egoism, very like in this to Chateaubriand, so self-absorbed that nothing outside himself seems worth desire or contemplation.   Chateaubriand has told us that "people wearied him by dint of loving him," and it was with a somewhat similar condescension to the solicitations of his friends that René at last consented to tell them "not the adventures of his life, for he had experienced none, but the secret sentiments of his soul," of which those of his kind were always replete to nausea.   He describes himself at the outset, very justly, as "a young man without force or virtue, who finds in himself his own torment, and has hardly any evils to bemoan save those that he had himself caused."   We know that Chateaubriand was uncongenial to his parents. René too has no sympathies in childhood, but it is because he has cost his mother her life and his father has died while he was still young. As Chateaubriand owed what he was pleased to imagine his conversion to the emotions attending the death of his mother and sister, so René receives from his father's death his first presentiment of immortality. The effect of religion, so called, on character was about equally absent in both cases. Chateaubriand could not describe that of which he knew nothing. His character never attained an adult development. It was neither Christian nor pagan, but hermaphrodite. And so was René's. In youth this young hopeful "used to go apart to contemplate the fugitive clouds or to hear the rain fall on the foliage." Naturally, therefore, when ne stood before "the entrance to the deceptive paths of life " he cared to enter on none of them. The monastic life, being the most obviously unnatural and apparently useless, attracted him most, but " whether through natural inconstancy or prejudice " he changed his plans and resolved to nurse his melancholy on the relics of antiquity till " he grew weary of searching in these grave-clothes where too often he stirred only a criminal dust."

At Paris René found he was only " belittling his life to bring it to a level with society," in the country he was " fatigued by the repetition of the same scenes and ideas." No wonder that after amusing himself by throwing leaves into a brook he reflects : " See to what a degree of puerility our proud reason can descend." René had reached this point in his mental and moral degeneration when he began to feel the desire of sharing it with another. His feelings, here too, are a curious perversion of mingled Christianity and paganism. " Oh, God," René exclaims, " if thou hadst given me a wife after my desire, if as to our first parent so to me thou hadst brought an Eve drawn from myself! Heavenly beauty, I should have prostrated myself before thee, then taking thee in my arms, I should have prayed the eternal to give thee the rest of my life."

This is Chateaubriand's ideal of romantic love. As Sainte-Beuve says (" Causeries," ii. 151), "what he sought in love was less the affection of any particular woman than an occasion of agitation and fantasy; it was less the person that he sought than the regret, the recollection, an eternal dream, the cult of his own youth, the adoration of which he felt himself the object, the renewal or the illusion of a cherished situation." This appears in the relation of Chactas to Atala, it reappears in the Velléda episode of *The Martyrs*, and especially in the astonishing later relation that unites René to Céluta. To this we shall recur presently. For the moment René finds in the kisses of his sister, Amélie, the Lucile of fact, the nearest approach to contentment of which his distorted heart was capable. "In this delirious state," he says, " I almost came to desire to feel some evil, that I might have at least a real object of pain." His sister shares his feelings, but, with more perspicacity and decision than Chateaubriand would have thought sympathetic in his blasé hero, she takes refuge in a convent. She writes to him, painting to him the charms of matrimony with a quivering pen that almost betrays itself at the close. But her separation from her brother is only for a time, the same cradle held them in childhood and the same tomb shall soon unite their warm dust. " If I snatch myself from you in time it is only that I may be joined to you in eternity." Meantime she makes the sensible proposition that he should adopt some profession, a suggestion that he must have received with a languid smile. He visits the convent as Amélie is making her monastic profession, and hears her ejaculate beneath her shroud: "God of mercy, grant that I may never rise from the funeral couch, and crown with thy blessings a brother who has not shared my criminal passion."

René now resolves to abandon civilisation, but while waiting for his ship he "wanders constantly around the monastery," reflecting that "here religion lulls the sensitive soul in sweet deception. For the fiercest loves she substitutes a sort of chaste glow in which the virgin and the lover are fused in one." But Amélie finally died, very much as Atala had done, and René seems to have thought it proper to spend the rest of his life in diffusing a general atmosphere of unhappiness around him. Of this we learn chiefly from *The Natchez*.

The Natchez, it may be explained, are a tribe of Indians, now extinct, into which René has been adopted. This has compelled him to take a wife, Céluta, from among them, but nothing could compel him to act like a Christian or even like a gentleman to her or to their child. Such a conversion as Chateaubriand describes his own to have been implies far less depth of heart than shallowness of mind. "I became a Christian," he says in his preface to the *Genius;* "I did not yield, I confess, to any great supernatural illumination; my conviction came from my heart; I wept and I believed." So it was with René, and, as Sainte-Beuve says, his letter to the wife he has abandoned, dated "from the Desert on the thirty-second snow of my existence," is on this subject the confession of the author's own heart. He tells this mother of his daughter that he does not love her, that he has never loved her, that she does not and cannot understand a heart "whence issue flames that lack aliment, that would devour creation and yet be unsatisfied, that would devour thee thyself." When he is gone, he tells her, she may marry, but he adds in the next paragraph that he knows she will not, "for who could environ you with that flame that I bear with me even though I do not love." Of course this is the height of fatuousness, but more than one woman seems to have loved Chateaubriand's disdain, though he certainly would not have classed his own spouse with the gentle Céluta.

As for René he assures his long-suffering wife that the trials of his life, which seem to us to be mere figments of a morbid fancy, are such that "they might win a man from the mania of life." He would like, he says, "to embrace and stab you at the same instant, to fix the happiness in your bosom and to punish myself for having given it to you," precisely as Atala had desired "that divinity might be annihilated, if only pressed in thy arms I might have rolled from abyss to abyss with the debris of God and of the world." Again in another place René exclaims "Let us mingle sensuous joys with death, and let the vault of heaven hide us as it falls." Sainte-Beuve says that in writing thus Chateaubriand gave passion "a new accent, a new note, fatal, wild, cruel, but singularly poetic. With him there always enters into it a wish, an ardent desire for the destruction and ruin of the world." But this is merely to reproduce a phase of medieval satanism, and if satanism is poetic our sanity can only protest that that is so much the worse for poetry.

René finds the world so out of joint that "he is virtuous without pleasure and would be criminal without remorse." He wishes he "had never been born or might be for ever forgotten," even by his daughter. "Let René be for her," he writes to Céluta, "an unknown man whose strange destiny when told may make her ponder, and know not why. I wish to be in her eyes only what I am, a sad dream." Which after all is merely another way of saying what we knew before, that Chateaubriand preferred to charm the imagination than to win the heart, making even of filial sentiment a subject of self-glorification and vanity. That Chateaubriand's absent hero presently perished in a massacre of the Natchez was surely no loss to the world, though Céluta seems to have caught the contagion of his folly and drowned herself at the news of her release.

The daughter that René abandoned was by no means the only progeny of that melancholy hero. Years afterward, Chateaubriand, still posing as an *ennuyé*, wrote : " If *René* did not exist, I would not write it, and if it were possible to destroy it I would destroy it. A family of Renés in poetry and prose has swarmed. We have heard nothing but tearful, disjointed phrases." " Evidently," comments Sainte-Beuve, with a healthy scorn, " René did not wish to have any children," and to judge by the way in which Chateaubriand treats Rousseau and Bernardin, he " would have preferred in literature to have no father."

René and *The Natchez* are, then, as melancholy a travesty of Christian feeling as *Atala*. They are wholly morbid and essentially immoral, but also essentially autobiographic in their psychology. Their charm and their popularity depended on their morbidity, which flattered an exceptional state of the public mind, and on their imagination and style.

The stories that resulted from his visit to Palestine, *The Last Abencerage*, as well as *The Martyrs*, may be more briefly dismissed. The former is more plaintively morbid than the American stories, but the situation is the same as in *Atala* and *René*, namely, the conflict of passion with duty, or superstition, or convention. All are elegies of self-torture, of which the chief cause was lack of common-sense. And the same may be said for *The Martyrs*, where the two episodes that give it its character as a novel, the unrequited love and suicide of the druidess Velléda and the unfulfilled loves of the virgin Cymodocée and Eudore, are characterised by the same teasing sentimental toying with sensuality.

The purpose of the narrative, as of *Atala*, *René*, the *Abencerrages*, and *The Natchez*, but on a broader field than they, is to bring two modes of life or of ethical conception into juxtaposition and contrast. As there it had been the civilised and the savage or the Christian and the Moorish, so here it is the epic of rising Christianity and sinking paganism that he sings in rhythmic prose. Indeed *The Martyrs* is *The Genius of Christianity* in action. The time is that of Diocletian. The real subject is the contrast between Christian and pagan morality, and, what is more interesting to Chateaubriand, between the ways in which this morality manifests itself in ceremonial and sacrificial worship. For it is much less important to him that the faith he advocates should be true to salvation than that it should furnish occasion for esthetic pleasure and pathetic emotions, that it should afford him what he describes in *Atala* as "the secret and ineffable pleasures of a soul enjoying itself." The various scenes and descriptions are bound together by the tale of the chaste loves of Eudore, the Christian, and Cymodocée, the descendant of Homer, a priestess and late convert. There is also a druidess of less uneasy virtue than Cymodocée, Velléda, whom passion leads to suicide, for Chateaubriand seems to think no hero or heroine of interest who does not somehow make shipwreck of his life or fortune in some sort of crusade against common-sense.

The nearest antetype of *The Martyrs* is Fénelon's *Telemachus* (1699). Like that work it is made the vehicle of much chronology and geography. We are carried from the Netherlands to Greece, from Rome to Egypt, we are introduced to nearly all the prominent characters of the Ante-Nicene church and, by a daring anticipation, to some of the philosophers of the eighteenth century also. But the great fault of the book is its rhythmic style, that hovers between prose and poetry in a way most exasperating to the modern reader. Chateaubriand may have meant to show us "the language of Genesis beside that of the Odyssey." As a matter of fact his invocations to the Muse, his scenes in heaven and hell, and his spice of the marvellous, supposed to be necessary to the making of an epic ragout, seem singularly flat to modern taste, while on the other hand it must be admitted that certain passages, especially the *Patriotic Cantos* (Chants de la patrie), give us perhaps the high-water mark of Chateaubriand's prose style.

It is this art of language that is Chateaubriand's chief title to literary remembrance. His thought was very largely morbid. It is hardly worth while to inquire how far he was sincere or capable of sincerity. In society and in ethics he was a *poseur*, whose fatuous conceit is endurable now only to those who have ceased to take him seriously. But he was an incomparable artist in words. And if he fell sometimes on the side to which he inclined and erred by excess of ornament, his genius was guided, guarded, saved from itself, by critical friends, whose taste he trusted and whose discreet counsels he accepted, much to the gain of his artistic reputation. His remarkable gifts of vivid description and eloquent appeal, thus restrained from too obvious excess, produced a style of which the effect can be felt

throughout the century.   Thierry tells us how passages from
the *Patriotic Cantos* in *The Martyrs* inspired him to write
his *Merovingian Tales* (Récits des temps mérovingiens,
1840), and even declares that all the typical thinkers of the
first third of the century "had had Chateaubriand at the
source of their studies, at their first inspirations."   Nisard,
too, thought that "the initial inspiration as well as the final
impulse of all the durable innovations of the first half of the
century in poetry, history, and criticism" were due to him;
to Villemain he was "a renovator of the imagination," and
to the cautious Sainte-Beuve "the first, the most original,
and the greatest imaginative writer" of his day.   The fruits
of this stylistic emancipation of individualism may be seen
even in our time.   Chateaubriand is the essential prelude
not only to Thierry, but to Lamartine and Vigny, to the
young Hugo, to George Sand, to Michelet, to Flaubert, to
Loti, and to many others.   It was the example of his daring that taught men to break boldly, perhaps too boldly
sometimes, with literary tradition.   For he is the source,
not of beauties alone, but of those exaggerations of language
in pursuit of emotional effect that mar the writing even of
such romantic masters as Hugo.   There was an affectation
of simplicity in Chateaubriand that was the very antithesis
of classic restraint, though this last had itself become a
mannerism during the eighteenth century.   By his anxious
striving for originality, his studious discarding of classic mythology and modes of thought, he invited a reaction from
the sixteenth century as well as the seventeenth, from Ron-
sard as well as from Racine, and so became the herald of
the romantic generation.

It has been said that if the style of *Paul and Virginia*
resembles a statue of white marble, that of Chateaubriand

is a statue of bronze cast by Lysippus. The former is more
polished, the latter more brilliantly coloured. Saint-Pierre
would choose a well-lighted landscape. Chateaubriand
takes for his matter, sky, earth, and hell. The style of the
one has a fresher and younger air. That of the other is
more ancient, as though it were the style of all time.
Saint-Pierre seems to choose what is purest and richest in
the language; Chateaubriand takes from all, even from
vicious literatures, but he makes them undergo a veritable
transformation. Like that famous metal which at the burning of Corinth was formed from the fusion of all others, so
the language of Chateaubriand fuses all his thoughts in
poetic fire.

It may be admitted that the limitations of his genius
were almost as striking as that genius itself. His imagination gave a wonderful utterance to the feelings of his own
and the following generation. It did little or nothing to
direct or develop their thought. But yet his novels are a
cardinal point in the evolution of the French literary spirit
and of French fiction. They mark perhaps the most important date since the renascence. For, as Madame de
Staël prepared the way for the romantic school in the realm
of thought, philosophy, and criticism, so Chateaubriand
became its master in the realm of art and of creative
imagination.

The only influence comparable to his during the first
and second decades of the century was that of Madame de
Staël; and though this influence was exercised on her successors and a few of her female contemporaries more by
her criticism than by her novels, yet *Delphine* (1802) and
Corinne (1807) mark dates not to be neglected in the story
of the development of fiction.

Madame de Staël was the daughter of the Genevese banker and French finance minister Necker. She was brought up in the midst of a brilliant literary society that included the best of the philosophers of the pre-revolutionary generation. Thus as a child she was breathed upon by the spirit of liberty from America, with its indomitable hopefulness and restless daring, while at the same time she was acquiring the well-bred, sentimentally virtuous, flowery and smiling style of her elders, with their benevolent optimism, their amiable cheerfulness, and their brilliant iconoclasm. There is probably no writer of the Consulate and the Empire in whom these characteristics persist as they do in Madame de Staël. She is an optimist in spite of everything. The Revolution and its horrors, even her own exile, do not shake her militant faith in the constant progress and final perfectability of human society, though perhaps we should attribute this attitude as much to her vigorous physique and virile mind as to any process of ethical reasoning.

In 1786 Mademoiselle Necker married the Swedish ambassador Baron de Staël-Holstein, and under the protection of his flag she remained in Paris, not without dabbling in politics, till 1792. The years of the Terror she spent at Coppet near Geneva, but in 1794 she returned to Paris, where both instinct and vanity led her to oppose Napoleon, and she was banished from the capital in 1803. Already she had written *Delphine* (1802). Now, in Germany and in Italy, her critical and esthetic faculties received a fuller and more cosmopolitan inspiration, that was reflected in *Corinne* (1807) and in her famous essay on Germany. She did not return to France till the fall of Napoleon. She was already an invalid, and died in 1817.

On her youthful sentimental essays in fiction there is no reason to dwell, nor on her private life and more or less intimate relations with the literary men of her time. What has been said will suffice to suggest what training and what experience she brought to the writing of her novels, and how the chances of her life aided her genius to sow the century, as has been said, with fertile literary ideas. For *Corinne* and *Delphine* are the links that bind Rousseau's *New Héloïse* (1761) to *Indiana* (1832) and the long series of the novels of George Sand. From her youth Rousseau had been an admired model and one of the first objects of her independent criticism. But while the *New Héloïse* fascinated her she confesses that she drank eagerly of the sentimental outpourings of Madame Riccaboni, and enjoyed the delicate analyses of Madame de Tencin and Madame de Lafayette. She read Miss Burney, too, and dipped into Fielding, but after Rousseau what seems to have interested and inspired her most was Richardson's *Clarissa Harlowe*. It will be observed that all these writers have more or less of that moral sentimentality that characterised the reign of Louis XVI.; and in an essay on fiction written in 1795, as well as in the preface to *Delphine*, she states frankly, what Rousseau had implied, that to her the novel was " a sort of veiled confession made to those who have lived, as well as to those who have life before them." To her the end of the novel was to reveal us to ourselves by holding the mirror up to our moral nature. Her novels are analytical observations of good society by a member of good society; and, since it is easier and safer to observe one's self than others, *Delphine* and *Corinne* are drawn in large measure from the author's inner life. Thus Madame de Staël was the first to give in

fiction a fairly complete psychic portrait of a woman.   But
to this psychologic interest she added a moral purpose.
Dreading lest individuality should degenerate to egoism,
she imposed herself on those of her own social station as
pedagogue and counsellor in her fiction, just as she was wont
to do in her conversation.   Like Chateaubriand she was an
aristocrat, and her novels are distinctly aristocratic.   These
are stories of serious moral purpose, and in signing them
with her distinguished name she contributed very essentially
to win for fiction the place beside the drama in France,
and above it elsewhere in Europe, that it has maintained
during the entire century.   By placing the interest, not in
intrigue, but in a picture of soul-life that is its own interpretation, she gave to the novel a new source of power and
a higher place than Rousseau could claim.   That she took
up and carried on this part of Madame de Staël's work is
the peculiar honour of George Sand.

In *Delphine* we are shown what Madame de Staël herself possessed, a highly accomplished mind and an undis-
ciplined heart, "civilised in her accomplishments, almost
savage in her qualities," type doubtless of many in this
strange generation.   But Delphine, choosing to guide herself by theory rather than by social experience, finds her
private life involved in troubles corresponding to those in
which like political ideas had involved the French State.
The moral of it all is that, for a woman in society, upright-
ness and good intentions are not enough.   "A man should
know how to brave public opinion, a woman how to
submit to it," she says.   Delphine tries to follow an inner
light without regard to the prejudices or the conventions of
society, and society finds itself forced to condemn her in
its own defence.

Obviously enough, this novel is the literary precipitate of Madame de Staël's relations with Benjamin Constant, who has given us his ideas on the same subject in *Adolphe* (1816). At intervals ever since 1794 she had loved, or thought that she loved, that talented man. Her husband had died in 1802, the year of *Delphine*, and at this very time we find her asking the rather striking question if talent in a woman "has any other purpose than to make one a little more beloved." But though her marriage with Constant was a subject of common talk, neither wished to feel bound, and they parted at last in mutual vexation, "he at not having been instantly accepted, she at not having been forced to consent." Then in *Delphine* she freed her mind. It was a confession, but, like George Sand's *She and He* (1859), it was also an apology, and so, naturally, the man of Delphine's choice is not given a sympathetic part. It was said that in externals he resembled Guibert, an old admirer of Mlle. Necker, but in character he had much of Constant's egoistical timidity, and in sacrificing his love at last to public opinion he did what she wished men to think Constant had done. She let him be arrested and shot for incivism, and in the first edition she made Delphine cut the knot of existence by suicide; in the second, however, she borrowed a sentimental touch from Chateaubriand and let her pine away, languishing of unrequited love, a concession to a popular taste vitiated by *Atala*.

Delphine was distinctly the novel of Madame de Staël's youth. There is in these letters a passion as full-blooded as that of Mlle. de Lespinasse. When men criticised, and justly, the details of her style she could reply that style is the colour and movement that language gives to ideas, and·

that, whatever she might lack, her pages had eloquence, imagination, and feeling. And she was right. Her incorrectness is that of passionate speech and of an overflowing heart. It seems palpitating with feeling, spoken rather than written. A contemporary critic, Fiévée, said that Delphine " speaks of love like a bacchante, of God like a Quaker, of death like a grenadier, and of the future like a sophist." Madame de Genlis and others thought the book morally dangerous, but it could be so only to the ignorant, and should have been useful to the experienced, for it helped to clear the air of the artificial sentiment that glorified excess of passion and emotion, and, if we may trust some of the novels of the period, caused women to " weep copiously " quite as often as they ate a full meal.

In 1803 Madame de Staël was exiled from Paris, and a change of environment changed the nature of her inspiration. She now began the study of German literature, visited the literary lights of Weimar and Berlin, and found in German metaphysicians a good antidote for the French philosophers. Then after a short stay in Switzerland she went in 1804 to Italy, and this roused in her a love for the fine arts, and with it an increasing appreciation of nature. Thus intellectually stimulated she returned to Switzerland, and there wrote *Corinne* during 1806, in the midst of feverish journeyings that betrayed her longing for the homage of literary Paris. The success of *Corinne* on its appearance was immediate and universal. Indeed it is the crowning point of her literary career, for it is here that she gives to her ideals their most complete expression. Corinne, as Chénier said, is still Delphine, but perfected, independent, giving freer wing to her faculties, and still doubly inspired, by her talent and by love. This, too, is a story of an uncomprehended woman, another link to bind Julie to Lélia. Like Delphine, Corinne presumes on the superiority of her mind and heart to seek emancipation from social conventions, and, like her, she dies a victim to her own glory, which as Madame de Staël pathetically says, is only "the bright shroud of happiness."

This novel has several curious points of psychic contact with Madame de Charrière's *Caliste* (1794). The heroine, who unites Italian to English blood, has gone to Rome to seek a freer artistic life than English society admits. But it is in vain that she abandons her dignity to her love. She dies a victim to social conventionality. Thus the general scheme of *Corinne* is almost identical with that of *Delphine*, but here the details are better elaborated and the art is admirable with which Italy is set off against England, ideal love against smug calculation, nature against respectability, passion against cant, the glory of the ideal against material wealth and comfort, the Colosseum and the Capitol against the Bank and the Four-o'clock tea. To Corinne all thoughts, passions, delights are but ministers of love. Glory, to her, is but a means to love, and if love fail glory has no charm. There is a deep pathos in this conception of woman's genius as the victim of passion, in whom every talent is a new occasion of suffering. And whatever exaggeration there may be in such a conception, it is surely less morbid than the posing pessimism of René, and a healthier factor in the formation of the romantic school.

As her own relations to Constant were the prototype of those of Corinne to Oswald, so the minor characters also were taken from life, but it is clear that her interest centres with ours in the heroine alone. For, though she admits at times historical or moral digressions, even the scenery is treated by her, not, as by Bernardin or Chateaubriand, as an object of description for description's sake, but solely for its reflection of, or concord with, the state of soul of her characters. Very curious is the contrast between her treatment of Rome and that of Chateaubriand in the nearly contemporary *Martyrs*. She is always the emotional thinker, he the conscious artist. But her melancholy, which she shares with Chateaubriand, is only a part of her optimistic idealism. Happiness is always hovering before her and beckoning her on, and it is this that made *Corinne* for a whole romantic generation the book of generous passion and of ideal love.

But it was not by *Corinne* alone that Madame de Staël acted on the fiction of the immediate predecessors of romanticism and on the masters of that school. By her essays on literature and on Germany she gathered up what was most fruitful in the eighteenth century and passed it on vivified by new esthetic ideals and by a new cosmopolitan spirit. All the Latin literatures, French, Italian, Spanish, had been till then essentially objective, rationalistic, artistic, and often materialistic. She more than any one else introduced into French fiction the English and German idealism and individualism. The reawakening of the *ego*, heralded by Rousseau and Bernardin, is accomplished in the next generation. That reawakening, that regeneration through the romantic school is in large measure the glory of Madame de Staël.

One of the first signs of this reawakening is the increased number of women that seek a literary expression for their feelings. Besides those who belong rather to the closing years of the preceding century, in spirit if not in time, such as Madame de Genlis, Madame de Charrière, and Madame de Souza, there was Madame de Krüdener (1764–1824), a German from the Baltic, who wandered over the face of Europe and finally died in the Crimea, but who belongs to French literature both by her writings and her associations. For a brief time after Waterloo she played a part in French politics to which, as to her mysticism, it is possible only to allude here. Our interest in her is for her *Valérie*, which to the readers of 1803 seemed a French *Werther*, the worthy rival of *René* and of *Delphine*, and even to-day is not without its charm. *Valérie* is the first conscious effort to blend the English, French, and German spirits into a cosmopolitan one. The style throughout is good, remarkable in a foreigner, and there are some bits of description, such as the shawl-dance, that were once regarded as masterpieces. The story as a whole, in spite of some sentimental excesses, deserves to be read still, for its own sake and because it is one of the most interesting of the early utterances of the " misunderstood woman."

Following closely in time on the five ladies already named were Pauline de Meulan (1773–1827) and Madame de Cottin (1773–1807). The former, who later became Madame Guizot, won more fame for her writings in journalism, ethics, and pedagogy than for her novels, in which a sane wit covers a sober observation, that makes *The Contradictions* (les Contradictions, 1800) or *Ayton Chapel* (la Chapelle d'Ayton, 1801) pleasant though small oases in the waste of contemporary sentiment. But they are not characteristic of their time and met with small success. The vogue of Madame Cottin was much greater, and her *Exiles of Siberia* (les Exilées de Sibérie, 1806) won the praise of imitation from Xavier de Maistre in his *Young Siberian Girl* (la Jeune sibérienne, 1825). Its vogue passed, however, as rapidly as it rose, and in the next generation Sainte-Beuve tells us that Madame Cottin's books were read only " out of curiosity to learn the emotional moods of our mothers."

In 1802 another lady conspicuous in Parisian society, Madame Sophie Gay, conceived the idea of writing *Laure d'Estell* to show how much she liked Madame de Staël and disliked Madame de Genlis. The mock melancholy of this book was far more in the spirit of the time than in her own, which found its natural voice in *Léonie de Montbreuse* (1813), an admirable study of the straw-fire of youthful passion, leading to the thoroughly French conclusion that the sure way to happiness for a girl is to marry the choice of her father. During the Restoration and the Orleanist monarchy Madame Gay wrote a vast number of novels that reflect so well the taste of their several dates as to call for no notice, and much the same may be said of the novels of her daughter, Delphine Gay (1804–1855), who became Madame de Girardin and was a voluminous writer of society novels, of which the best is doubtless *The Eyeglass* (le Lorgnon, 1831).

A more marked individuality is Madame de Duras (1778–1829), who belonged to the literary generation of the Empire, though she wrote later " with the emotions of great catastrophes behind her," and never quite recovered from the terror that had blighted her youth. So both her *Ourika* (1823) and her *Édouard* (1825) deal with social inequalities and prejudices. In the former the heroine is a gentle maid from Senegal, of French nurture and negro blood; in the latter we have an anticipation of George Sand's *Miller of Angibault* (1845) in the love of plebeian and noblewoman. Through both novels there runs, however, as would hardly have been the case a little later, a deep spirit of Christian resignation. Here priests are once more confessors, austere spiritual guides, and the convent is still a refuge for storm-tossed lives. So while these books are marked by the Terror, they are marked also by the *Genius of Christianity* and by the resigned melancholy of Lamartine's *Meditations*. Thus her work, though slight, has great interest for the literary psychologist, because, while she represents the best phase of the culture of the Restoration, she represents also, as Sainte-Beuve has noted, by her oscillation between passionate revolt and Christian resignation, by her style and by her life, " something of the most touching destinies of the seventeenth century."

Many other women there were who sought literary utterance at this time, among whom it may be well to note Madame de Montolieu and Madame de Remusat; but the fact that they wrote is more significant than their writing. Meantime, among men, Senancour and Constant had taken up, each in his way, the melancholy burden of *René*. Senancour is known solely for his *Obermann* (1804), a novel in letters, that strikes the deepest note of despair and reveals the profoundest pessimism in this disillusioned age. " René says : ' If I could will I could do.' Obermann says : ' Why should I will? I cannot.' " This epigram of George Sand exhibits a new phase of despair. No writer had pushed pessimism to such blank negation as Senancour, nor will any writer of the century, save only Vigny, give it more eloquent expression; for these reveries of impotence are conducted with admirable literary skill, in spite of an apparent lack of system and co-ordination.

Obermann is cast in the form of a novel, but it is rather a series of melancholy reflections on nature and society exactly suited to the morbid sentiment of the romantic generation, so that after a period of comparative neglect the book became exceedingly popular during the days of Charles X. and Louis Philippe, and like feelings have made it again a favourite in our day in a narrow circle of minds too delicately organised to brook our modern life. It should be noted, however, that it is isolated, that it did not translate, as did *René*, the spirit of its time, but rather that of 1830 and of our own day.

Another novel stands in isolation at the close of the period we are considering, the *Adolphe* (1816) of Benjamin Constant (1767–1830), which was the literary precipitate of the author's relations with Madame de Staël, as *Delphine* had been hers. It was the sole novel of this versatile politician, and is a clear, keen, relentless, and realistic analysis of the mutual degradation that results from an ill-assorted union. The story is brief, almost cruelly simple, and told in a style as precise and dry as that of a mathematical demonstration.

The feeble egoism of Adolphe may seem contemptibly romantic, but the novel is a faithful piece of psychic auto-biography. Externally the story may be taken from the relation of Chrétien de Lamoignon and Madame Lindsay and the author has been gallant enough to dissociate Ellenore from Madame de Staël. But Adolphe is Constant, his father is Constant's father, his former lover is Madame de Charrière, his officious lady friend is Madame Récamier; and the best commentaries on this true cameo of romantic psychology are his correspondence, his journals, and indeed all that we know of a life spent, as Sainte-Beuve says, in seeing emotion always without ever attaining to passion.

One would not quite do justice to this pre-romantic

generation if one failed to note that, together with the vociferous despair of René, the voluntary ataxia of Obermann and Adolphe, and the hyperæsthesia of Madame de Staël's sentiment, a clear though slender plea for common-sense was raised by Xavier de Maistre (1763–1852) whose work began with that genial afterglow of eighteenth-century wit, the *Journey around my Room* (Voyage autour de ma chambre, 1794), and culminated in *The Lepers of the city of Aosta* (les Lépreux de la cité d'Aoste, 1811), though *The Young Siberian Girl* (1815) and *The Prisoners of the Caucasus* (les Prisonniers du Caucasse, 1815) have maintained for two generations their eminence as models of vigorous and direct narration. They combine, as does all the fiction of Maistre, an observation and power of description almost as exact as that of Mérimée with a sentimental affection that suggests Sterne, or perhaps rather Marivaux. Thus he stands apart, not wholly of the eighteenth nor of the nineteenth century, and wholly aloof from that romantic school whose fall he lived to see and whose rise we shall presently consider.

CHAPTER II

THE NOVELS OF STENDHAL

HENRI BEYLE, who called himself and is more generally called "Stendhal," took pleasure in posing as an isolated and peculiar nature born out of due time, and though doubtless there was much affectation in his attitude, yet we too must consider him so, though not, indeed, because he languidly affected to detest his family, his parents, his teachers, his native province, and even his fellow-countrymen *en masse*, and pretended to feel at home only in Italy, where, as he said, "the human plant lives more vigorously than elsewhere, for it is the sole country of art, of poetry, and of love."

As a critic, Stendhal was perverse and contradictory. Whatever Frenchmen agreed to admire he assumed to slight, and he chose their greatest aversion for his admiration. It was as though in literature and art he had said: "Evil, be thou my good; and good, my evil." Molière had for him no great comic genius, Chateaubriand would be soon forgotten, Hugo's sound and fury signified nothing, Vigny's gloom was silly pessimistic posing. On the other hand, the exiled Emperor was his ideal liberal in government, and Racine utterly unworthy of comparison with Shakspere. Many of these views have a very considerable element of truth in them. Some seem almost commonplace to-day, but during the Restoration, at least in its first decade, they seemed perversely iconoclastic. And the

man himself irritated opposition rather than evoked sympathy. Endowed by nature with a most commonplace
physique, his efforts to distinguish himself in dress and
manner served only to give him the repute of a ridiculous
affectation. Thus it happened that his personality was little esteemed and his writing little admired in his lifetime.
Balzac alone seems to have recognized in him a kinship
to the analytical side of his own manifold genius. In the
next generation Sainte-Beuve ventured to caution Taine,
who, in his *French Philosophers* (Philosophes français, 1857),
had pronounced Stendhal " a great romancer, the greatest
psychologist of the century." To Sainte-Beuve his novels
were "never quite satisfactory, in spite of pretty portions,
and take them all together, they were detestable." Gradually, however, as the memory of the man has receded, his
works have seemed to draw nearer. He had said himself
that he " would be understood about 1880," and curiously
enough this date does represent the period when his reputation reached its culmination with the rising prominence
of the psychological school in fiction, who joined with the
naturalists in claiming him as their legitimate ancestor.
Bourget, for once, could echo the sentiment of Zola and
accept Stendhal as " the father of us all."

To understand the unique place of his fiction, it is necessary to have in mind both the chief facts of his life and also
of his social philosophy. He is the only novelist with
whom we shall have to deal who brings to his writing the
experience of active participation in the Napoleonic campaigns. This alone would tend to give him a place apart,
but the experiences of his youth had already segregated
him from the common type of his generation. He was
born in 1783 and found the influences of the household

in which he passed his childhood so irritating that he was impelled to oppose anything that they seemed to approve. Did his family seem devoted to church and king? Then he would be sceptic and jacobin, would find the reign of Terror mild, and "feel the liveliest joy" at the execution of Louis. The only sincere prayer of thanksgiving that he seems to have uttered was when, on hearing of the death of his aunt, he threw himself on his knees "to thank God for that great deliverance." From the clergy who superintended his early education, and for whom he entertained very similar feelings, he was delivered also, somewhat later, when in 1799 he went to Paris, whence in the next year he was enabled to go to join Bonaparte in Italy and to take up the life of action to which he had so long aspired. He tells us that he "was so absorbed in the excess of joy" at this departure that he cannot recall and analyse his feelings, though his character appears delightfully in a little scene thus recounted by his biographer Rod : —

"He faced fire for the first time under the fort of Bard, . . . but all that he could recall afterward was this remark of a captain, whom he had asked, 'Are we within range?' 'Look at the fellow who's afraid already,' said the old veteran. As there were seven or eight persons present, the remark had its full effect. Beyle exposed himself as much as he could, exhibited his courage without however attracting particular observation, and that evening asked himself in all sincerity, 'Is this all?' This disappointed exclamation was to escape from him often in the course of his existence, active and filled as it was. There was always a disproportion between events and what he expected of them. To his hunger for emotion, war and love, which he preferred, remained always beneath his desires, yet he never ceased to seek and to enjoy them. During the Russian campaign by the bivouac fire he used to ask as before the fort of Bard, 'Is that all?' This phrase was always the melancholy refrain of his life, the *Leitmotiv* of his experiences."

That Italian campaign was, he says, "the best period of his life," and one sees it reflected in the enthusiasm of his posthumous *Life of Napoleon* (1876), and in his best novel, *The Chartreuse of Parma* (la Chartreuse de Parme, 1839). This period of active ambition lasted, by his own account, till 1811, and was succeeded from 1811 to 1818 by love for a woman who deceived him, and then by more transitory affections and jealousies, on which he has left curious comments of self-analysis in his *Love* (Sur l'amour, 1822), and still more in his *Journal* (1888). Ill health had constrained him to leave the army somewhat before the battle of Leipzig. He withdrew to Milan, always his favourite residence, and watched with apparent calm the abdication and final struggle of his old chief. Expatriated by choice, he remained in Italy, with brief visits to Paris, until his death, isolated thus socially, as he was also morally and esthetically. He was absolutely out of sympathy with his age and with romanticism. The revamped medieval Christianity of Chateaubriand affected him much as it would have done Voltaire. The sentimental self-torture of René disgusted him much as it does us to-day. To him emotions were objects of study, not occasions of sympathy. He made himself and his friends the subject of constant relentless analysis, in which he would suffer no embellishment and no intrusion of the imagination. He notes on hearing the death of his father that "during the first month I sought in vain to be grieved. The reader will think me a bad son, and he will be right." Elsewhere he says that his life has been filled with unhappy love-affairs, and notes eleven names of ladies with the reflection, " I was not gallant, not enough." Again he resolves to achieve the reputation of being the greatest poet of France, " not by intrigue like Voltaire, but by deserving it." Elsewhere we shall find him admiring " the inimitable physiognomy of my conversation" and " the reflection, à la Molière, that I made at that moment." But we shall be in danger of colouring our judgment if we dwell too long on the facile fatuousness of his *Journal.* The best that is in him, all that concerns us here, is in his novels, and to these we may turn, recalling only the wide experience and habit of indefatigable analysis that he brought to their composition at the ripest period of his mind's development.

These novels are *Armance* (1827), *The Red and the Black* (le Rouge et le noir, 1831), *The Chartreuse of Parma* (la Chartreuse de Parme, 1839), two novels unfinished at his death, *Lamiel,* and *The Green Chasseur* (le Chasseur vert), as well as some rather insignificant short stories. In all these works the end proposed by the author is the same, to discover the sources of happiness in human life by the analysis of the motives and means of its pursuit. Thus he is philosophically the disciple of the optimistic encyclopædists of the eighteenth century, most of all perhaps of Condillac. This is more clearly seen in the later novels, but it is obvious even in *Armance,* where Stendhal has paid his passing tribute to the spirit of the time and of René. He has placed his scene in the aristocratic Faubourg Saint-Germain, and he has striven to paint this background accuratèly from observed data; but it is doubtful if he understood or penetrated beneath the surface of the society he attempted to describe, and it is certain that the characters whom he places against this background are thoroughly romantic and Byronic. Octave is a creature of fate, desperate and declamatory; Armance is a noble girl, too proud to yield to her love for him or even to confess it, though she die of her secret. Surely it needs little penetration to see René and Amélie here, as well as a little of Stendhal himself in the self-tormenting fear of each lover that he or she may be the dupe of the other, with the result that both, but especially Octave, become singularly irritating. What shall we think of a young man whose life is so intensely unreal that he is "impatient of society because it distracts and draws him importunately from his dear reverie," and who is so frightened at discovering that he is growing fond of his fair cousin that he is guilty of such utter fatuousness as the exclamation: "I love. I! To love! Great God! . . . I had in my favour only my own esteem. I have lost it!" Whereupon he breaks out in "transports of rage and cries of inarticulate fury." Evidently Octave loves himself too much to love another with his whole heart. But with Armance love is checked by fear both for herself and for his constancy, so that she becomes distrustful, restless, inconsequent. In both characters Stendhal seems to be analysing himself, though we know that the first suggestion of the situation came to him from *Olivier*, an unpublished story of the Duchess of Duras, and there is in him no masquerade of Christian ethics as in Chateaubriand. Given these natures, the course of love in the two is traced with remarkable and minute perspicacity till Octave terminates it by a jealous suicide, an end that we may call happy by contrast to the broken, dolorous life that stretches before the personages of Stendhal's later novels as we turn the last page.

Stendhal's biographer Rod is probably right in thinking that Stendhal put most of himself, as was natural, into his first novel. Later he became more distrustful of his own sentiments. The work becomes harder and colder, the analysis more pitilessly minute. The result of extending the circle of his psychological observation becomes obvious three years later in *The Red and the Black* (1830), where we bid a last farewell to René, and are shown in Julien Sorel a new and typical novelistic creation, of such strength that one cannot but be surprised to find that it required ten years and the trumpet call of Balzac to rouse France to a recognition of its merits. Till then, if we may judge from Stendhal's correspondence, the greater part of its few readers had sought only autobiography and sniffed only scandal. Stendhal no doubt put into Julien somewhat of himself, but, in the main, Julien is rather his aversion. He is incarnate democracy, seeking to make for itself a place in society by its wits. Stendhal was by nature an aristocrat, and one of the first to see the ultimate effect of general suffrage. He sees in France a generation whose school-days were filled with the triumphs and defeats of the Empire, whose eyes had been dazzled by changes of fortune that till then had seemed to belong only to the dreams of *Arabian Nights*. They had, Stendhal tells us, " the example of the drummer Duke of Bellune, of the petty officer Augereau, of all the lawyers' clerks who had become senators and counts of the Empire," and they felt themselves irritated beyond bearing by the resuscitation of the Old Régime attempted at the

Restoration. Of such men Julien is an intensified type, as Augier's Giboyer of the proletarian of the second Empire. This is the significance of the rather enigmatic title, — *Red* for democratic liberty, for the opening of all careers to all ambitions, and for the reflection of the sun of Austerlitz; *Black* for the monarchical and jesuitical reaction of Charles X. and the Villèle ministry, till an outraged nation drove him from the throne he darkened and the country he was stifling.

The scene of *The Red and the Black* opens in Franche-Comté at the house of a royalist mayor who has a simple but pretty wife and is seeking a tutor for his two children, being moved thereto by a desire to show his superiority to a rival for social distinction, — a motive that marks the age. They have chosen for this office Julien Sorel, a carpenter's son, who has studied for the priesthood, that being apparently the line of least resistance to the "struggle-for-lifers" of that day. Now, Julien is devoured by passionate and envious ambition, he is educated beyond his station, and hates those who help him, because he needs their help. Vanity and pride rather than any form of love urge him to seduce the wife and to dishonour the husband. "Here," reflects the self-satisfied Julien, "is a woman of superior mind reduced to the depth of misfortune because she has known me."

Having profited by this first essay in hypocrisy, and having taken for his moral guide in life the maxim "never to say anything that did not seem false to himself," Julien returns to his seminary, where he finds himself in the presence of past masters of the art he is attempting to acquire. The description of this seminary is among the most effective things in the book, and entitles it to rank, as some one has said, as "a veritable breviary of hypocrisy." The next portion of the book, Julien's relations with Mathilde de la Mole, is less satisfactory as a whole, though the culmination of their intrigue is perhaps the best single episode of the novel. In her Stendhal endeavoured to present the female counterpart of Julien, but the analysis of motive is pushed to a wearisome virtuosity. Zola says that Stendhal here reminds him of those billiard-players who create difficulties just to show that there is no position of the balls in which they cannot make a carom. At every moment Julien, Mathilde, and others too, examine their consciences and listen to their thinking, with the surprise and delight of a child who holds a watch to his ear.

The climax of the novel is decidedly overwrought. Julien has brought matters to a position where the Marquis, Mathilde's father, is constrained to desire their marriage. The proletarian's social ambition is about to be crowned, when the mayor's wife writes a letter that breaks off the match. With an Italian fury such as always hovered before Stendhal as an ideal, Julien seeks out the traitress, finds her kneeling in church, and shoots her as she prays. He is arrested, tried, guillotined, but not until he has left us fifty pages of reflections on the last days of a condemned man, a defence of passion as the supreme arbiter of destiny that is intended to make us look on Julien's execution as his apotheosis. "Leave me my ideal life," he says to those who seek his rescue. "Your little chicaneries, your details of actual life, more or less repellent to me, would draw me from the sky. One dies as one can. I will think of death only in my own fashion. What matter the others to me? My relations to the others will soon be cut short. Please talk to me no more of those people. It is enough to see the judge and the lawyer." There is here a pride of egoism, a power of self-justification, that mark the Napoleonic mind.

Stendhal's last finished novel, *The Chartreuse of Parma*, is said to have been written immediately after *The Red and the Black*, during the year 1830. It was not published, however, till 1839, for Stendhal always liked to pose as a literary dilettante and affected indifference to his literary fame. His contemporaries generally accepted this as his best work; and that is still the usual opinion, though some naturalists see a more faithful reflection of their methods in *The Red and the Black*. But both novels are heterogeneous and difficult to classify. In both there are pieces of naturalistic description worthy of Zola, and touches of human pettiness worthy of Flaubert, with bits of psychic analysis that might delight Bourget, and, especially in *The Chartreuse*, a plentiful dose of romantic passion; while to all these elements *The Chartreuse* added still another, — the first serious attempt in French fiction to paint not alone foreign scenes but foreign ideals and foreign life, though indeed it was a life as familiar and, as he thought, more congenial to him than that of France itself. Whether the picture of the Italy, or rather the Milan of Napoleon, is any more true to nature than that of the Faubourg Saint-Germain in *Armance*, might be hard to discover. The book gives the impression of crude colours and melodramatic exaggeration. The Italy of his ideal seems rather that of Benvenuto Cellini or the Borgias than that of the nineteenth century. Four persons fill the book with the intensity of their passion. The Duchess Sanseverina, poisoner, almost incestuous, — quite after the author's own heart, so little trace remains in her of commonplace humanity, — is the worthy sister of Balzac's

Countess of Cadignan, loving with her whole though rather
shop-worn heart her nephew Fabrice, for whose sake she
kills one man, marries a second, and gives herself to a
third; a lady withal whom the author has delighted to
endow with his own wit and an aureole of beauty. Her
nephew Fabrice has in him much of Stendhal himself, like
Sorel, but with a less original flavour, a sort of Macchiavellian
type compounded of unscrupulous shrewdness and of
intense energy. The collapse of the Empire leaves the
spirit of Fabrice cribbed and confined. Waterloo has
closed to him the career of military ambition; he turns
instinctively to the Church, and, more successful than Julien,
ends his career of adventures in an arch-episcopal see. His
ethical ideas and ideals are, however, too different from our
own to allow us to follow with sympathetic interest the life
of one who behaves, as Sainte-Beuve observes, "like an
animal given over to his appetites or like a wanton child
who follows his caprices." One may feel a certain curious
interest in his conduct, but his motives are too foreign to
our range of experience, and the excessive resort to duels,
dungeons, poisons, and other such chimeras dire of romance
provokes a repletion of melodramatic effects.

Another noteworthy character in *The Chartreuse of
Parma* is Count Mosca, in whom Balzac saw a sort of glorified Metternich, "to create whom and to prove the creation by the acts themselves of the creature, to make him
move in an environment fit for the development of his faculties, was the work not of a man but of a fairy and an
enchanter." All of which seems to mean little more than
that Stendhal gave an admirable description of the court of
Parma and of the tactics of a shrewd and unscrupulous
courtier in striving to reconcile his duties with his lusts, his

office and his mistress. The ingenuity of the intrigue here is admirable, but it is almost painfully tortuous and accords with no reality that we know. Then, finally, in this Italy of cypress and myrtle, of poison and stiletto, Stendhal has painted for us in Palla the romantic political outlaw who becomes highwayman by necessity, and explains to the duchess that he has followed her "like a savage fascinated by her angelic beauty. It was so long since he had seen two white hands." This philandering highwayman is methodical, however. He keeps a memorandum of the persons whom he robs, and after reserving twelve hundred francs as a reasonable living due him from society, he returns the rest if he can. To the duchess he seems "a sublime man," especially after he has agreed to oblige her by killing an acquaintance; to us he seems another impossible Hernani.

So in these four characters we have the whole novelistic scale, ultra-romantic passion, adventure, minute realism, delicate psychology, each in turn, seldom combined, and all used to illustrate Stendhal's ideal of love omnipotent, unreasoning, fatal, one is almost tempted to say animal, which is the dominant note also in his shorter stories, such as *The Abbess of Castro* (l'Abbesse de Castro, 1832) or *San Francesco a Ripa*, stories that he averred he had drawn from old family records of the fierce passion of former Romans, — that love which was, he said, "a delicious flower, that was granted to him alone who had the courage to go gather it on the edge of a fearful abyss." Here, too, there is a needless "supping full of horrors" that the reader is glad to miss in the unfinished *Green Chasseur*, which promises more than any of Stendhal's completed novels realise.

In *The Green Chasseur*, as in the other novels, the hero is Stendhal himself projected by the novelist's imagination into a new environment. Suppose Henri Beyle had been born an aristocrat? he seems to ask in *Armance*, and having worked out that psychological problem, he asks himself, But suppose he had been an educated plebeian? and he writes *The Red and the Black*. Then, as he is living in Italy, he naturally lets his imagination picture himself as growing up in that environment, and we have *The Chartreuse of Parma*. But wherever he goes in the Europe of his day he is confronted with a plutocracy, self-assertive, cosmopolitan, and he asks himself: How if Henri Beyle had been a banker's son, how if he had entered the army for very ennui at a time when he knew it could offer little but the daily round of garrison duties? And to answer this question he writes *The Green Chasseur*. And if *Lamiel* were less fragmentary, we should doubtless find there also a like impulse.

Sainte-Beuve calls Stendhal a romantic hussar. He was a sort of literary skirmisher, a dilettante, who belonged to no school and has been claimed by all. When he is content to deal with normal human nature, his analytic powers produce admirable results, but, like every dilettante, he has an instinctive desire to exhibit his literary virtuosity on abnormal characters that appeal rather to psychologic curiosity than to broadly human sympathy. He did not see life steadily nor see it whole, but what he saw he described with a marvellous minuteness that roused the admiration of men so great and yet so different as Balzac and Mérimée in his own day, and Zola and Bourget in ours. Never widely read by the public, he is still closely studied by those writers of fiction who take their vocation seriously.

His influence on the style and general spirit or pervading ideas of French fiction has been slight. His importance in the evolution of novelistic processes is perhaps greater than that of any writer of his half-century, except of course Balzac.

CHAPTER III

THE romantic movement in France was less the result of individual genius or of a combination of cosmopolitan influences than of a national state of mind. The environment of gestation and childhood surely affects genius. It is not without significance that of the writers who gained eminence in fiction between 1820 and 1840 three were born before the ascendency of Bonaparte, twelve during the Consulate, and nine others during the four triumphant years that culminated in the interview at Erfurt; while the seven years that separate Erfurt from Waterloo, the descending action of that gigantic drama, count but five distinguished names, and the first five years of the Restoration but one. Of the novelists born before the fall of the Empire seven stand out clearly as superior in genius, though not necessarily in popularity. Of these Stendhal had been old enough to take active part in the Napoleonic campaigns. He looked at the romantic spirit from outside, and made it the subject of his psychological analysis. Balzac had been segregated in his youth, and did not therefore affiliate himself completely with the romantic movement, though he did not wholly escape it. Vigny, Hugo, and Dumas were the sons of soldiers, and could not but inherit the spirit of those epic days. George Sand, too, was the daughter of an officer and first-fruit of a marriage that was

itself a romance ; while Mérimée, who stands a little outside
the romantic current, was of civilian and partly English blood.

These five grew up in an atmosphere of magnanimous emotions, of the great Napoleonic épopée with its
soul-stirring messages of victory and defeat, and from this
they passed, when already old enough to feel it, into an
atmosphere of political repression where their overwrought
imagination naturally sought a vent in fantastic ideals. " I
belong," says Vigny, " to that generation born with the
century, that was fed by the Emperor with bulletins and
had before it always a naked sword which it was about to
seize at the very moment when France re-sheathed it in the
Bourbon scabbard. . . . Even our schoolmasters read us
constantly bulletins from the Grand Army, and our hurrahs
for the Emperor interrupted Tacitus and Plato.   Our
teachers were like heralds at arms, our studies like barracks,
our recitations like manœuvres, and our examinations like
reviews. . . . Even now I am not far from a relapse, so
deep are the impressions of infancy and so well was the
burning mark of the Roman eagle engraved on our hearts."
But Musset and Gautier, who were four and three years old
when the Restoration came, felt this less, and more of the
foreboding of catastrophe.   So it seems to Musset, in his
Confession, as though " during the Empire, while husbands
and fathers were in Germany, anxious mothers brought into
the world a pale and nervous generation," to grow up after
Leipzig and Waterloo, " weighted with care in a ruined
world " and " struggling to fill their lungs with the air
Napoleon had breathed." So Musset makes shipwreck of
his life in a passionate effort to grasp an illusive ideal, and
Gautier seeks escape from the real in the realm of art and
phantasy.

Of course it would be easy to overstress the power of this political environment, of which the effect varied with the personality. Yet it is an element not to be neglected, and to it must be added the natural reaction toward royalism and medievalism after the intense modernity of the Napoleonic political life. But as a popular state of mind this reactionary sentiment yields under Charles X. to a general warmth of democratic sympathy that finds its natural expression in the Revolution of 1830. Add to this a third element, the result in part of the other two, and we shall have the main factors of romanticism. This is the " world-pain " of Chateaubriand, modified somewhat perhaps by *Werther* and *Childe Harold*, but still essentially the woe of René, the heart-sickness of all who can find in the real world nothing to correspond to ideals that they are alike impotent to attain or to banish. " We are your true sons, René," says Sainte-Beuve. " Our infancy has been troubled by your dreams, our youth agitated by your restlessness, and the same north wind has borne us upward."

Now, to be a child of René is to allow one's imagination to be guided more by feeling than by reason ; and this the typical romanticists illustrate in their treatment of nature and in their style. Nature to them is no longer, as it had been to Rousseau and to Bernardin, " material for sensations and a pretext for descriptions, a sort of magnificent cradle prepared by God for his privileged creatures." In Chateaubriand first, but still more in the poet-novelists and in George Sand, creation takes on an independent life, the material world becomes a symbol of an ethical or hedonistic ideal. And since this view of nature is the product of individual fancy, the fabric of a vision, it will find its natural expression in lyric declamation, in strained or gro-

tesque imagery, and in weird or exotic scenes in which the
fancy can riot at will. So the romantic imagination will
eagerly sup full of horrors and cast itself with delight into
the vortex of crime.

The germs of this "world pain" were in the French
Revolution, but their development was aided by foreign
influences. This was a generation in which, as Goethe has
told us, Ossian had supplanted Homer and Macpherson's
wildly grandiose visions passed for current coin of "emotion in its state of nature." This influence, combined with
the melancholy morgue of Young, affected poetry more
than prose, but is obvious enough, for instance, in Hugo's
Han of Iceland (Han d'Islande, 1823). Much more wide-
reaching, however, was the development of the historic
sense that the French owed to the Waverley Novels, those
picturesque re-creations of the past to which the French
echoes are *Notre-Dame* (1830) and *Cinq-Mars* (1826).
Then, too, Byron by his heroic devotion and death had lent
a dignity to romantic despair that Chateaubriand could not
give to René because he did not have it to bestow.

Byron had died in 1824, and from 1826 onward the
tendency to the fantastic already obvious in Nodier was
strengthened by the increasing vogue of the German ro-
manticist Hoffmann, whom in 1828 the *Globe*, the literary
organ of the romanticists, hailed as the *ne plus ultra* of "the
bizarre and the true, the pathetic and the terrible, the
monstrous and the burlesque." Hoffmann, as later our
own Poe, attracted the French because his racial qualities
enabled him to excel the Latins on the side to which for
the moment they inclined. Hoffmann had more readers
in France than Goethe or Heine. He probably has more
there to-day than in Germany. Naturally popularity pro-

voked imitation. One finds it, tacit or avowed, in Hugo, Gautier, Musset, Sand, Balzac, to be silent of a host of minor writers and feuilletonists. For the decade of 1830 Hoffmann directed French romanticism. He greatly furthered its inherent tendency toward a confusion of moral and esthetic ideas. What was to him a nebulous dream became to them a sharply defined vision. What in him had been grotesque or eccentric becomes in them ghastly and monstrous. To see, however, that Hoffmann did not originate the movement that he accelerated, one need only consider the striking combination of all the elements we have been considering in the later novels of Nodier and in the fiction of Victor Hugo.

If a group of writers can be called a school whose only bond of fellowship is a general union of total dissent, the schoolmaster of the romanticists would be the genial Charles Nodier (1783–1844), and their schoolroom his librarian's salon at the Arsenal, where from about the year 1823 the leaders of that movement were wont to gather. At first the more prominent members were the critic Sainte-Beuve, the poet Vigny, and those diligent translators the brothers Deschamps. Later Hugo allied himself to them, and from about 1826 this group, calling itself the *Cénacle*, became a more or less purposeful "log-rolling society," from which Sainte-Beuve thought it wise to withdraw, while they drew to themselves the less steadfast and thorough-going adhesion of Musset and Gautier.

Nodier was by far the oldest of this group, yet in his sympathy he was ever young, and so he could form a rallying-point for all, and he helped all with sympathy and counsel to the last. His novels are less interesting to us than his personality, yet they are not without interest.

Others before him had shown clear marks of the influence
of English fiction, but he was the first to make the fiction of
Germany and more especially the *Sorrows of Werther* felt in
France. His literary talent seems to have been dispersed
rather than arrested by the influences of the Napoleonic
epoch, and the result is a puzzling mixture. Naturally
gifted with a fanciful imagination, he was constrained to
pass the formative years of his genius in a time of repression, when the only great writers, Staël and Chateaubriand,
are those whose minds were already formed, whom the Empire could not bend and did not break. So it happened
that Nodier became a polygraph. He wrote, and wrote
well, on science, history, criticism, philology ; and already
as a youth he seems to have meditated fiction and found
absorbing delight in *Werther* and Shakspere.   When, in
1800, he left his native Besançon for Paris, he had already
begun two imitations of Goethe's novel, *The Exiles* (les
Proscrits, 1802), and *The Salzburg Artist* (le Peintre de
Saltzbourg, 1803), the latter aptly characterised by its second title, " Journal of the Emotions of a Suffering Heart."
But though both novels are more declamatory and more
fatalistically romantic than *Werther*, we must not be the
dupe of Nodier. He was quite capable of writing in the
same year *Meditations from the Cloister* and the lively, not
to say Pantagruelistic *Last Chapter of my Novel* (Dernier
chapitre de mon roman, 1803), to afford us a reassuring
witness that he was safe from all morbidity. Except for
this, however, his novels written during the Consulate are in
the key of *René, Delphine*, and *Obermann ;* but his sentimentality has in it more of the German, which he derived in
part from the translation of *Werther* that had been made in
1776, and in part from other translations preserved to liter-

ary memory only because of their contribution to forming the new cosmopolitan emotion that Nodier expressed.

For in these early novels he preaches with graceful languor the desperate melancholy that he mocked with such verve in the *Last Chapter*.   Yet all of them have the sterling mark of a studied style, and there are passages in them that would surely be commonplaces of the anthologies if Rousseau or Chateaubriand had had the good fortune to write them.   But by 1818 Nodier had thoroughly outgrown *Werther*, and had ceased to nurse his fancy on suicides and funerals.   So *Jean Sbogar* (1818), a tale of a chivalrous Illyrian brigand, has in it much more of the fresh breezy spirit of *Rob Roy* than of the conventional melancholy of *René;* and the stories that follow, *Ruthwen* (1820), *Smarra* (1821), *Trilby* (1822), are thorough bits of romantic fancy, conceived in the spirit of Fouqué's *Undine*, of Bürger's *Leonore*, and of the fantastic tales of Hoffmann.   Thus they are the forerunners of what is most charming in the work of the romanticists of the thirties, while Nodier himself continued to sound the keynote in such exquisite little masterpieces as *The Crumb-Fairy* (la Fée aux miettes, 1832), *Sister Beatrice* (Sœur Béatrix, 1838), *The Chandelier* (la Chandelier, 1839), and *Brisquet's Dog* (le Chien de Brisquet, 1844).   But while these stories stretch out one hand to the romanticists, they reach back the other to Voltaire.   In Nodier the short story that had been neglected since the rise of Rousseau returns with all its insinuating grace and quite without its sting.   This, then, is the significance of Nodier, that he unites in himself and transfers to the fiction of the romanticists the Voltairian *conte*, the English romance, and the German sentimental tale, working by example, by personal counsel, and by printed criticism, to stimulate in their first efforts Lamartine, Hugo, and the brilliant train that followed, whose fiction we have now to consider.

The father of Victor Hugo (1802–1885) was a bold general of the Republic and the Empire, his mother was a Breton Catholic, and thus he inherited an imagination at once emotional and grandiose.   These predispositions were fostered in his youth, first by his stay in Spain and the weird experiences of his life there in a convent school, of which there are traces in his work from the *Bug-Jargal* (1818) to *Torquemada* (1882), and second by several years spent in romantic yet urban retirement with his mother in the abandoned convent of the Feuillantines at Paris, of which he has left a beautiful account in his poems.   So it happened that at fourteen he showed an unmistakable aversion from mathematics, technological studies, and indeed from any facts of which his imagination could not make its sport, and recorded in his diary his aspiration "to be Chateaubriand or nothing."

Seldom was the wish of youth more completely fulfilled. He had more than Chateaubriand's poetic power, he could touch deeper and stronger chords of feeling, his style was capable at once of grander heights of eloquence and of gentler strains of pathos.   But with these qualities he had also their faults, — a veritable gift of inaccuracy, that makes him almost valueless as a witness in regard to the facts or dates of his own productions, an almost comic sincerity of conviction that his exclamatory eloquence is orphic wisdom, and a profound conceit whose fatuousness can be surmised rather than fathomed by a line in which the aged poet invites the Deity to discuss a matter with him for their mutual edification.

As a school-boy Hugo won distinction for his poetry, and

became associated with a group of literary friends of his brother Abel. In 1818 he wrote, or at least he says that he wrote, his first novel, *Bug-Jargal*, a story of the Haytian revolution of 1794, which, after being expanded to some four times its original length, was first published in 1825. The earlier story has the exaggeration and the grotesque gruesomeness that belong to the romantic conception of fiction, but it lacks what was to be the mainspring of the longer tale, as of nearly all the fiction of Hugo, — a passion so ill-assorted as to lead inevitably to tragedy. In this earlier version both composition and style are in their infancy; but it is the infancy of Hercules, a fancy running glorious riot in scenes of wanton horror.

The second *Bug-Jargal* is keyed to a higher pitch, but it is more mature. New motive and intensity is given to passion, and contrast between grotesque and pathetic is pushed to the uttermost, marking a decided advance on the *Han of Iceland* (Han d'Islande) of 1823.

This last is a story of Norway, and an attempt at historical evocation in the manner suggested, as Hugo expressly tells us, by Scott. The scenes were to be " pictures in which description should supply the decoration and the costumes." But the effort to produce this vivid visual impression is too obvious. The diction pants and heaves. The confusion of genres is pushed here, as afterward in Hugo's dramas, to a point where it aims to add to epic effects not alone those of lyric and drama but of the plastic arts as well. In this attempt failure was certain, and the story is far inferior to the final *Bug-Jargal*. And yet this tale of a double-skulled monster and his hardly less human consort, a polar bear, who together destroy piecemeal a regiment, after which Han burns himself to death that he may consume in flame the castle of his captors, has a force that proclaims a coming master in tales of terror and daring. It has also the humour that comes from the grotesquely incongruous; and if its pathos seem painfully morbid and false, this was a fault of the time rather than of Hugo. "Few men," said Nodier, "begin with such errors, and leave for critics only those faults that they have voluntarily committed."

Such criticism as this was then most welcome, for classicism still predominated among reviewers, though romanticism was gaining control of the stage and of fashion. Classical writers were more praised, but romantic books were more read. Nodier notes that "the most distinguished work of the good school does not for a moment share the irresistible vogue of the often very extravagant reveries that swarm in the bad." The fashion was set already toward the strange and exotic, toward "gilded chivalry, the pretty medievalism of chatelaines, pages, and god-mothers, the Christianity of chapels and hermits." During the years between *Bug-Jargal* (1825) and *Notre-Dame* (1830), this medievalism with its symbolic treatment of nature developed very rapidly in Hugo, and found its most remarkable expression in this latter work, the finest prose of his early period, and the only other novel written before his exile save for the short pieces of criminal psychology, *The Last Day of a Condemned Man* (le Dernier jour d'un condamné, 1829) and *Claude Gueux* (1834), both pleas, as eloquent as they were impracticable, for the abolition of the death penalty,—a subject to which Hugo recurred in season and out of season during his whole literary career.

Notre-Dame is a novel gothic in subject, in imagination,

in treatment, and in style. It mingles the noble and the base, the heroic and the grotesque, as though the aim of the author were to cover the whole range of human sentiment and to discover a physical symbol for every human feeling and passion. The story is of the slightest, hardly as elaborate as *Bug-Jargal*, and the characters are essentially the same. Here the preferred lover is the gay Phœbus; Frollo, the priest loving with furious hopeless fatality of passion in spite of learning and vows, replaces Bug, the negro prince; and the hunchback Habribrah of the former tale becomes the hunchback Quasimodo, the bell-ringer, who also loves desperately in despite of deformity. And to all these the gypsy girl, the daintily romantic Esmeralda, is what the aristocratic planter's daughter was to those, though of course the situations here are managed with far higher art and more complete tragic pathos. For Marie found satisfaction in her love, while the devotion of Esmeralda was unscrupulously exploited by the gay light-o'-love soldier, until she perished at last as a sorceress through the jealous intervention of an old hag, who discovered too late that she has compassed the death of her own child, — a situation that in its essential features recurs several times in Hugo's dramas.

But it is not in the story that our interest lies. Far more real, far more living than any of these characters is the great cathedral, the ever-recurring symbol of the society over which it broods, throwing over all its weird and sombre shadow. This device, essentially epic, has never been managed with greater effect in fiction, though it has been attempted by Zola and Daudet with great effect, as well as by Huysmans and Loti. But besides this foreboding presage in the cathedral, the grotesque side of medieval life is unveiled in that strange Miracle Court (*Cour des miracles*), a social cesspool of beggars and criminals, where the lame grow nimble and the blind see, that they may share in nightly orgies in which Hugo combines the superstitions, the customs, and the thieves' talk of the submerged of many nations to give us the illusion of a realistic, exotic phantasmagoria, approached in French literature only by some chapters of Gautier's *Captain Fracasse* (le Capitaine Fracasse, 1863).

It is here, where author and reader alike forget the thread of the story, that Hugo is at his best; and his best is so good, so vivid that we hardly pause to ask whether it is true. No scholarly investigations can undermine the structure of Hugo's fancy, nor can the dust of documents mar its bright colouring. For us and for generations to come the Paris of Louis XI. will be the Paris of Esmeralda. The popularity of the story was immediate and great, and its effect has been lasting, for it is from *Notre-Dame* that we may date the revival in France of that interest in ancient buildings and monuments, to arouse which Hugo then regarded " one of the chief ends of his book and indeed of his life." Of course there is in *Notre-Dame*, as always in Hugo, an occasional ring of false declamation, and a straining or even a panting for effect; but it is less felt here than in the novels of the later period, and as a piece of reproductive imagination *Notre-Dame* deserves not only the first place in Hugo's fiction, but a high rank among the novels of the world.

An interval of thirty-one years separates *Notre-Dame* from Hugo's next contribution to fiction, *Les Misérables* of 1862, which was succeeded in 1866 by *The Toilers of the Sea* (les Travailleurs de la mer). *The Man who Laughs* (l'Homme qui rit) followed in 1869, and the list is closed by *Ninety-Three* (Quatre-vingt-treize) in 1874. But all these stories are of this later period in date alone. In their manner, rhetoric, and diction they are as romantic as *Notre-Dame*, and belong to a type of fiction even more discredited in their day than it is in ours. As has been well said, here as in his poetry, Hugo "barred the current of evolution, he did not deflect it;" and it is more fitting to consider these novels of the sixties and seventies with those of the thirties than with their own contemporary fiction.

Yet between *Notre-Dame* and such historical novels as *The Man who Laughs* or *Ninety-Three*, and even more between that prose epic and the novels of contemporary life, *Les Misérables* and *The Toilers of the Sea*, there is sharp contrast in political views and social sympathies. The young Hugo had been more or less royalist, Catholic, medieval; the political experiences of a decade made him a social democrat. Like Antæus thrown to earth, he gathered new strength of conviction and of utterance from his exile; though his enthusiasm, like that of the Revolution of 1848, was as vague as it was intense, as untrained as it was generous. He seemed to imagine that he had a gospel of social salvation to proclaim to the world, and he proclaimed it with such serious emphasis that many were found to take it at his valuation. "So long," he says in his preface to *Les Misérables*, "as there shall exist through the fault of our laws and customs a social condemnation that creates artificial hells in the midst of our civilisation and complicates a divine destiny by human fatalism; so long as the three problems of the century — the degradation of man by the proletariat, the fall of woman through

hunger, the arrested development of the child by ignorance
— are not solved ; so long as social asphyxia is possible in
any place, — in other words and from a wider point of view,
so long as there shall be ignorance and misery on earth,
books like this cannot be useless."

Hugo is doubtless in earnest, but his work can hardly be
regarded seriously. It is a chaos of all genres and all
subjects. Taking for his philosophic background the not
precisely original idea that voluntary expiation and repentance will produce a moral regeneration and so reveal to
the soul a higher life, he uses this background to set off
humanitarian declamations and a sentimental social democracy. Not content with this, he imports into his novel
antiquarian lore, political reminiscences, studies in dialect
and slang, emotionally realistic slumming, scenes of battle
and riot, the most impassioned lyric appeals, the most
insipid idyllic banality, and the most puerile symbolism.
The whole is a chaos in ten volumes of passion, beauty,
aspiration, and of a bathos that is simply cyclopean.

The characters, as we should expect from such a lyric
novel, are not based on observation nor correlated to the
life of this planet. Its hero, Valjean, ex-convict, manufacturer, and philanthropist, is a thoroughly romantic self-
contradiction, a Utopian without wisdom or prudence,
whose magnanimity would be as unnatural and as futile in
real life as it is surely wearisome in romance. And just as
in Hugo's dramas characters enter proclaiming, " I am
Murder and Vengeance," so here we are told that the
grisette Fantine is a symbol of joy and modesty ; Marius is
always posing for what Hugo pretended he had been in
1830 and was not, — a type of youthful energy, nursing
democratic aspirations on imperial memories ; Enjolras is

the typical intransigent, whose fundamental imbecility it was left to Flaubert to exhibit *ad nauseam* in his *Sentimental Education* (1869). Javert is the incarnation of social order, and Cosette is the ideal romantic young lady, somewhat childish in her sentimentality. Not one of them all has the life of the scoundrel Thernardier or of that precious street urchin Gavroche.

As in *Notre-Dame* it is the digressions and sermons that best reward the reader in this chaplet of scenes loosely strung on the life of Jean Valjean. The psychology is feeble, but we are shown with much feeling the veil of ostracism that separates the discharged prisoner from society and almost forces him to crime. The early volumes seem most deeply felt, and on the whole are the best. In the body of the work, in the account of the youth and student days of Marius, there are touches of autobiography, and from this the novel sinks to its lowest depth in the prolix senility of the loves of Marius and Cosette. But no one of its ten volumes is without individual scenes of great power, and the escape of Valjean from Thernardier, his flight through the sewers, the defence of the barricade, and, above all, Waterloo, reveal the poetic genius of Hugo in its glory. Yet, if one take the work as a whole, one must agree with Flaubert that it has neither truth nor grandeur.

The Toilers of the Sea (les Travailleurs de la mer) is rather a prose poem than a novel. Its interest is almost wholly epic and lyric, and its inspiration is obviously the poet's residence on the Channel island of Guernsey. Here he informs the reader it is his purpose to show how the fatality of inanimate nature " is mingled with the supreme fatality, the human heart." As a matter of fact the desperate love of Gilliat for Deruchette, his devotion and suicide, show no such thing, but only her lack of common honesty and his lack of common-sense. As in *Les Misérables*, the interest is neither in the story nor in the psychology, but in the marvellous descriptions of the sea, where Hugo's prose throbs and thrills with the far-sounding waves. But for this it was not necessary to write a novel, and as a whole *The Toilers* is as inferior to *Notre-Dame* or *Les Misérables* as it is superior to *The Man who Laughs* (l'Homme qui rit), where with strange perversity Hugo imported to the court of the English Elizabeth the manners of *Han of Iceland* and produced an abortion which it is but charity to bury in silence.

On the other hand Hugo's last novel, *Ninety-Three* (Quatre-vingt-treize), is in many ways his best, for here at last he found a period suited above all others to his genius, and of which he had as it were an hereditary knowledge. The scene is Vendée in the crucial year of the first Republic, and into it Hugo has put a more intense palpitating life and a truer tragic catastrophe than he ever attained elsewhere, though the novel is marred by the mannerisms of age and his usual looseness of construction. It was a time that produced and justified the extreme natures and sharp contrasts in which Hugo excelled ; and if Cimourdin is still a lifeless type, Gauvin and Lantenac are flesh-and-blood men, neither too heroic nor too sentimental for their time. Yet here, as always in Hugo's novels, what leaves the deepest and freshest impress on the mind are the episodes and the minor characters, pictures of Paris in revolution, the weird procession of the guillotine, the cannon aboard ship broken loose and dealing destruction, battle scenes, the grisly old trooper Radoub, and the peasant woman's children whose prattle runs like a golden

thread through these scenes of fire and blood. Judged by
the canons of fiction, both for what it is and for what it
avoids, this is the best of Hugo's novels ; judged as a combination of epic, lyric, idyllic, realistic, didactic, oratoric,
and philosophic story-telling, it is less unique than *Les
Misérables*, and it never attains that novel's highest reaches.

In historic fiction Hugo's only important rival among
the romanticists was Alfred de Vigny, who published between 1826 and 1835 three volumes that represent the
rising tide of romanticism and also the unique personality
of their author. He was of noble blood and strongly
royalistic sympathies. Therefore at the Restoration he made
haste to enlist in the army, and remained connected with
it for thirteen years, during which his nearest approach to
the active service that he ardently desired was a period of
guard-duty in the Pyrenees during the brief Spanish war.
In 1827, weary of piping peace, already a noted poet and
the author of *Cinq-Mars* (1826), but grieved perhaps that
others did not surround him with a halo quite so brilliant as
that with which he glorified himself, he resigned from the
army and turned to literature, finding for the moment his
closest affinities in Hugo and Sainte-Beuve, though his
sensitive and passionate royalism afterward estranged him
from both. He felt keenly the Revolution of 1830. *Stello*
(1832) was marked by deepening pessimism, and in *Military
Servitude and Grandeur* (Servitude et grandeur militaires,
1835) he voiced with subdued sadness the tragic fatality
of conflicting duty in the soldier's life. Then he wrapped
himself in gloomy silence, and published no word until his
death. Vigny was afflicted with the "world-pain" of his
generation in one of its last stages. In the beginning and
to the end his fiction is the expression of a dignified mel-

ancholy.   He tells us that he was "disenchanted before he had tasted illusion and fatigued with life before he had lived."

Cinq-Mars (1826) is the elaboration of a hearty diet of Walter Scott and Chateaubriand in a mind strong but reserved and coldly pessimistic, and by an imagination stimulated through military service in the legendary valley of Roncesvalles.   Its subject is a triple tragedy, the tragedy of the dying Louis XIII., humiliated by the daily filching from him of his regal authority, the tragedy of the dying Richelieu, clutching his power over life even as he is passing to death, and the tragedy of Cinq-Mars, his brave, magnanimous, though criminal victim.   Scott had used history as a picturesque background, Vigny thought he saw in it the possibility of a deeper revelation of human life. To him, as to Carlyle, illustrious men seemed symbols of the universal mind of society.   Thus, when he took histori- cal persons for his characters he projected into them his own ideas, and so *Cinq-Mars* inevitably became, for all its three hundred authorities, a falsification of history and a distortion of character.   But though these faults were obvious enough to such critical historians as Thierry, Thiers, and Guizot, they were less felt by the public then than they would be to-day.   The book attained immediate and very great success, partly because it was the first evocation of a national past toward which the reaction from the Revolution naturally impelled the romantic mind, partly also because of its limpid style and poetic charm.   But if it be judged by modern standards, *Cinq-Mars* must be pronounced dull, artificial, and false, without historic insight or historic feeling.   The plot lacks action, and the charac- ters lack life.   Its delicate descriptions and occasional elegiac beauties do not raise it to the rank of *Notre-Dame* (1830) or even of *The Three Guardsmen* (1844). Yet it is right to remember that Vigny was first in the field, and that he led where others followed.

Stello is a novel only in the sense that we give that name to *James the Fatalist* (Jacques le fataliste, 1796) or to *Tristram Shandy*. The historical methods of *Cinq-Mars* are here applied to André Chénier, and the author seems to have been both surprised and hurt that that poet's relatives should prefer their truth to his fancy. The other victims of his idealistic philosophy of history were the long-dead English poets Gilbert and Chatterton, who had no relatives to protest for them.

Time, that tries all things, will probably grant a longer life to the three short stories that illustrate *Military Servitude and Grandeur* than to *Stello* or to *Cinq-Mars*. In *Stello* he had, he says, lamented the condition of the poet in our society; here he will show that of the soldier "another modern pariah," for to him as to Madame de Staël it seemed that all moral greatness carried with it a servitude to be the shroud of its happiness. The construction of the stories may still be faulty, but there is a nobility in the fundamental conception that we miss in *Stello* and *Cinq-Mars;* and though the poet's vision certainly still distorts and falsifies history, yet, as Sainte-Beuve says, it is rather by over-anxious thought than by wantonness. Like an alchemist, he is seeking to transform metals, to make gold of clay and diamond of carbon. Vigny says he will be content if men "believe and weep," but unfortunately readers do not weep to-day as they did in 1835, though none can fail to remark the admirable rhetorical art in the dialogue between Pope and Emperor in *The Malacca Cane* (la Canne de jonc) ;

and the noble conception of honour as "the faith that all still share" gives to the whole a dignity of abnegation and resignation hardly surpassed in modern fiction.

All the members of the first *Cénacle* attempted fiction, even Sainte-Beuve, who published, in 1834, his sole novel, *Pleasure* (Volupté), as "an indirect way of loving and of saying so," like the youthful verses that had preceded it. Sainte-Beuve's learning and broad sympathies were destined to make him the greatest literary critic of the world; but his whole life was, as he says, only "a long course in moral physiology," and *Volupté* is an effort of self-analysis in a man who from being an eager medical student had become a love-sick Werther, had then developed "a pronounced vein of religious sensibility," and had at last recovered his normal balance of mind. His story is to be, he tells us, "an analysis of an inclination, passion, or perhaps a vice, and of all the part of the soul that is dominated by that vice and takes its tone from it, that is, all that is languid, idle, clinging, secret, private, mysterious, furtive, subtly dreamy, effeminately tender, in short, voluptuous." His Amaury is himself in the sense that Werther is Goethe. But while Sainte-Beuve became a confirmed epicurean, Amaury "attributed to himself a mystic illusion to colour and shade his epicureanism," and so finally turned priest, as Lamartine's Jocelyn was to do under somewhat similar circumstances. The novel, once much talked of, is to-day interesting chiefly as illustrating a phase of romantic morbidity, and for the light that it throws on the ethical and intellectual process by which this remarkable mind came to clearness.

Of far higher rank is the fiction of Alfred de Musset, *The Confession of a Child of the Age* (la Confession d'un enfant du siècle, 1836), and the admirable short stories of various dates from 1836 to 1853.   Musset, like Hugo and Vigny, was greater as a poet and as a dramatist than as a novelist, yet we shall not understand him as a poet if we fail to take account of this *Confession*, the literary precipitate of his love for George Sand and of his estrangement from her. The ghouls of criticism have recently stirred this malodorous affair with eager industry, but there is no reason to follow them into the *latrinæ* of literature.   It is sufficient to know that Musset's naturally weak moral nature was incapable of constant attachment to anybody, but he cared for George Sand more than he ever did for any other, and their estrangement was a shock from which he never recovered.   Musset was indeed "a child all his life and a spoiled child."   He was also a showman of his emotions, eager to exhibit his torn heart and to invite all the world to the spectacle.   That is the purpose of this rather morbid "confession," which opens with a discussion on the social psychology of the nineteenth century by which the author seeks to make us comprehend and excuse that melancholy that had befallen him as the result of a somewhat vulgar and commonplace adventure.   One lays aside the book with a strange mingling of admiration and contempt, and with the feeling that Musset's genius cannot hide his fatal weakness.   Like his hero, Octave, Musset had allowed the zeal of his heart to consume him.   For the moment he had lost all joy of life and hope in life for love of George Sand, who is Octave's Brigitte, even to her clothes.   But as the wound scarified with time, at intervals during the next eight years he wrote ten lively, delicate, graceful, and fascinating sketches of young love, to which during the rest of his life he added but one, *The Beauty-Spot* (la Mouche, 1851), which has hardly more than a pathological interest, as of a flickering imagination blazing brightly a moment before its final extinction. We may not care for the sentimental psychology of simultaneous love in *The Two Mistresses* (les Deux maîtresses), but the dash of *Croisilles* is as brilliant as its historic colouring, *Frederic and Bernerette* is a piece of exquisite pathos, a unique blossom in the literature of virginity of heart, *Mimi Pinson* takes us on a charming excursion to the coast of Bohemia, and *The White Blackbird* (le Merle blanc) is the high-water mark of Musset's melancholy irony, a transparent allegory, first of the nipping of his boyhood's aspirations, then of the blighting of his heart at the vanishing of the ideal George Sand that his fancy had conjured for his intoxication. These and nearly all the other tales are founded on observation, and in a sense are human documents; but in his moments of inspiration Musset saw reality with a poet's vision that is all his own.

The oldest of the romantic poets and the first to make his mark in literature was the last to write novels; nor was it by his novels that Lamartine exercised the greatest influence on the development of fiction, but rather on its emotional tone by his *Meditations* of 1820, and on its technic by his epic *Jocelyn* of 1828, while his first and best prose tales date from 1849. *Jocelyn* deals with the loves of the bewitching Laurence for her affinity Jocelyn, a candidate for the priesthood and so vowed to celibacy before he had learned to know the joys that he had forsaken. It is thus, in all but form, a psychologic novel, and its descriptions of country life unmistakably affected the pastoral fiction of George Sand. Moreover, it was from *Jocelyn* and from personal experiences already treated in the *Meditations* that Lamartine drew the materials that he recast, late in life and under stress of circumstances, not at all to their advantage, into the prose tales of *Lucy, Graziella*, and *Raphael*, which he wove into his autobiographical *Confidences* (1849), to be followed by a great number of novels and tales, made to sell and not to read, of which it is charity to be silent.

Raphael and *Graziella*, when they are detached from the setting of fatuous self-admiration in which they were first presented, are seen to be sentimental paraphrases of his verses. He had treated the theme of *Raphael* in the first *Meditations*, and that of *Graziella* ten years later. It is true that Lamartine dates the prose *Graziella* 1829, but also true that, like Hugo, he had " the gift of inaccuracy " and tells us in his preface that he wrote it in 1843. It records an experience of 1821, as *Raphael* does one of 1816, with a curious unconsciousness that his part in them could seem contemptible, and that the fate, at least of Graziella, could provoke indignation as well as pity.

Raphael is the warmed-over gruel of the poet's love for Elvire as told in *The Lake* (le Lac), though with inaccuracies of date and otherwise. Worse than this is the drop of sensual tar in the jar of sentimental honey, and worse than all, the author's fatuous delight at the contemplation of perfections that made his autobiographic hero resemble at once Raphael, Canova, Job, Tasso, Shakspere, Byron, Cæsar, Demosthenes, Cato, and some unnamed " great musician." In short, he was " a Titan of emotion," who required a background of lake and mountains against which to set off his sentiment, and who describes this environment to us with a detail that he ingenuously remarks he was too preoccupied to notice at the time, so that it is plainly both superfluous and impertinent. Lamartine does not make his landscape illustrate emotion, and the story is psychologically unsatisfactory. To know the truth about this poet's young love would aid greatly in understanding his genius, but *Raphael* is meant to mislead rather than to guide us.

Graziella transports us to a fisher's hut on a little island near Naples, where the author is cast ashore and passes the winter evenings in innoculating the weeping family with the sentimental virus of *Paul and Virginia*. There are those to whom the story seems instinct with gentle purity. There are others to whom this narrative of a deliberate seduction by sentiment, ending, after the fashion of *Atala*, in the death of the heroine, seems a sickly aftermath of that intermingling of sentimentality and cerebral voluptuousness in which the eighteenth century produced so many masters. The ethical tone of Lamartine's tales was already in Bernardin, and one is not surprised to learn that this was his favourite author.

Both these tales were praised for their poetic grace and melody, and to a sober taste they seem surcharged with both. But for a time some thought them destined to renew among the youth of 1850 the effect produced on the generation of 1820 by the *Meditations*. Times had changed, however. The weary idealism of 1820 was yielding to an eager materialism that was determined to possess the good things of this world and to enjoy them, a temper that soon translated itself into that social corruption and literary frivolity which provoked the satire of the naturalistic school. Thus in the development of the fiction of the Second Empire Lamartine, like the elder Hugo, changed nothing and checked nothing. Their novels never outgrew the youth of their authors, and were old even when they were new.

CHAPTER IV

BESIDES the literary artists and poets who in various directions enlarged the borders of the romantic novel there was a considerable group of men to whom fiction was less an art than a trade, while others, having achieved a passing success, either suffered eclipse or turned their talent elsewhere. They were often men of genius; some attained a popularity unapproached by any of the writers whom we have as yet studied; and one of them is still probably the most universally read story-teller of the world, though by no means among the great artists of fiction.

Many of the faults that the author of *Monte Cristo* shares with those of *The Wandering Jew* and of *The Memoirs of the Devil* are due to the invention of the *feuilleton*, which was first introduced, possibly by Sue, in the early thirties, and has become an indispensable part of every French journal. This is not the place to inquire the reasons that make Frenchmen desire daily fragments of novels, but that they do desire them is certain, and the effect of that desire on minor novelists and even on the greater caterers to the public was obvious from the first. Where each day demands its "copy" hasty production becomes the rule, and when each fragment must have independent interest and artistic effect the whole suffers from the accentuation of the parts, the attention of the reader is concentrated perforce on details, and this can but influence the author in the conduct of his story. In search of a market for his work he becomes a sort of novelistic restaurateur, serving literary meals daily to order and spicing each dish to suit the palate of his customer.

The passion for the *feuilleton* culminated in the forties, when, as Jules Janin said, "France was overwhelmed by some five or six huge compositions that embraced in their sombre frame-work, earth, heaven, and hell, with all the most deadly passions of the human race." It seemed as though general satiety had challenged the spirit, wit, and invention of the best story-tellers of the time to rival one another in unwholesome studies, each of which effaced the transitory impression of the foregoing. The amount produced was immense. Dumas alone boasts to have issued under his name twelve hundred volumes. Kock, Sue, Soulié and others show lists of portentous length. But what was once easy writing now makes exceedingly hard reading. The most conscientious historian of literature will not subject himself to the futile labor of reading the complete works of Souvestre or of Karr, of Janin or Bernard, or even of Sue and Dumas. It is enough if he have read sufficiently to catch the tone and spirit of these authors, and if he be able to direct the reader to the more characteristic products of their genius.

Unquestioned king among the feuilletonists of this generation, "the greatest inventor of stories in the Western world," the most universal in his interests and sympathies, was Alexandre Dumas, father of the noted dramatist, and son of a gallant general of Napoleon who served with distinction in the Tyrol and in Egypt, but died in neglect in 1806. His grandfather was the Marquis de la Pailleterie,

but his father's legitimacy is not altogether clear, for Dumas
was the name of a full blooded Domingo negress whom the
marquis is said to have married in 1760.   General Dumas
was therefore a mulatto, who returned to France from the
West Indies about 1780, and when his aged father persisted
in a foolish marriage with a woman from the servants' hall,
enlisted in the Queen's Guards under the name of his
mother, Dumas.

Many wonderful tales are told of this man's courage, im-
petuosity, and physical strength.   He married in 1792 an
innkeeper's daughter at Villers-Cotterets, became a general in 1793, provoked the jealousy of Napoleon, was retired in 1801, and returned home to close his adventurous
life with five years of restless inaction.   It was under these
exceptional conditions that his son Alexandre was born,
July 24, 1802.   The child inherited much of the negress-
grandmother's appearance and nature, but also much of the
aristocratic spirit of his marquis grandfather, a contrast and
combination that one notes constantly in his novels.

Dumas's boyhood was passed at Villers-Cotterets.   His
first impressions were of his soldierly father, and then of war
and of the Cossack invasion after Leipzig.   He has painted
his awkward boyhood and calf-love both in his *Memoirs*
and in *Ange Pitou*.   There was talk for a time of educa-
ting him for the Church; but in 1819 he received a strong
literary impulse from a performance of Ducis's version of
Hamlet at Soissons, where he had been apprenticed to a
notary.   Instantly he set about writing a play and schemed
a visit to Paris, which he reached at last in 1823 with
twenty francs and hope for all his patrimony.

In Paris he presently found a livelihood in the household
of the future king, Louis Philippe, and in the next year

his son Alexandre was born, though he had no regular
domestic life till fortune had ceased to smile on him. To
a young author the drama then offered the best opportunity,
so to this he devoted himself almost exclusively, and was
first to ring the tocsin of romantic revolt on the stage with
his *Henry III.* in 1829. His dramas brought him notoriety and wealth, which he spent as soon as won and often
before. He was in the fore-front of the Revolution of
1830, but was too ebullient a republican to find favour with
the Orleanists. He resigned his post in the royal household, and presently began to contribute to the since famous
Revue des deux mondes the first of his historical novels, *Isabelle of Bavaria.* Here his theme is the years that preceded
the coming of the Maid of Orleans, and were to degrade
the French crown to the point where it should owe its
survival to a shepherd girl. But even in such a crisis of
history Dumas does not base his story on any careful study
of anything, but on hasty impressions of the memoirs of
the time, decked out by his exuberant imagination into
scenes that he hoped might resemble those of Scott; and
presently there arose in his mind a scheme for turning the
whole history of France to similar account in a sort of
Comedy of History that should be neither romance nor
history, but something between the two, history for those
who could or would read only romance, and romance for
those who liked, as he said, "to exalt history to the height
of fiction," and let their fancy play around the evidences
of the past.

These historical novels, published under the collective
title of *Chronicles of France*, are decidedly the best work
of this prince of improvisatores. They have no grasp of
character and no psychological insight, but they show

a prodigious imagination, and a wonderful dramatic instinct that fused and recast all materials that fell into the furnace of his imagination. He is a true Jongleur, linking together by the slenderest thread of narrative chaplets of episodes that are by turns frolicsome and wild, extravagant, breathless, and impetuous. They are "chronicles" rather than novels, and consist, as such primitive writing is apt to do, largely of dialogue. In them all women are subordinated to men, character to plot, and everything to action. Milady, his best female character, is so because she is most virile. He skims the surface of history like a light-hearted boy to the last, yet with a power of story-telling that never fails to absorb the reader and excite an intense curiosity.

Arranged in their historical order these "chronicles" begin with *The Bastard of Mauléon* and *Duguesclin*, pass in *Isabelle of Bavaria* to the days of Joan of Arc, and thence in *Queen Margot* to the St. Bartholomew. From that point they succeed one another with comparatively brief intervals through the closing years of the Valois in *The Lady of Monsoreau*, and the early days of the Bourbons in *The Forty-Five*, to Louis XIII. in *The Three Guardsmen*, and the days of Mazarin in *Twenty Years After*, while *The Viscount of Bragelonne* brings us to the early reign of Louis XIV. The setting of that royal sun occupies *The Chevalier of Harmental*, and *A Daughter of the Regent* brings us to the disintegration of society under the childking Louis XV., a subject pursued in *Joseph Balsamo*. Then *The Queen's Necklace* shows us the prosperous days of Marie Antoinette, while in *Ange Pitou* and *The Countess of Charny* we are carried on to the Revolution, with varied aspects of which Dumas deals in *A Chevalier of the Maison-Rouge, The Whites and the Blues, The Companions of Jehu,* and *The Red Rose*, that closes the series of well-nigh an hundred volumes.

In his *Memoirs* Dumas tells us that about the time when he first achieved success as a novelist he was trying to pose as a gloomy René, but suddenly discovered that he had an irrepressible gaiety of style, so that his brightest fancies were stimulated by the hardest labor and came on his dreariest days, — a fact testified to by his *Impressions* of a journey undertaken in 1832 chiefly because his methods of adaptation and annexation of the works of others had made his absence from Paris for a time desirable.

These *Impressions* belong in good part to fiction; they are filled with anecdote, and they have an instinct for the romance of history, seizing instantly on the effective legends of each locality and decking them out with a picturesque humour that is rarely strained or excessive, though the volumes are outrageously padded and betray a rudimentary and perhaps racial notion of literary honesty.

On Dumas's plagiarism volumes have been written, and something must be said of it in any account of him. He was accused of keeping a "novel factory," of buying the work of unknown authors or translators and selling it to publishers under his own name, though in some cases he had not so much as read what he signed. In Quérard's *Literary Cheats Unveiled* (les Supercheries littéraires, 1859) the literary iniquities of Dumas are pursued through the bulk of an ordinary-sized volume, though with an envious injustice that defeats its own purpose. The truth seems to be that Dumas was always willing to buy ideas, and if he used these in novels or plays he regarded himself as their sole author. More than this, he was willing to buy novels and plays written out, and when he had rewritten them

he also claimed their authorship because of the new spirit
and matter that he had infused into them. Thus he bought
sixty pages on *The Chevalier of Harmental* and made from
them four volumes. But more even than this, he was
willing to supply the ideas and let others do the journey-
man-work of composition. Later he became even less
scrupulous, but his multitudinous volumes published during
the forties, including nearly all now read, would fall in one
or another of the categories above, and might be claimed
as in some sense his own. Certain it is that none of
those who claimed to share his honour as well as his profits
were able to produce anything like them, and we know
that Dumas was as facile a composer as he was an industrious penman. " He lived," says Jules Janin, " without a moment's rest. Even while travelling he wrote,
composed, planned. . . . He was a slave of story-telling.
His youth, his whole life, passed in obeying this task-
master — the ogre that swallowed up his genius." There
was no period of his life when he was incapable of intense
application and rapid production. If he employed assis-
tants, at least he got far more out of them than they could
get out of themselves. He gave more than he received.
" Gentlemen," he could proudly respond to his detractors,
" the doors are open for you, the columns are ready. . . .
Write us a *Three Guardsmen*, a *Monte Cristo*. Don't
wait till I am dead to do it. With all the books I have
to write, give me the relaxation of reading yours."

The vanity that Dumas had as an inheritance from
his negro grandmother no doubt made him over-confident
in this squandering of his reputation, powerfully stimulated
as it was by the urgent demands of the Parisian press. Six
newspapers at once besought him for stories after *The*

Chevalier of Harmental had won him fame in 1843, and it was precisely in the three following years that he produced his best work, *Monte Cristo, The Three Guardsmen, Twenty Years After,* and *Queen Margot,* work that he never equalled, and approached only in the next four years with *The Memoirs of a Physician, The Forty-Five, The Viscount of Bragelonne,* and *The Black Tulip,* and later never, save perhaps in the last flash of his genius, *The Whites and the Blues,* of 1868.

In one way or another, by plan, spirit, or creative breath, Dumas was inspirer, adapter, author, or sponsor of some 1200 volumes, which in their present more closely printed form still number 298. The taste of the time was for long novels in daily morsels, where, as Gautier said, "people found the characters so regularly and so long every morning at their bedside that they came to regard them as a part of daily life. . . . I used often to hear men say: 'Monte Cristo has done this or that; I think he was right,' or possibly wrong, just as one would praise or blame the acts of one alive." Thackeray, in a playful letter to Dumas, alludes to this advantage of length: "I like your romances in twenty-one volumes. . . . I have not skipped a word of *Monte Cristo,* and it made me quite happy when, having read eight volumes of the *Three Musqueteers* (*i. e. The Three Guardsmen*), I saw Mr. Roland bring me ten more under the title *Twenty Years After.* May you make Athos, Porthos, and Aramis live an hundred years and treat us to twelve volumes more of their adventures. May the Physician whose Memoirs you have in hand, beginning them at the commencement of the reign of Louis XV., make the fortune of the apothecaries of the revolution of July by his prescriptions."

But if in *feuilletons* the novels gained by length they lose by it when read in volumes, for here their lack of structure and proportion is more obvious, and the " spinning of copy " is seen to be at times mere charlatanry. It is the simple truth to say that Dumas was always willing to sacrifice art to money. He made no secret of it. He was ready to contract for the future delivery of his imagination at fixed date in quantities to suit all purchasers. The childlike frankness of his shamelessness is almost amusing. Pleading in one of his innumerable lawsuits he said in 1847 : " There are forty Academicians. Let them contract to supply you with eighty volumes a year. They will bankrupt you. Alone I have done what never man did before nor ever will again." Or consider this little scene : " Mr. Veron came to me and said : We are ruined if we do not publish in eight days an amusing, sparkling, interesting romance." " You want one volume," I said ; " that will be six thousand lines, thirty-five sheets of my handwriting. Take this pile of paper. Number and head the pages." And the work was done.

As to the quality of such work, Dumas did not for a moment deceive himself. Toward the close of his life he wrote to the Emperor (1864) : " There were in 1830, and there are still, three men at the head of French literature, Hugo, Lamartine, and Myself. Hugo is proscribed, Lamartine ruined. . . . The censorship is against me. I know not why. I have written and published twelve hundred volumes. It is not for me to appreciate them as literature. Translated into all languages they have been as far as steam could carry them. Though the least worthy, these volumes have made me in five continents the most read of the three, perhaps because . . . I am only a vulgariser." Thus

Dumas is a quantity rather than a quality with which we have to reckon, not an artist but an entertainer, a nation's Scheherazade, who greatly extended the domain of French fiction and contributed more than any other to give it a cosmopolitan audience in the great middle class.

His popularity brought him enormous returns, but he was a phenomenon of thriftlessness and was preyed upon in ways that seem almost incredible, for, as his son says, he had the generosity that made him a millionnaire to others and a beggar to himself. He became involved in lawsuits, as costly as they were dishonourable, in regard to contracts that he had signed with thoughtless levity. His palace, Monte Cristo, built at a cost of half a million francs in the heyday of his prosperity (1847), was sold in 1851, and he himself was constrained to seek refuge in Brussels from his creditors. From that year till his death he became a pathetic wanderer in search of peace and " copy," visiting England in 1857, Russia and the Caucasus in 1858, Italy in 1860, and again in 1866. Then came four years of senility and precarious poverty. He was saved from a sordid end only by the persistent solicitude of the son whose boyhood he had neglected and whose youth he had misguided, but who took him rather as a warning than as an example, and, with a genius more steady though less brilliant, came to be the representative of uncompromising morals and unbending probity.

He died in a country house near Dieppe, whither he had been taken from the excitements and dangers of Paris in war time, on the very day of the Prussian occupation (Dec. 5th, 1870). He was solemnly interred in April, 1872, at his old boyhood's home in Villers-Cotterets.

Into a detailed examination of his novels it is impossible

and unnecessary to enter. *Monte Cristo* (1844–5) and *The Three Guardsmen* (les Trois mousquetaires, 1844) typify what is best in all. Here the first impression is of ease and fluency. His work seems, as Michelet said, to move like a natural force; he has an easy and seemingly unnecessary fecundity; he creates needless characters and squanders in a chapter incidents that might suffice for a volume. Ideas come to him as readily as words. The reader soon feels sure that the author's imagination will never leave him in the lurch, and then first begins to note what movement he gives to his story, how lightly he touches and passes, what an instinct he has for the telling situations that will mask his shallow handling of character, for which indeed the mass of his readers cared and care but little.

The Three Guardsmen, that "Iliad of the *feuilleton*," is based on the *Memoirs of Artagnan*, written by Courtils de Sandras early in the eighteenth century, and in themselves by no means dull reading. But though Artagnan is the thread of connection, he is no more the centre of action than Achilles is of the Iliad. That centre, as the new title suggests, is the triple-linked devotion of the Three. "Of your heroic heroes," says Thackeray, "I think our friend Monseigneur Athos, Count de la Fère, is my favourite. I have read about him from sunrise to sunset with infinite contentment of mind. He has passed through how many volumes? Forty? Fifty? I wish for my part there were an hundred more, and would never tire of his rescuing prisoners, punishing ruffians, and running scoundrels through the midriff with his most graceful rapier. Ah, Athos, Porthos, and Aramis, you are a magnificent trio." What matters it that the best scene, Milady tempting her guards to treason, is adapted almost bodily from *The Tower of Nesle* (le Tour de Nesle, 1832)? We feel it was worth the repetition, and the whole story is so full of rush and excitement as quite to disarm sober criticism.

History as we see it here is a phantasmagoria of facts romantically discomposed and distorted, yet we feel that this man, so full of verve, brio, and genius, believed in himself and in his work, over which friends say he showed at times an almost pathetic enthusiasm. Two years before his death his son found him reading *The Three Guardsmen*. "It is good," said the old man, with feeling. "*Monte Cristo* is not up to the *Guardsmen*." And in spite of ourselves we share his enthusiasm. His situations are improbable if not impossible, but he never gives us time to realise it. We are hurried from one hair-breadth 'scape to another. Wanton feats of daring, chivalrous fellowships, bold tricks, jolly pranks bubble through the whole, set off against the sinister background of Milady's plots till she is done to death with healthy thoroughness by the great Three. The morality may not be elevated, but it is sound, hale, and hearty. There are touches of a finer nobility in *Twenty Years After*, and the stealthy step of age introduces a vein of pathos into *The Viscount of Bragelonne*, where the dying Artagnan says "Au revoir" to Athos and Porthos, and to Aramis "Good-bye for ever." And yet for all that they cannot match *The Three Guardsmen*.

Monte Cristo, like the story of Artagnan, was founded on an earlier novel, Penchet's *A Diamond and a Vengeance*, in itself, as Dumas said, " an idiotic tale," whose possibilities he elaborated with the aid of Maquet, one of his novelistic journeymen. The island of Monte Cristo was a real one that he had examined in 1841 when cruising as the guest of Jérôme Bonaparte. The hand of Maquet lies heavy on

the opening chapters of *Monte Cristo*, but the spirit of
Dumas enters with Dantès into the prison of the Château
d'If, and from that moment the whole pulses brisk with
excitement, dramatic situation, chivalry, gallantry, and wit.
He gives free rein to his imagination to picture an orgy of
wealth, as though to outbid Sue and Soulié at their own
game.   He conceives a society in which gold shall be the
universal factor, only to drive his hero to the conclusion
that matter is unconquerable, so that Monte Cristo is fain
to take refuge in hashish, as Sue's hero does in opium,
from the weariness of satiety.   Thus *Monte Cristo* has a
less tonic moral than *The Three Guardsmen*, and the central figure is not psychologically consistent.   A Dantès
could never have become such a man as the Count, who
forfeits the sympathy he had won when he pushes a righteous vengeance beyond the verge of spiteful cruelty.   Our
first wish, as some one has said, is that the last five volumes
had been condensed to two ; our afterthought a regret that
they were written at all.

When Dumas began to write fiction the historical novel
was budding with brilliant promise at the hands of Vigny,
Mérimée, and Hugo, under the inspiration of Walter Scott.
Dumas blighted it, for it is a genre that cannot bear vul-
garisation.   That was the extent of his contribution to the
development of fiction as an art.   But his success in the
trade of novel-writing evoked a cloud of imitators who have
strutted and fretted for brief hours of popular applause, and
passed away forever to the limbo of the back shelves of the
provincial circulating libraries.

The best of these was surely Marie Joseph (Eugène)
Sue, a man of great though ill-balanced genius, and second
only to Dumas among the heroes of the *feuilleton* in

rapidity of production, fertility of imagination, and prodigal carelessness of execution. In 1831 he had launched on the crest of the romantic wave *Atar Gull*, a novel of the sea, a subject little cultivated in France since Gomberville. For this he had gathered his inspiration, and the then indispensable "local colour" on a three years' naval cruise. He had a gift of story-telling, a vivid and popular style, but from the first he wrote in a sort of romantic vertigo, recklessly mingling tragic and comic, the pathetic and the grotesque, with an inexhaustible fund of gaiety and rapidly growing power of picturesque description.

About 1835 Sue, who had been hailed as the French Cooper, had his head so turned by aristocratic adulation that he caught the infection that came from contact with Chateaubriand. In *Cécile* (1835) he shows the first symptoms of the sickness of the age, and he passed the next five years in an intermittent fever of snobbery, that reached its crisis in *The Marquis of Letorières* (1839). This was followed by a violent democratic reaction, due in part to his disgust at his equivocal position in a society that patronised him, in part to his debts, in part to the socialistic propagandism of Proudhon and Fourier.

He turned his conversion to good commercial account, and it is the work of this period alone that survives. His long socialistic novels in the cheap newspapers won such hold on the masses that the government actually sought to check or control his activity. As a critic of the day said, he was entering on an unexplored path, he was undertaking to paint the sufferings and needs of the working classes with the intent of influencing them politically. "M. Sue has been called the novelist of the sea. To-day he has named himself the novelist of the people." Thus he gave the novel an audience and an interest that it had never yet had in its history.

His enthusiasm in his new task was indefatigable, and in *The Mysteries of Paris* (les Mystères de Paris, 1842), he has created popular types, Fleur de Marie, Le Chourineur, the Schoolmaster, La Louve, and the rest, that still have power to horrify or to charm, though perhaps none of them have the uncanny fascination of Rodin, the dirty, shrewd, relentless, chaste, and diabolical Jesuit of *The Wandering Jew* (le Juif errant, 1844–5). It is curious to note, however, that, throughout, Sue's humanitarianism is paradoxically associated with a sort of cynical hedonism, as we see at the close of *The Wandering Jew*, and with a belief in the saving power of the five-franc-piece as strong as that of Balzac ; and it is probable that this reacted on the novels of Dumas, especially on *Monte Cristo*.

In one regard, and in one only, Sue is Dumas's superior. He has greater command of the resources of terror. As careless in style, as melodramatic in situations, as prolix as Dumas, he is, at least in later novels, more earnest, but he is far inferior to Dumas in variety of interest, in vivacity of dialogue, and in geniality of conception. Together Dumas and Sue made the *feuilleton* an integral part of the French newspaper ; but before we trace its further fortunes we may remark in passing that the socialistic novel, inaugurated by Sue and glorified by Hugo in *Les Misérables*, had violent hands laid on it by Félix Pyat, and is now barely convalescent under the gentle nursing of Léon Cladel, while the satirical aspects of the agitation that culminated in 1848 found voice in Reybaud's two novels, *Jérôme Paturel in Search of a Social Position* (1843) and *Jérôme Paturel in Search of the Best Republic* (1848). These stories, now almost forgotten, are among the most interesting efforts of our century to turn the novel to political account, and suggest in many ways the *Tales* of Voltaire.

The oldest of the group of writers who without high literary ideals or care for literary art aided Dumas and Sue in popularizing the novel was Paul de Kock, whose name, like that of Pigault Lebrun, an earlier successor of Restif de la Bretonne, carries with it a suggestion of frivolity but also a savour of gaiety, of the quips and cranks and wanton wiles of youth, that must have been a welcome refreshment to readers weary of the descendants of René and of Obermann, whose melancholy had threatened for a time to eclipse the normal Gallic spirit. Socially, too, the novels of Kock are in sharp contrast to those of Chateaubriand, Staël, and the romanticists. They are bourgeois, democratic, vulgar even, but they are not immoral. They demand no literary training, they gratify no delicate taste. His hundred volumes passed almost unnoticed by the critics, but they were very popular during the Restoration and the Orleanist régime, that period of well-fed ease in which the commercial class sought repose rather than stimulus in fiction, as they did in the dramas of Scribe. As typical of the bourgeois taste of their time *The Barber of Paris* (le Barbier de Paris), *André the Savoyard*, *Gus the Unruly* (Gustave le mauvais sujet), and *The Milkmaid of Montfermeil* (la Laitière de Montfermeil), still merit the attention of the student.

Another voluminous novelist, whose work falls between 1837 and 1860, is Joseph Méry, whose specialty is exotic landscape, done with such lively fancy that it is said many were lured by the mirage of his imagination to visit India and China, countries that the novelist had never

seen.   Even more rapid was the production of Frédéric
Soulié, who may be justly called a victim of the *feuilleton*,
for he had talent.   He gives us in his *Memoirs of the Devil*
(les Memoires du diable, 1837) the extreme of romantic
horror and barbarity, after the manner of Hugo's *Han of
Iceland*, and was for a time very popular, though his work
contains nothing to promise or justify a revival of his
reputation.

A more deplorable victim of the *feuilleton* was Léon
Gozlan, among the most fantastic and eccentric of the
romantic novelists, with a fancy stimulated by foreign travel
and a vein of delicate satire.   His *Aristide Froissart* (1843)
and *The Emotions of Polydore Marasquin* suggest that he
would have done more had he done less, and might indeed
have achieved a permanent place in French literature.

Perhaps the best representative of the individualistic
vagaries of romanticism, whether we regard his style or his
thought, is Jules Janin, whose later novels still have charm
for dainty spirits.   The author calls them " idylls with
court-plaster patches."   Stories like *The Nun of Toulouse*
(la Réligieuse de Toulouse, 1850), or *Country Gaieties* (les
Gaietés champètres, 1851), seem like Dresden china reproductions of the days of Louis XV., fragile, not natural,
yet charming.   His earlier novels are trivial and ultra-
romantic.

Another prodigy of fecundity is Émile Souvestre, who
from 1835 to his death averaged three volumes a year of
almost unvarying mediocrity.   He comes to us burdened
with the title of the schoolmaster in literature, for he
strove to make his novels useful, and naturally made them
prosy.   At his best, when dealing with his native Brittany
in *The Last Bretons* (les Derniers brétons, 1835–7) and *The*

Breton Hearth (le Foyer bréton, 1844), he is still readable, but he has more of the seriousness than of the poetic fancy of his race.

In such early stories of Alphonse Karr as *Under the Willows* (Sous les tilleuls, 1832) we feel something of the romantic passion of George Sand's *Indiana*. Sentiment is pushed to morbid intensity. His later and very numerous novels, of which any volume taken at random will give the tone, show rather a fantastic and stinging humour that half justified the comparison he invited with the Aristophanes of *The Wasps*. His earlier manner was continued by Arsène Houssaye, who produced a huge mass of individually insignificant novels. They all have some wit, but their common characteristic is rather a sentimental smile that degenerates easily and frequently into a tearful smirk.

Decidedly more robust, perhaps because less prolific, are Bernard and Sandeau. The latter had much in common with George Sand, with whom he had collaborated, but to her romantic talent and psychologic intuition he added a keener sense of humour and a greater faculty of patient observation. He took for his domain the rich bourgeois whom the revolution of 1830 had brought to the front politically, while leaving them still aspirants for social recognition by a poor but proud aristocracy. This conflict between the emigrant nobles and the purchasers of their confiscated estates, and its effect on their character, is the common subject of *Mlle. de la Seiglière* (1848), *Green-bags and Parchments* (Sacs et parchemins, 1851), *The Mansion of Penarvan* (la Maison de Penarvan, 1858). This social conflict still interests, because in altered form it still exists; and so, though Sandeau never achieved a brilliant success as a novelist, his reputation has shown a vigorous life. He is soundly virile yet sunny, cheerful, and charming, and a delightful painter of landscape. His morality joined to his graceful and sympathetic irony have commended him particularly to the feminine arbiters of the novelist's fate, but to all who wish to understand the social movement under Louis Philippe he will be an essential supplement on a single side to the universal genius of Balzac.

The first avowed disciple of Balzac was Charles de Bernard, but he was so inapt a pupil that he resembles rather Paul de Kock. His novels and tales show a curious intermingling of the romantic hair-breadth 'scape, the hidden closet, the secret drawer, and the solitary horseman with realistic pictures of the society of 1840. He has good intentions, but no insight into character, little patience and less genius. One thinks of him less as a great novelist than as a pleasant time-killer, yet he cannot be passed over, for he helped to prepare the public for the radical naturalism of the next generation. His longer novels do not hold the attention, and they irritate at times by a moral callousness, but his five volumes of short stories have proved a mine to later novelists, who have read and used more than they have acknowledged.

It is said that when, in the heyday of romanticism, the more sober of its friends urged Xavier de Maistre to reproduce for them the charm of his *Young Siberian Girl*, he called their attention to an obscure professor of rhetoric, Rudolphe Topffer of Geneva, who, he said, might spare his labour and satisfy their desire. This stimulus produced the *Genevese Tales* (1840) and two novels, all simple and yet artistic in construction, somewhat archaic in style, as befits the city of Protestant refugees, witty and sound, yet with a childlike fancy and play of sentiment as fresh as Alpine hay.

Topffer's shrewd observation is salted with humour and inter-penetrated with Christian grace and charity, so that to read him is, as Sainte-Beuve said, one of the sweetest, most winning, and healthiest of literary pleasures.

A curious interest attaches to the fiction of Barbey d'Aurevilly, most eccentric of romantic degenerates, full of obscure and bizarre affectations and aristocratic virtuosity, but falling at the close of his literary activity under strange hallucinations of moral perversion of which the interest is pathological rather than literary. Of his earlier manner, *The Bewitched* (l'Ensorcelée, 1854) may serve as a type; of the latter, *The Possessed* (les Diaboliques, 1874).

It remains to speak of two one-volume novelists, Claude Tillier and Xavier Saintine. The former is remembered solely for *My Uncle Benjamin* (Mon oncle Benjamin, 1843), a book whose circle of readers, never large, shows no signs of diminution. It is a piece of genial satire, neither strong nor deep, but not unworthy to be classed with Topffer's *Genevese Tales*, as of like though not equal merit. Saintine was a far more productive writer, who during twenty-eight years of tireless writing had a brief moment of inspiration in which it was given him to conceive *Picciola*, a story that brought him a decoration, the Montyon prize, and a place in the gentle hearts of his generation, who have handed down its fragrant memory as a tradition to ours. It is the story of a prisoner and a flower, tender yet sound in its pathos, sentimental but not mawkish. It has been immensely popular, and is perhaps still much read, though like many other popular books it has not influenced the writers who influenced in their turn, and so the effect of its thousands of readers on the development of fiction is almost as imperceptible as that of the fairy tales of Laboulaye.

CHAPTER V

BALZAC is the greatest novelist of France, and perhaps of the world. In greater measure than it is given to most writers to realise their ideals, he was what he aspired to be, — "the secretary of society;" and the fifty volumes of his *Comédie humaine* are indeed "an illumination thrown upon life," or rather on three lives, — on the life of the Empire, of the Restoration, and of the Orleanist monarchy, in all their varied manifestations both of ages and of states. With certain reserves and obvious exceptions it may be said that his Scenes of Private Life are studies in the psychology of normal youth, those of the Provinces are typical of middle life, while the few studies of country life seem concerned with old age. But all his types are influenced by occupation, and Balzac's *Comédie*, beginning thus as a comedy of character, turns in the Scenes of Parisian Life and still more obviously in the Scenes of Military and Political Life into a comedy of states, while both are supplemented by the analytic studies on the conjugal relation and by the much more numerous "philosophic studies," in which the author deals with various forms of mental and moral divagation and monomania.

To produce this social comedy Balzac created something more than two thousand characters, all of whom seem to have had as real an existence in his mind as the men who lived and moved about him. There are times when he seems almost under an hallucination, a clairvoyant in whom the imagination has taken possession of the senses and the visions become more real than the reality. That story of Jules Sandeau telling Balzac of his sister's illness, to whom the novelist listens for a time only to interrupt with the remark, "All that's very well, my friend, but let's come back to reality; let's talk about Eugénie Grandet," can be paralleled by a score of passages from his familiar correspondence. Thus his characters become so real to him that their least actions are characteristic of their nature, and recall all that we know of them. Their fortunes are so interlinked with one another that they seem to constitute of themselves a complete microcosm, of which it is possible to compile in all seriousness, as Christophe and Cerfbeer have done, a biographical dictionary.

Of course in a work so vast all is not completed nor is all of equal merit. As Zola has said in a finely sustained metaphor : —

"The *Comédie humaine* is like a Tower of Babel that the hand of the architect did not have and would never have had time to finish. Some of its walls seem as though they would crumble for age and cumber the ground with their débris. The workman has used all materials that fell under his hand, plaster, cement, stone, marble, even sand and mud from the ditch ; and with his strong arms and with these materials taken at hazard he has erected his edifice, his gigantic tower, without always heeding harmony of lines or balanced proportion in his work. You seem to hear him panting in his workshop, cutting the blocks with heavy mallet-blows, indifferent to grace and delicacy of outline. You seem to see him mounting heavily the staging, building here a great, bare, rough wall, and there erecting colonnades of a serene majesty, making porticos and peristyles, of plaster and of marble, that human pride has sought to raise to heaven, and whose unfinished walls already cover the ground. Black cavities appear in this series of superposed storeys. Here and there a cornice is gone. A few winter rains have sufficed to make the plaster crumble that in his haste the workman too often used. But all the marble stands firm, all .the colonnades, all the friezes are there intact, widened, whitened by time. The workman has built his tower with such an instinct of the great and eternal that the body of the edifice will probably remain always entire. Walls may crumble, floors may sink, stairways may fall, but the stone courses will resist still, the great tower will rise as clear, as high, supported on the broad bases of its giant columns. Little by little all that is mud and sand will pass away, and then the marble body of the monument will appear still on the horizon like the silhouette of a great city."

In this truly titanic task Balzac lived absorbed in great measure, though his recently published correspondence shows that he found time, how we can hardly conceive, for various other attachments, as well as for the love for Madame Hanska that began in 1829 and lasted till his death in 1850. Nor do the fifty volumes of fiction produced during this period, though representing an average production of six hundred words a day, besides the labour of proof-reading, which Balzac made almost equivalent to re-composition, represent by any means his whole literary productivity. There are still to be reckoned the two volumes of dramas, a large number of critical articles and letters, the Rabelaisian *Droll Stories*, and some thirty volumes of unsigned youthful fiction, part of which was produced in collaboration with others, and none of it acknowledged by the author or now included in his works. And yet, though it might seem that here, if ever, it could be said that a man's writings were his biography, we shall find in the circumstances of Balzac's early life some elements essential to the comprehension of his novels; and to this therefore we first turn.

Balzac was born on the sixteenth of May, 1799, at Tours, and of typical Touranian stock, epicurean, pantagruelistic, except for the humour, and not at all literary. The family was in comfortable circumstances. Honoré was the first of four children, one of whom died young, and another " left his country for his country's good " and fades from sight in the colonies. The third and the only one important to us is Laura, the first intimate friend of Honoré, and to the last the most sympathetic of all, the confidante to whom, at least in early life, he pours out his whole heart; and it was she who rescued his memory from ghoulish gossip and to whom we owe a rational knowledge of his arduous beginnings. It is she who tells us that Honoré's father was a combination of Montaigne, Rabelais, and Uncle Toby, and that his mother, who was rich, beautiful, and much younger than her husband, had " a vivacious imagination, a tenacious will, and unwearied activity," which seems to be a dutiful way of saying that she was nervous, domineering, and fussy. The first four years of his life were spent with a foster mother in the country. When he returned to Tours he showed no cleverness at school and found no appreciation at home. At seven he went to a clerical school, where he remained till he was fourteen, when he was brought home, apparently in a state of nervous prostration, with which, however, his teacher averred that study could not possibly have had anything to do.

Of this school life Balzac has left us an interesting and, in places, pathetic picture in *Louis Lambert*. He had him-

self while there written that essay "On the Will" that he
attributes to his friend, and he never quite forgave the
teacher who burned it, to punish him for his neglect of pre-
scribed duty.   At home he became for a time a diligent
pupil of the Truant School (*l'école buissonnière*), interpene-
trating his nature with the placid breadth and rich fertility
of the Touranian landscape, with its sparkling river Loire,
its terraced vineyards, the noisy cooper-shops of Saint-Sym-
phorien, and the ruin of Plessis, that he was himself to do
so much to make a familiar word to all readers of the *Droll
Stories*.   The influence of these years can be felt through all
his work, and it was never stronger perhaps than at the
very last.

It was in these years at Tours that he began to have what
his sister calls the intuition of renown, that is, the consciousness that he had a literary vocation ; and he had no sooner
reached this stage than a kind literary providence took him
with his parents to Paris (1814), which remained his residence for the rest of his life, though his father was constrained to leave it in 1819.   Here he continued his education, and presently came into contact with the intellectual
lights of the Sorbonne, Guizot, Villemain, and Cousin, who
stimulated greatly his literary activity.   For three years he
studied law, an apprenticeship without which he could
hardly have written several of his novels, and more especially *César Birotteau*.   But he refused to practise, much
to the chagrin of his father, who had lost his post and the
greater part of his property.   The family relations became
strained as the first efforts at literary expression proved
quite without success.   His parents lost faith and patience.
The pressure of poverty evokes from him a pathetic cry.
He does not doubt his vocation, but he doubts his power.

" I am young and hungry," he writes, " and there is nothing on my plate. Laura, Laura : — my two boundless desires, my only ones — to be famous and to be loved — will they ever be satisfied ! "

And now follows a period of ten years (1819–1829), which so far as accomplishment is concerned is negligible, but not so if we would watch the development of the writer's genius. They taught him his trade, the manipulation of the novelistic tools. Of thought he never had lack, but fluent expression he was slow in acquiring, and the careful reader will feel that, though he took infinite pains, he rarely satisfied himself. " Do not read that," he said to a friend who had one of these early volumes in his hand, " I have in my head novels that I think are good, but I do not know when they may be able to get out of it." The fourteen romances of these years appeared under various pseudonyms, and were classified by contemporary criticism with those of Pigault-Lebrun and Restif. Perhaps the most interesting thing about them is the premonition in a preface to the *Vicar of Ardennes* in 1822 of the co-ordination of a series of novels such as he afterward realised in the *Human Comedy*, as well as the stubborn persistency that such a conception of the novel implies. For here he invites his readers to note well the characters that he introduces, since, as he tells them, they will have to follow their fortunes through thirty novels to come ; and though this was in that case without even the beginning of a fulfilment, yet it shows the cyclopean character of his imagination, that after these years of prodigal effort suddenly revealed itself capable of lofty and sustained flight.

Of the struggles, hardships, and disappointments of these ten years the letters preserved in the correspondence bear an often pathetic witness. He writes under pressure always, and always with the feeling that there is in his mind more than he has power to express. Yet even in poverty and while harassed with debts, he shows himself at times the victim of overmastering caprices, though at times capable of a sustained intensity of labour that is quite marvellous. He begrudges the time that he spends in letter-writing, and still more the time that he must devote to the care of his bachelor household, " economising his steps" that he may have more time to write and gradually to attain a position where he can sign himself " Honoré, public scrivener and French poet at two francs a page." His unsigned novels, in four volumes each, begin to pay him two, three, even four hundred dollars, but always in notes not readily negotiable. He got no cash for his work till toward the close of this period, and meantime he had got himself deeper in debt than ever, so that in 1827 we find him working on *The Chouans* (les Chouans) " with a tired brain and an anxious mind," with eight or ten business letters that he must write every day before he could sit down to his work, and feeling that the demands of his family were " as unreasonable as it would be to disturb a founder during a casting." " Postage and an omnibus are extravagances that I cannot allow myself," he writes ; " I stay at home so as not to wear out my clothes. Is that clear?" he says with vexation as late as 1827 ; and though during the next two years his letters show that he is beginning to form stimulating literary friendships, it was as an author rich only in hope and with thirty-five mediocre volumes to outlive that he made his first acknowledged literary venture.

In *The Chouans* the unique genius of Balzac was first apparent, more apparent than in work written during the

two succeeding years, if indeed it be true, as he states, that
the book was finished in 1827. A greater gulf separates
it from anything printed before 1830 than from anything
that follows. And yet the novel has glaring defects, and
not a few of them. The attempt to imitate Scott is more
obvious than successful, the descriptions are far too long
and too numerous, and the plot, though said to be founded
on fact, is almost ludicrously romantic, — a fact that has
made this novel one of the most popular with the masses.
What shall we say of a heroine, a republican spy, who " had
seen life pass till then like an unattainable shadow that she
had always wished to seize. Having sown with full hand
and reaped nothing, she remained a virgin, irritated by
a multitude of deceived desires. Then, weary of a contest
without adversaries, she came in her despair to prefer good
to evil when it offered pleasure, evil to good when it offered
poetry, misery to mediocrity as something more grandiose,
the unknown future of death to a life poor in hopes or even
in sufferings." This is romanticism reduced to the absurd.
And as though this were not enough, there is the impossible
lover, Montauran, and Corentin, the police agent with the
basilisk green eyes, as the readers of our dime-novels know
him, a warning example unheeded even by the great Hugo,
not at all the grandiose conception of the same character in
later novels.

But on the other hand, in its resuscitation of the Brittany
of 1799, *The Chouans* is one of the first and best of the
historical novels of France. Some scenes, with not a few
conversations and observations by the way, are of the best,
and quite worthy of Balzac's genius. And yet, in spite of
this success, Balzac turned resolutely from the battle-fields
of history to those of domestic life, convinced that for the

task he already felt before him he must pass through an apprenticeship in the miniature work of a Memmling or the petty realism of a Gerard Dow before he could presume to paint the gigantic frescos of passion.

So in November, 1829, we find Balzac writing to his publisher: " I work all day on the *Physiology of Marriage*, and give only six hours of the night (from nine to two) to the *Scenes of Domestic Life*, of which I have only to correct the proofs. . . . I am ready to send the necessary copy to finish the 15th if you wish, but we should have committed the most odious assassination on a book. . . . It's a matter of selling inked paper at seven or at fifty francs a ream. I work as zealously and as steadily as any human creature can, but I am only the very humble servant of the muse, and that minx pouts sometimes."

To this intense labour Balzac was constrained by debts, amounting in 1828 to 120,000 francs, and discharged with scrupulous honour, though constantly renewed by the extravagant whimsicalities of the now popular author. He was hardly ever free from the pressure of debt until the closing years of his life. At times he had been perilously near bankruptcy, and in 1828 had been saved from it only by the generous aid of Madame de Berny, a woman who exercised perhaps the strongest moral influence, after his mother and sister, on the early development of his character. " In my greatest troubles she sustained me by words and deeds," he writes: " that which she had already roughly moulded in me I work now to complete." Madame Firmiani and, above all, Madame de Mortsauf in *The Lily in the Valley* are monuments of pious love erected to her memory. For she passed speedily from Balzac's life, falling sick in 1834 and dying in 1836.

Balzac regarded the *Physiology of Marriage* then and for several years later with a complacency that his critics cannot share. It is a rather shallow monograph on adultery, redeemed by a few keen observations and well-told stories, adding nothing to the reputation of the author and interesting chiefly for its early date. But at this very time he was doing in the *Scenes of Domestic Life*, six stories published in April, 1830, work of a far higher order, while he had begun also a novel on Cardinal Mazarin that he never found occasion to finish.

In January of 1830 Balzac printed *El Verdugo* (Spanish for " The Executioner "), a brief contribution to the shudder in literature, from the war of Spanish independence. The conception of a family feeling so overmastering that a father shall beg his son to be a parricide, that brothers and sisters shall join in the prayer, and that the son shall accede to their wish, to save the family name, is an idea so romantic that only the greatest artistic restraint could make it tolerable. Balzac has made it worthy of admiration.

This was followed by *Gobseck*, the first of those marvellous studies of avarice, morbid visions of the power of wealth and of its cancerous grip on the soul, that resulted not unnaturally from his financial anxieties and hungry imagination. Even old Grandet, though painted in more detail, is hardly a more remarkable picture of miserly degeneration than this Dutch Parisian Jew, while in the death-bed of Count Restaud Balzac has given us one of the most ghastly scenes of horror to be found in all fiction.

Together with *Gobseck* during February, 1830, Balzac had been writing his first *Study of Woman* (Étude de femme), a little story of feminine pique that calls for no further notice, and April brought five scenes of private life to make up with *Gobseck* the two volumes first published under that title. These bear various dates, from July, 1829, to February, 1830; but as we know that Balzac changed much in his proofs, suggesting in one case to his publisher that it would be cheaper to have the whole work composed anew, it is wiser throughout to follow the order of publication, for, so far as we can see, Balzac never finished anything till it was published, and felt his reputation in peril if he did not see two or even three sets of proofs.

Of these five scenes, the first in time, *Domestic Peace* (la Paix de ménage), dated July, 1829, seems to have been composed under less sombre conditions than *Gobseck* or *El Verdugo*, for, though it is the first of Balzac's many studies of the effect of adultery on domestic life, we have here, what is quite the exception with him, an attempt at comedy and a happy ending. Perhaps we are to attribute this to his growing intimacy with the Duchess of Abrantès, to whom he now begins to write familiarly.

The Cat and the Racket (la Maison du chat-qui-pelote) of October, 1829, stands in striking contrast to anything that the author had at that time done or attempted, and witnesses also to a mind less racked and strained than the crowded productions of 1830, '31, and '32. Its opening scene is a masterly description of a draper's shop under the still simple conditions of commerce in Napoleon's day, when clerks dined at the master's table and left it humbly before the dessert was served, while, as in the Germany of Freytag's *Soll und Haben*, each member of the household had an active share in the business. The heart of this story is in the relation of the artist, Sommervieux, to Angélique, whose love he first returns, then tolerates, then spurns, as she had done the love of her father's clerk Joseph, who marries her sister Virginie — and the business. This sensible couple " live happy ever after," while Angélique, afflicted by the counsels of mother, sister, and rival, sinks faithful and sorrowing to an early grave. The story is brief and admirable in its restrained strength. It has flashes of insight that in one of Balzac's then age and experience seem clairvoyant. He was to plead often for conventional marriage, but seldom with more eloquence than in this story, which alone should have revealed him to his generation as their master in social psychology.

A far slighter thing is *The Ball at Sceaux* (le Bal de Sceaux), weak in its analysis of overweening girlish pride, but interesting as the first of many attempts to bring the new social ideals into effective contrast with those inherited from the old social régime. Then in *The Vendetta* the cloud that we felt in *Gobseck* casts its shadow over a sad tale of the struggle of love with poverty and with the satanic intensity of Corsican passion. As markedly romantic and even more luridly intense is the later part of *A Double Family* (une Double famille), of which the earlier portion had drawn a prettily romantic picture of the ideal grisette and the primrose path of unrecognized connections. This opening, however, sinks into insignificance beside the strength of the close, where with terrible concision we are shown the poison that a bigoted wife and a meddlesome priest can cast over domestic life. The analysis may be no keener here than in *The Cat and the Racket*, but the flashes of genius are more frequent and the author seems to grow more conscious of his power.

Almost at the same time with these scenes of private life there was published *The Two Dreams* (les Deux rêves), said to have been written in 1828 and now forming the third part of *Catherine de' Medici* (Sur Catherine de Médicis). This defence of the Massacre of Saint Bartholomew is curiously interpenetrated with the spirit of the Italian renascence, but it calls for no extended notice. Then in May appeared *Adieu*, a masterpiece of tragic pathos, and containing in its picture of the passage of the Beresina during the retreat from Moscow one of the four or five great military pictures in all French literature, a picture whose accumulated horrors might·well have produced the pathetic madness of its heroine. She recovers only to die and to leave her lover no escape from memory but suicide. Here at the outset of his mature career the gloomy strength of Balzac's genius already touches its climax.

Amid a mass of journalistic work, of which the titles alone occupy two octavo pages, Balzac produced also during this year in October *The Elixir of Long Life* (l'Elixir de longue vie), a fantastic story adapted from the German of Hoffmann just at that culmination of French romanticism when, as Balzac says, "every author was ' doing the atrocious ' to please the young ladies." His Don Juan was meant to be a universal mocker, and the story, as an orgy of fantastic hypocrisy, is a *tour de force* of considerable power.

November brought *Sarrasine*, of which it may suffice to say that its scene is Italy and its subject the unnatural love of a French sculptor for a *castrato* singer, a situation possibly suggested by the memoirs of Casanova. Then in December comes an equally curious study of unnatural love, *A Passion in the Desert* (une Passion dans le désert), a subject to which Balzac recurred again in *The Girl with the Golden Eyes* (la Fille aux yeux d'or, 1834).

The former tale was originally intended to form part of a novel on the French in Egypt. Its description of the desert, "all and nothing, God without mankind," renders superbly the moral oppression of solitude, and the little tale as a whole is a cameo that intensifies our regret that it must remain a fragment. Of the same month (December) is *An Episode during the Terror* (une Épisode sous la terreur), a philosophic study of the effect that such a death as that of Louis XVI. might produce on the mind of his executioner, and also of the purification of religious feeling by persecution. Balzac had as yet written nothing so exquisite. His sympathies, here as always, were with throne and altar, for if in *The Two Dreams* he had seemed to condone for a moment the crimes of the Terror it was only that he might show the admiration of talent for unswerving will and the instinctive hatred of genius for mediocrity.

During this year, especially through the influence of the noted journalist Girardin, of his wife Delphine, and of her mother Sophie Gay, Balzac was extending his acquaintance among the aristocrats of literature and the young romantic royalists who united in dislike of the bourgeois king and the Revolution of 1830. In the Salon of the Girardins Balzac met Hugo, Vigny, Lamartine, George Sand, Thiers, and other men and women of note, then or later, and contributed with others to the literary feast there. With these allies he ventured on journalism, an experience that he put later to excellent use in the *Lost Illusions*. Toward the close of the year he had won a foothold in the staff of the *Revue de Paris*, to which he presently joined the *Revue des deux mondes*, and by the spring of 1831, though he relaxed nothing in the intensity of his labour, he felt justified in indulging his talent in a little of that love of luxury that seemed to him essential to the evoking of his highest powers.

An important influence entered his life during this year, in the form of an anonymous correspondent who proved to be Madame de Castries, a complete aristocrat and semi-invalid, whose character Balzac has given us without much flattery in the *Duchess of Langeais*. It was through her that he came to know that part of the unreconstructed aristocracy that remained faithful to the ideals of the Old Régime more even than to those of the Restoration, just as the intervening aristocracy of the Napoleonic period had been represented to him by the Duchess of Abrantès and Madame Gay. It was at Madame de Castries' suggestion that he made in the next year (1832) a journey to Switzerland, which resulted in a cooling of their relations; but this is to anticipate, for Balzac did not come to know Madame de Castries personally till March, 1832.

Madame Gay and the two duchesses helped Balzac socially; the more steadfast Madame Carraud exercised at first a very considerable political influence upon him. It was at her suggestion that he now began to study social politics, and even became at the close of 1830 a candidate for the Assembly. It was with her that he discussed by preference and most ingenuously such books as his *Country Doctor*. Meantime, amid these varied influences, and vexed by quarrels with publishers whom he vexed, he was pouring out a mass of work that may seem incredible if one regards its quality and its elaboration. To accomplish this he was obliged to deny himself to visitors and even to correspondents for considerable intervals, and to remain in seclusion for long periods. Of his daily life the correspondence gives frequent hints, and his publisher Werdet supplements them with a picture of his daily life as he saw it in Paris. "He usually went to bed at eight after a very light dinner, and would almost always be sitting at his desk by two in the morning. Till six his quick lively pen (he always used a quill) ran full speed over the paper with an electric sputtering. . . . At six he entered his bath for an hour. At eight he took a cup of coffee without sugar. Then I was admitted to bring him proofs or take away the corrected ones and to get parcels of manuscript from him if I could. Composition was then taken up with like zeal till noon," when he breakfasted frugally and worked from one to six. From seven to eight he would see friends, and so he would live for six weeks or two months, and then plunge into society again, like a bee among flowers.

When away from Paris he worked with equal intensity. We hear of him in 1831 at Nemours, the scene of *Eugénie Grandet*, and with Madame Carraud at Saché. He spent the larger part of 1832 here and at Angoulême, Lyons, and Switzerland, even planning a journey to Italy, which pressing proof-sheets compelled him to abandon. In 1833 we find him again at Angoulême, and later at Neuchâtel, where he first met Madame Hanska, who was finally to be his wife and had been an anonymous correspondent since 1829. Indeed he is constantly travelling, again in Switzerland in 1834, at Vienna in 1835, in 1838 in Sardinia, and in 1839 in Italy and Austria.

We are now in a position to study Balzac's work with such light as the correspondence may throw upon it from 1831 to his quarrel with the *Revue de Paris* in 1836. This work begins, so far as it concerns us here, with fragments of *The Woman of Thirty* and parts of *The Accursed Child* and of *Droll Stories*, all to be noted later. Then in February came *The Recruit* (le Réquisitionnaire), a sad story of hope deferred, of agonising suspense and mocking despair, ending in heart-broken death, very good of its romantic kind, which is still that of *The Elixir* and *Adieu*, while its subject associates it with *An Episode under the Terror*. This was followed in May with *The Exiles*, where the mysticism of Dante and of the French philosopher Sigier is interpenetrated with a wonderfully vivid evocation of the Paris of 1308 and its university life. The story has always been "caviare to the general" though it is one of the strongest works of Balzac and one of the most profound; and it is doubly interesting to the critic because here first we see the gate ajar that he was to open into the spiritual world in *Louis Lambert* and in the ecstatic visions of his wonderful *Séraphita*.

The Unknown Masterpiece (le Chef-d'œuvre inconnu), that followed in July and was revised in 1837 with the collaboration of Gautier, takes up the psychic fact that Zola was afterward to make the theme of his *Work* (l'Œuvre), that an artistic ideal by its very intensity of conception may defeat its own execution. Thus this little sketch forms a prelude to *Gambara*, of 1837, and in a more general way to *The Search for the Absolute*. It was indeed of minor interest, but August gave to the world two of its psychic masterpieces, *The Red Inn* (l'Auberge rouge), and *The Wild Ass's Skin* (la Peau de chagrin). The former has its scene at Andernach in the days of the first French Republic. Its subject is the psychic suggestion of a crime that shall be imagined by one and executed by another. He in whose brain the murder originated is convicted of it and executed. Was he wholly innocent? To the material murderer the crime is a source of great wealth. Was he wholly guilty? Had he atoned for his guilt by a life-long remorse and a mental degeneration culminating in death? Could one who knew the truth honourably marry his daughter and enjoy his fortune? Such are the questions that Balzac leaves half answered in this story, where the execution yields little if at all to the striking originality of the conception.

The central figure of *The Red Inn* reappears in *The Wild Ass's Skin*, which, as the correspondence informs us, was written together with the other, and is the longest and the most remarkable of all the so-called "philosophic tales," and the one into which the author has put most of his life's philosophy. Using the marvellous, as Goethe had done in his *Faust* and Shakspere in his *Hamlet*, he makes his story the symbol of the eternal conflict of duty and will, of the ideal that dashes itself to fragments against the disenchantments of the material life. The early struggles of Raphaël, its hero, are partly autobiographical, but presently he comes in possession of a bit of wild ass's skin, by which all material wishes are fulfilled, though always at the cost of a fraction of life ; for Balzac believed, what his own life illustrated, that the spirit could grow rich only at the body's cost and that "the sword would wear out the scabbard." Raphaël's intense soul seeks satisfaction in love and in a fantastic orgy of debauchery and wit, then makes a desperate effort to prolong life by ceasing to will at all, and perishes at last in a revolt of his animal nature. The conception is most curiously profound, and the execution, though uneven, contains passages among the best in fiction. To the inexhaustible subject Balzac returned the next year in *Louis Lambert.*

But Balzac's protean genius was still to show itself this year in two other forms: as a medieval mystic, and as a medieval materialist. *Jesus Christ in Flanders* (September, 1831) is a brief piece, but it is full of significance for the comprehension of Balzac and of his work. He himself so conceived it, as we may see from his first letter to the Duchess of Castries, where we find that as early as October, 1831, he wishes all his novels to be regarded as parts of a not yet fully elaborated plan, and utters a just warning against any partial judgment of his work or its ethical bearing. The general system of his fiction, he writes to Baron Gérard, "is beginning to unveil itself," and he begins to feel the weight of an immense task to be accomplished, "enough to occupy three or four men." In *Jesus Christ in Flanders*, under the veil of a Flemish legend we are to see the moral philosophy of the *Human Comedy*. The scene is a ferry-boat. On it are representatives of all social classes, with a sober minded realist for pilot and a stranger from the spirit world. A tempest reveals the nature of all. Among the wealthy in the stern are avarice, pride, worldly wisdom, vice, crime, scepticism, and terror; in the centre sits the pilot, himself his own providence, opposing his strength of mind and body to the force of nature. In the prow are the little ones of Christ, the faithful and the poor, and with them sits the stranger, and gives to each words of mystic comfort. Borne up in spirit they follow the master from the sinking ship and walk on the waves to land. The pilot, sound at least in head, is washed alive to shore. The others perish, "weighed down by crimes perhaps, but still more by incredulity and faith in false images, heavy with devotion, light in charity, and in true religion." In a brief second part comes the appli-

cation of the tale. "A short time after the revolution of
1830 " the author tells us that he was weary of living, when
a vision came to teach him that Belief is Life. " I have
seen," he says, "the burial of the monarchy. We must
defend the Church." And this the *Human Comedy* does
directly or indirectly in every page. All that is realistic,
tragic, sordid in life Balzac will show us relentlessly, laying
bare society's spiritual sores, like a skilful confessor of
souls, but behind Balzac the realist we shall see always the
stout upholder of human self-conquest, the believer in the
eternal power of the unseen, a social philosopher, if not
always profound, at least always earnest, hopeful, honest,
purposeful and sincere.

It is not without its suggestiveness that *Jesus Christ in
Flanders* should be followed immediately in the list of
Balzac's fiction by *Master Cornelius* (Maître Cornélius),
like Gobseck a study of soul-destroying avarice, in which
the miser, finding that in somnambulist sleep he is robbing
himself with such diabolical ingenuity that when awake he
cannot recover his treasure, "succumbs to the horror of
the torture that he has created for himself." This Cornelius was a friend of Louis XI., and plays a part in the
Droll Stories also. Artistically, then, the story affords
occasion for some fine descriptions and a portrait of the
favourite king of the romanticists that shows, what *Catherine
de' Medici* was to prove, that Balzac had in him the potentiality of a greater historical novelist than France has yet
produced.

But if the work of this year was varied, that of 1832 was
so in a far more remarkable degree. For in that twelve-
month were published four volumes, parts of two others,
and eight short stories ranging from the depth of horror in

in *The Great Bastion* (la Grand bretèche), to the philosophic heights of *Louis Lambert*, with studies in the psychology of rage, of long suffering, and of delicate analysis
of "the woman of thirty," sinned against, and sinning,
abandoned, and betrayed.   And to set off all this there is
the graceful pastel of *The Purse* (la Bourse), and the
Rabelaisian laughter of the *Droll Stories*.   Did ever writer
manifest himself in such protean shapes in the space of
twelve months?   We may learn at least from the works
of this year the task that awaits him who would write a
general essay on the works of Balzac, and may understand
the relative failure of all who have yet attempted it.

Madame Firmiani (February, 1832) is a rather romantic
little story of love and honour with something perhaps of
Madame de Berny, in the central figure, but the same
situation was handled with far more art and power in *The
Interdict* (l'Interdiction) four years later.   Then *The Message* (February, 1832) seeks to sound the depths of tragic
grief, and is followed in March by the pitiful tale of *Colonel
Chabert*, who returns from a German military hospital like
a ghost to trouble joy, to find the wife for whom he had
longed married to another, and bent on disproving the
identity of her first husband.   In his desperate struggle
with the meshes of the law the poor colonel wrecks heart
and brain.   So this story is the first, as it probably remains
the best, of the group of Balzac's legal novels, — *The Interdict*, *A Start in Life*, *The Marriage Contract*, and *A
Mysterious Case*, — that introduce us to the soul-wearing
chicanery of the courts.   Chabert himself, however, a
spectre from the Grand Army, is a figure of the most tragic
grandeur, and his account of the battle of Eylau is one of
the masterpieces of military fiction.

Of the ten *Droll Stories* published in April, to be followed by a second ten in 1833 and a third in 1837, it may
be well to speak here once for all.   They stand apart in his
work.   All are intended to imitate the language, the manner, and in some degree the spirit and the view of life of
Rabelais and his Pantagruel.   Balzac himself speaks of
them as his recreations.   Here he found expression for that
joyous animal nature that the seriousness of his task has
almost wholly suppressed in the *Human Comedy*.   If there
at times he had denounced a decaying and degenerate civilisation based on democracy and materialism, and at times
had let his mind bear him into idyls of the ideal, into
pseudo-philosophic speculations, or into spiritualistic ecsta-
sies, here he showed himself possessed by the jovial spirits
of love, wine, and laughter, and so rounded out for us the
complete circle of his genius, that regards life from every
side, comprehends alike the ascetic and the sensualist, sym-
pathises with all expressions of human beauty, the spiritual
and the sensuous, and enjoys all expressions of human will,
the vulgar and the exalted ; showing, too, with the frankness
of an infant, that pleasure which far more men feel than confess in mentioning the unmentionable, and the laughter that
holds both its sides when a jest is pointed at the abdomen.

For this reason it is obvious that no detailed analysis of the
thirty *Droll Stories* should be expected here.   They formed
a part of a larger scheme, of which he announced twenty ad-
ditional tales as " in press " in 1838, though of these only
The Spinner (la Filandière) has ever seen the light.   They
therefore coincide in time with the medievalistic phase of
romanticism, and are simply Balzac's reflection of it.   Yet
while the *Droll Stories* have thus many elements in common,
within their limits they show a variety almost as great as

the *Comédie humaine* itself. We have first in *The Fair
Impéria* an evocation of Constance in the days of the coun-
cil (1414–1418), a phantasmagoria of theology, love, lust,
trickery, and jollity, a picture of the contest for facile favours
between the wealth and power of age and the simple passion of youth. Here the future Lucien, Esther, and Nucingen of *Splendours and Miseries of Courtesans* are transposed
as it were, from the realistic, modern tragic key to the
comic and the medievally grotesque. *The Venial Sin*, that
follows is a scene of private life, where again the elements
of tragic, comic, pathetic, and grotesque are mingled with
romantic intention, while beneath all there is the beginning of the psychological analysis that was to produce the
Woman of Thirty and the group of studies co-ordinated
with it. Inferior in kind, though not in execution, is *The
King's Leman*, a practical joke played on a senile husband
for the benefit of Francis I. Again the manner changes,
and in *The Heir of the Devil* we have a bit of picaroon
fiction with just a dash of sorcery, while *The Jokes of King
Louis XI.* is one of the very best pictures of that royal favourite of the romanticists since Scott had discovered him in
Quentin Durward. Then in *The Constable's Wife* there is
the tragic irony of a woman yielding to the solicitation of
one lover, even while another is perishing to obey her sum-
mons. This is followed by *The Maid of Thilhouze*, a
rather commonplace tale of mock modesty, and this by
The Brother in Arms, a medievalised Joseph and Madam
Potiphar. The first Ten is closed by *The Curé of Azay-
le-rideau*, a good-humoured pantagruelistic priest, such as
Balzac imagined Rabelais might have been, and *The Apos-
trophe*, a tale of feminine wiles in the manner of the old
fabliaus.

The second Ten opens with *The Three Clerks of St. Nicholas* and *The Fast of Francis I.*, both relatively commonplace. *The Pleasantries of the Nuns of Poissy*, also, is a mere bit of ingenious and amusing scatology, and *The Castle of Azay* only an amorous adventure of the daughter of Louis XI. told with much verve. A far higher place must be accorded, however, to the tragic *False Courtesan*, in which there is a diabolical ingenuity of moral perversion breaking itself in vain against simple virtue that dies unstained. From this height we descend to the smoking-room jest, very good in its kind, on " *The Danger of Being too Innocent*," and the fatal adventure of *The Dear-bought Night of Love*. This is followed by a supposed sermon of Rabelais, a political and satiric allegory, and by the longest and most remarkable of the *Droll Stories*, *The Succubus*, an astonishing reproduction of the medieval attitude of mind toward the spirit world, and of the legal procedure of 1271. The vision in the third part of this tale is one of the most vertiginous passages in Balzac or in any literature. *Despair in Love*, with which the second Ten closes, would have pleased Stendhal more than it is likely to do a modern reader. It is a tale of Italian passion so intense that it changes coquetry to love by violence.

The third Ten is inferior to the others. *Perseverance in Love*, a story of romantic devotion, affords a curious illustration of the possible complications of medieval vassalage, and the tale of *A Justice who Remembered Things* is only a clever after-dinner jest. There is more art, though not more verve, and much the same spirit in *The Monk Amador*, who "became a glorious abbot" for qualities hardly consistent with the monastic profession. Of a higher excellence is *Bertha Repentant*, in which the situation suggests somewhat that of *The Venial Sin*, though both the pathetic, elegiac and the grotesquely weird are pushed to a greater extremity of contrast. None of the succeeding pieces reach this height. *The Fair Maid of Portillon* and *Fortune is always feminine* are mere clever vulgarities; *The Old Tramp* is a bit of fantastic slumming; *The Incongruities of Three Pilgrims* is a commonplace story, and *Naïveté* a trifle. The last of the *Stories*, *The Fair Impéria Married*, alone rises to the level of *Bertha*. It is an elegy of passion that at the close becomes so absorbingly intense as to find no issue save in self-destruction. While, then, it is obvious that some of the *Droll Stories* are, as Balzac calls them in his correspondence, the recreations of a tired brain, others, and especially *The Succubus*, are worthy to take a place among the best of the *Philosophic Stories* in the firmness of their emotional psychology, while at the same time they are stylistically perhaps the very finest work of their author.

Soon after the first ten *Droll Stories* Balzac published three of the original six parts of *The Woman of Thirty* (la Femme de trente ans), begun in 1831, finished in 1834, and rewritten in 1842 with an attempt at fusion of the parts that did not attain to entire homogeneity. It is most suitable to speak of it here because of its close connection with two other stories of this year, *La Grenadière* and *The Deserted Wife* (la Femme abandonée). All three are studies of conjugal infelicity and all teach in different ways the same stern truth that, given society as it is, women must submit to social rule, even though it stifle the most imperious voice of the heart. *The Woman of Thirty*, as has been said, is very uneven, it has passages almost grotesquely romantic and others of admirable realism. The story opens brilliantly with a description of a review in the heyday of the Empire, minutely vivid and quite out of key with that part of the narrative that tells how a little girl killed her half-brother, and presently eloped with a pirate while her mother was enduring the petty miseries of conjugal incompatibility, or the dust and ashes of adultery. Morally the book is stern, yet not unjust in its even-handed condemnation both of the present social order and of those who being in it will not be of it. But it has less artistic charm than *The Abandoned Wife* (September, 1832) that takes up from another side the psycho-physiological problem of *A Double Family* and asks how the memory of years passed in a passionate liaison will affect the capacity of a man for the joys and duties of home, while in *La Grenadière* (October, 1832), which Balzac says that he wrote in a single night, we have a picture of child life in Touraine that is really exquisite.

Stronger, however, than any of these, and perhaps the best sustained piece of work that Balzac had yet done, was *The Curé of Tours*, conceived and planned, as he tells us, in ten days of intense thought. Here he first essays to expose the ecclesiastical intrigues, the occult influence of which had been felt throughout the reign of Charles X. and had made the Church at once dreaded and hated by the liberals. This, then, is Balzac's contribution to a cause that Sue sought to serve in his *Wandering Jew*, and Michelet in his lectures on the Jesuits. But Balzac's attitude was more generous and catholic-spirited than theirs. Abbé Birotteau is but one of his series of noble clergymen, and it is because such priests as Troubert undermine the spiritual power of the Church that they are hateful to Balzac. These two abbés epitomize the French clergy under the Restora-

tion with the clearest vision and most delicate touch that
have ever been brought to the task, and in his Sophie Gamard we find also an interesting anticipation of Balzac's later
reflections on *The Old Maid* (la Vieille fille).

But if the *Curate of Tours* is in its way the best work
that Balzac had yet done, so, too, in another way is that
little masterpiece of horror *The Great Bastion* (la Grande
bretèche), afterward incorporated in *Second Study of
Woman* (Autre étude de femme). Here an injured husband with diabolical deliberation has the lover walled up in
a cabinet, where he knows that he has taken refuge, inducing the terrified wife to declare that the closet is empty,
and leaving the guilty lover to reveal their common
disgrace or die a lingering death, a victim of Spanish
pundonor, of a woman's fears, and of a vengeance that in
satanic ingenuity of detail has perhaps no equal in fiction.
And, as though these two were not enough for a single
month, this May produced also *The Purse* (la Bourse), a
little idyl of true love, radiantly simple, and, though certainly not great, remarkable for the entire contrast that it
shows to all the other work of this year.

Balzac's next novel, *Louis Lambert*, if we may judge
from his correspondence, preoccupied him more than any
of these. In it he desired to put both a picture of his own
school-days and literary apprenticeship and also a sort of
introduction to his proposed treatise on the will. He says
that he " is in a mood for work and capable of marvels,"
that *Lambert* " will sell thousands of the *Philosophic
Stories*." " It is a work in which I have sought to contend
with Goethe and Byron . . . a last response to my enemies,
that should show an incontestable superiority," and yet
under such pressure is he now working that he thinks it

" has cost him dear " because he has given to it " six weeks persistent work at Saché and ten days at Angoulême."

The plot in *Louis Lambert* is of the slightest. The interest centres in the development of a spiritualistic theory of thought by which the will or soul is supposed to transmit movement to matter. This theory has in it elements of mysticism, Mesmerism, and Swedenborgianism, and it will be well to leave the analysis of these things to those who think they understand them. Balzac himself, writing in January, 1833, speaks of it as the saddest of all abortions, and the effect of his theory on Lambert, when coupled with a passionate love, was to induce a sort of philosophic insanity and an early death, before which, however, he wrote five letters to his beloved, in which there is a gradation of sentiment worthy of Stendhal.

Balzac closed this busy year with *The Marana*, another " philosophic study " but resembling *Lambert* only in that name. Here he takes up the parable of Hugo's *Lucrezia Borgia*, the redemption of the courtesan by maternal love, merging this at the close into a question of family honour, where a woman prefers to kill her husband rather than to suffer his criminal cowardice and the shame of his execution. The elder Marana is one of those queenly Italian courtesans of the renascence, such as Balzac had described so superbly in *The fair Impéria* of the *Droll Stories*, and here first we meet types of the imperial soldier of fortune, always favourite characters with Balzac as with Stendhal. The whole story is far more dramatic in treatment than is usual with Balzac, and has been turned to account several times by modern dramatists. Beside all this varied production his correspondence shows a brain teeming with projects of stories and novels that have never been published, though some of them seem to have been completely planned and partly written.   And all this time he was fighting what he calls the hydra of his debts, and disputing his rights vigorously with publishers.   While his mother acted as a sort of factotum in Paris, interviewing editors making contracts, and settling or renewing his obligations, he shut himself up in a country solitude, expecting to turn off twenty pages a day and to work fifteen or sixteen hours.

During the year 1833, though the number of works produced is less, the same arduous labour is continued.   He tells us that he lives in " an atmosphere of thoughts, ideas, plans, works, conceptions, that mingle, bubble, and sparkle in my brain, enough to make me crazy.   Yet nothing makes me thin, and I am the truest portrait of a monk that ever was seen since the last hour of the convents.   As for the soul, though, I am profoundly sad.   My work alone keeps me up."   His preoccupation, from September of 1832 until June of 1833, is *The Country Doctor* (le Médecin de campagne).   He writes in September that he has finished it by working three days and nights.   But as usual the correction took more time than the writing, and in the next March he complains that " it has cost him ten times more work than *Lambert*," though, he adds, " when one tries to attain the simple beauty of the *Gospels*, to surpass the *Vicar of Wakefield*, and to put the *Imitation of Christ* into action, one must 'pitch in' and hard."   His ambition is to rival the popularity of *Atala*, of *Paul and Virginia*, or of *Manon Lescaut*, to write a book that My Lady and her portress alike may read, that may be sold by the 100,000, that shall seem inspired by the Bible and the catechism. And the while he is relaxing himself with the second **Ten**

of his *Stories* and with the criminal novel *Férragus*, the
latter published in March and April, the former in July and
The Doctor in September.

If we may trust the letters to Madame Hanska, *Férragus*
was produced by working day and night to satisfy the exi-
gencies of the *Revue de Paris*, which after all disappointed
his perhaps unreasonable expectations.   But the story had
" an extraordinary success " in Paris, then more disposed
than now to such romantic extravagances.   For *Férragus* is
the chief of " The Thirteen," a band of pale, mysterious,
Byronic desperadoes, social Bonapartes banded to plunder
society in imitation of the Laras and the Corsairs.   He is
interesting to us now chiefly as a preliminary study for the
Jacques Collin of *Lost Illusions* and *Splendours and Miseries
of Courtesans*.   Like him he is an escaped convict, and, as
Jacques has a model son, so Férragus has a gentle daughter,
wife òf the respectable broker Desmarets.   In secret she
visits her fond father.   Suspicion arises in the mind of a
jealous lover, and he innoculates the husband with his own
moral disease.   The Thirteen mow a swath of corpses and
attain at last the delator, who dies in lingering agony, but
not until suspicion has slain its victim, and grief at her
death has transformed the dread bandit chief into a harm-
less imbecile.   The idea of the power of secret societies
seems to have been a favourite with Balzac, and the story
is good of its kind, but it is not the kind that gives him his
rank in the history of fiction.   Except for a wonderful
passage on the *Dies iræ* toward the close, the whole might
almost as well be from the pen of Eugène Sue.

The Country Doctor, as may be gathered from what has
already been said of it, is not, strictly speaking, a novel at
all.   The story is but a slight framework for a sort of tract

on social and moral economy, abounding in exquisite descriptions of scenery and such photographic reproduction of peasant modes of thought and attitudes of mind as to seem, especially if we regard it in connection with *The Village Curate* and *The Peasants*, simply marvellous in one who knew as Balzac did the provincial town and the capital. None should pass artistic or ethical judgment on the *Human Comedy* without weighing, beside the dramas of Parisian and provincial vice and crime, the stories of Benassis, the doctor, and of Bonnet, the curate.

The book recounts the experience of Genestas, a general of Napoleon and of the Restoration, who, before confiding his somewhat morbid ward to the country doctor, seeks occasion to observe, under an assumed name, his life and character. He accompanies him on his rounds among the people and learns to know them as they talk to Benassis, whose devotion to their interests has transformed sordidness into prosperity, by convincing them that "intellectual progress was involved in sanitation," and that there were fortunes in model farms. In this Balzac shows the effect on his vigorous but conservative imagination of the teachings of Saint-Simon and Fourier, reinforced later in *The Peasants* by those of Proudhon. But if the economics, though suggestive, are somewhat inartistically obtruded, the studies of peasant characters are wholly admirable and their fundamental egoistical shrewdness is relieved with a touch of romantic idealism here in La Fosseuse, as later in Farrabêche. Perhaps no one has caught the nature of the French peasant and small villager as Balzac has done, that small, narrow, materialistic soul, clinging to the soil like a mollusc to the rock, industrious and capable of great sacrifice, of the earth and therefore sensual, but surely not so brutally so as Zola has painted him in *Earth*. Yet the glory of *The Country Doctor* is not here, but rather in Napoleon, whose memory seems to brood over these country minds and rises to an epic utterance in the twenty-five pages where Goguelat, in his own savoury language, tells us what the great Emperor was to the men of that generation who lived far away from the ignoble strife of Parisian factions. No wonder that Madame d'Abrantès wept over it, as we are told in the correspondence, for nothing in the whole fifty volumes of the *Human Comedy* shows such astonishing power of self-projection and psychic vision.

The Country Doctor was not yet printed before the letters show Balzac's intense preoccupation with *Eugénie Grandet*, and before this is through the press he has begun work both on *Lost Illusions* and on *César Birotteau*, and is meditating *Séraphita*. He now goes to bed at six, rises at midnight, and works till noon, with proofs in the afternoon. "Poor pen," he writes, "it must be diamond not to wear out under such use." He has a lawsuit on his hands, also, about *The Country Doctor*, and threatens another about the as yet unpublished *Duchess of Langeais*. He is deep in journalism also, and, as though that were not enough, he has become a partner in a publishing enterprise. He is beginning to regret the abuse of coffee, and yet, in the midst of all this, he has advanced in the general scheme of his novels very near to the final conception, for in August (1833) he has already co-ordinated the groups of scenes of Private, Provincial, Parisian, and Country Life, under the title *Studies of Manners*, with the *Philosophic Studies*. That he did not add in terms Military Studies and Political Studies was only because he had not yet advanced in them sufficiently to warrant their inclusion. All that really remained for the ultimate conception was the title, *Human Comedy* (Comédie humaine), first used in 1838 in a letter to Madame Hanska, and the conception of social evolution that underlies the latter part of his work, as characters reappear in different ages and in their own children, a conception not grasped in all its consequences before 1842.

"*Eugénie Grandet* will astonish you," writes Balzac, with no unjust pride, for it is one of the most remarkable studies of avarice in all literature, and its heroine Balzac's most exquisite feminine creation. Yet the book was at first received with critical incredulity as *The Country Doctor* had been with sceptical indifference. The action of the story is a tragic conflict between the egoism of avarice and the generosity of love. Many of its scenes have become part and parcel of the literary consciousness, not of France alone, but of all well-read men. Grandet in his store-room, or mending his stair, or convicting Eugénie of romantic generosity, or dying in his strong-room, these are but a few of the imperishable pictures that every reader may evoke at will from this wonderful stage-setting and action of human comedy. Just as the serpent's eye fascinates its victim, so the glitter of gold drags Grandet to moral ruin and to monomania. "He would lie in wait," says Balzac, "watch his prey, jump on it — and then, opening the jaws of his purse, he would swallow a pile of écus and lie down tranquilly like a serpent in his digestion, impassive, cold, methodical." But more and more what he possessed came to possess him, until at last, a paralytic maniac, he clutches the crucifix to his lips in death, not because it is the Saviour who is nailed there, but because devotion has gilded the body and the nails. As he lingers on the threshold of the unseen world he gasps to his daughter with his last breath the menace and the warning: "You will have to give an account to me of all I leave to you." Has literature ever drawn for us a ruling passion stronger in death, or a more ghastly travesty of the spiritual tie that binds the living and the departed?

The composition of such a masterpiece as this must have cost intense effort, and from it Balzac seems to have sought relief in composing *The Illustrious Gaudissart* (l'Illustre Gaudissart), the story of a commercial traveller, told with all the gusto and vulgarity to which commercial travellers have accustomed us, and which we may read either in the broad jesting spirit in which it was written, or with curious wonder at the insight it affords into the mobility of Balzac's marvellous genius.

The close of 1833 found *Séraphita* "much advanced," but he guarded jealously this loftiest flight of his genius, and did not let it go finally till the close of 1836. Indeed in January of 1834 he complains that he is "dazed with ideas and hungry for rest." *Séraphita* seems to him "a work more cruel for the author than any," though "as far superior to *Lambert* as *Lambert* is to *Gaudissart.*" The output of this year is therefore less in quantity than that of the preceding. The *Duchess of Langeais* was finished in January and printed in March, part of *Séraphita* was given to the world in June, the *Search for the Absolute* (la Recherche de l'absolu) and further brief portions of the *Woman of Thirty* followed in October, and *Père Goriot*, finished in September, closes the year and in its serial publication reaches into the next. That is all for 1834, but he had been meditating also *The Lily in the Valley* (le Lys dans la vallée), and had been much occupied with new editions of older work and his usual financial distractions.

The Duchess of Langeais, offered as the second part of the *History of the Thirteen*, is such a novel as Balzac alone in his generation could have written, and as only his generation would have written at all. The "Thirteen" enter the tale only to enable Montriveau to rescue the duchess, or, as it proves, her corpse from a Spanish cloister, where she is the self-immolated victim of coquetry transformed to passion. The interest of the tale centres in its picture of the society of the Faubourg Saint-Germain during the Restoration, and in its analysis of intellectual coquetry, that supreme product of social artificiality. The duchess, who seems intended for Madame de Castries, was "a type of the nature of her caste, at once superior and feeble, great and petty, artificially instructed, really ignorant, full of high feelings, but lacking a thought to co-ordinate them. Spending the richest treasures of her soul in conforming to social conventions, ready to brave society, but hesitating and becoming artificial through her scruples, having more wilfulness than character, more infatuation than enthusiasm, more head than heart." But the whole of this long and subtle description must be read and pondered, and even then we shall not know wholly this woman, who could toy with love till she killed it, and then kill herself with ascetic macerations because her own too tardily proffered love was spurned. This psychic dissection is admirable, but the climax of the tale, the abduction and proposed branding of the duchess by the Thirteen, is too much in the spirit of its time to satisfy ours. The last words of the story have a biographical significance. At Geneva, in January, in the first months of his acquaintance with Madame

Hanska, Balzac writes: " It is only the last love of a woman that can satisfy the first love of a man." But even as early as October, 1831, he had written to this Madame de Castries, " If I should marry by and by, it will be with no one but a widow."

The Search for the Absolute is the first of a group of stories written during 1834 and 1835 that mark preoccupation with the hidden life of the soul, growing in intensity through *A Drama by the Sea-shore* (un Drame au bord de la mer) and *Melmoth's Reconciliation* (Melmoth reconcilié) and reaching in *Séraphita* an almost ecstatic climax of orphic mysticism. This *Search for the Absolute* is a strangely fascinating story of scientific curiosity growing into absorption, and thence to monomania. Balthazar Claës, in seeking for primordial matter, spends millions, ruins as far as in him lies his family, and dies with " Eureka ! " on his lips. Very curious also is the figure of the famulus Lemulquinier, ignorant and yet himself gradually caught in the net of science. But the long-suffering devotion of Madame Claës, like that of Chaucer's Grisildis, threatens to become exasperating, and his daughter Margaret, though apparently intended for a heroine, has inherited more than was well of the weaknesses of both her parents. The persistency with which these women ruin themselves for sentiment, and the iteration of the phrase " Margaret paid her father's debts," are irritating, though they may be essential if the ultimate social immorality of scientific egoism is to appear in all its potential horror. Here, however, the family is saved from the worst results of Claës' folly by the decidedly romantic financial talents of Margaret, and our regard for her filial affection that suffers her father to turn affluence to bankruptcy is diminished by the easy

facility with which the wand of her genius can transform
bankruptcy to affluence.   The critic will hardly agree with
the author, who writes with fatherly self-satisfaction that this
novel is " grandly constructed."

Like Shakspere, Balzac was not backward in self-approval,
and often in his letters judged his work more justly than his
contemporaries.   If we cannot agree with his judgment on
the structure of *The Search for the Absolute*, he is probably
right when he says a little later that *Père Goriot* is " finer
even than *Eugénie Grandet*," though indeed it is hard to
choose between two novels so different and so excellent.
Père Goriot is Balzac's King Lear.   He has been a successful manufacturer, and has retired from commerce with
wealth that enables him to procure for one daughter an
aristocratic, for the other a wealthy husband.   From this
moment his life becomes an elegy of paternal sacrifice.
Like the fabled pelican he tears his breast to feed his
children, who live a heartless life of leeches and of lechery.
The father dies at last, the impoverished victim of his
devotion.   This death-bed scene is among the great
chapters of fiction, and serves as an object lesson on
the necessity of balancing altruism with egoism to a
certain Rastignac, a type of the self-made man of those
days and the successful social struggler of ours.   Given
the world as it goes, worldly wisdom speaking by Bianchon
and cynical self-will incarnated in Jacques Collin, here
masked under the name Vautrin, both enforce the lesson
that, however society may be out of joint, it will avenge
itself implacably on all who contravene its laws whether for
better or for worse.   Even the giant genius of Vautrin,
after having in other novels felt, once and again, the
necessity of seasoning even criminality with devotion, is

obliged at last to place itself in the service of society; and if Rastignac climbs to wealth, station, and power, it is by shrewdly taking the world as it goes. But this is to anticipate. The primary purpose of *Père Goriot* is to show senile devotion and hideous ingratitude, and these have seldom found stronger literary expression.

In 1835 the only long novel published was *Séraphita*, and four short stories of varied excellence make up the work of the year, during which he began also *The Lily in the Valley*, over which he says he weeps, and trusts others will do so. Over-work is telling on him. He complains that the excessive labour of completing *Séraphita* has given him such neuralgia as to compel him to stop work altogether, though a few months later the necessities of his debts have inspired him with the desperate scheme of working twenty-four hours at a time, with one interval of rest between, thus securing "twenty-one and a half hours of work a day." " Men talk of the victims of wars and epidemics," he writes, "but who considers the battle-fields of art, science, and letters, and the dead and dying that fierce struggles for success pile up on them?" and yet his restless mind is thinking once more of journalism and of taking an active part in politics. He is encouraged, too, by the growing popularity of *The Country Doctor* and by flattering offers for the right to reprint what he calls his "youthful literary garbage." In November he makes a flying visit to Madame Hanska at Vienna, and "near that dear being recovers all his imagination and his verve," which he employs on *Séraphita* and on *The Memoirs of Two Young Wives* (les Mémoires de deux jeunes mariées). He closes the year much encouraged with his business prospects and buys a country house, " La Grenadière."

The publications of 1835 begin with *A Drama by the Sea-shore* (un Drame au bord de la mer), which bears a close relation as a study of remorse to *The Red Inn*. But here the murder is done by a father on his son to guard the honour of his family. The setting of the story is a very effective scene on the Breton coast, that Balzac was to paint so fondly in *Béatrix*, and the story is told by a native fisherman with a naked simplicity that recalls Flaubert. Another but much less satisfactory story of remorse is *Melmoth's Reconciliation* (Melmoth réconcilié), the idea for which was taken from the English Maturin's *Melmoth* (1820). The horrible melancholy that comes from supreme power in the world of matter and of thought, the Mephistophelian joy in doing ill, is the supposed subject, but our interest, save for the well-drawn figures of the courtesan Aquilina and of the dishonest cashier Castanier, is attracted mainly by the fine opening passage on " the feudality of money on which the modern social contract rests," " that sore of our civilisation that since 1815 has replaced the principle of honour by that of wealth."

Of *The Girl with the Golden Eyes* (la Fille aux yeux d'or) one need say only that, as *Sarrasine* had been a study of uni-sexual passion between men, so here a similar perversion draws the marchioness of Saint-Réal to Paquita Valdez, who falls at last victim to a jealousy that may be called unnatural, though both medicine and the law know many curious parallels that justify the artist ; for, as Balzac says, " my plan obliges me to be universal." The story opens with observations on " the soul of Paris," twenty pages summed up at last in a fine paragraph where the armorial bearings of the city are made to symbolise its

nature in a way that justifies to Balzac the title of "seer,"
le voyant. The boudoir in this tale is one of the famous
passages of sensuous description in French literature, and
there is a deep psychological interest in the analysis of
Marsay, that spirit of mocking corruption whose genius
permeates like yeast a large portion of the scenes of the
Human Comedy. This natural son of an English lord had
been trained by one of those priests "cut out to be
cardinals in France, or Borgias under the tiara," who "believed neither in men nor women, in God nor the devil."
This half-brother of the marchioness, and her rival in the
affections of Paquita, is one of the first *blagueurs* in literature and perhaps still the greatest, though the type was
more common under the third Napoleon than under Louis
Philippe, so that Balzac's insistence on this character seems
almost prophetic.

Of the same month as *The Girl with the Golden Eyes*
yet so different from it that no one pen but that of Balzac
could have drawn them from the same ink-bottle, is *The
Marriage Contract,* first known as *la Fleur des pois.*
This, as Balzac says, is "one of the great scenes of private
life," in which signing of the marriage contract reveals the
future of the parties in a situation whose "profound
comedy can be appreciated only by business men," and
perhaps no longer even by them, for it is based on a
struggle between the modern and the now obsolete ideals of
the "family notary." This was Balzac's first study of the
rôle of the dowry in French society, and of the conflict of
interests that it tends to produce between husband and
wife. The central figure is his greatest mother-in-law,
Madame Evangelista, with her terrible "bride's breviary,"
to which Marsay furnishes the natural masculine counter-

part by his brilliant pleas for selfish cynicism at the opening and at the close.

But if *The Girl with the Golden Eyes* and *The Contract*
stand at opposite literary poles, what shall we say of
Séraphita, that " door opened into the world of the invisible," save that it seems of another sphere than either?
This exquisitely mystic poem in prose is the first and
sublimest product of the author's spiritual communion with
Madame Hanska, a hymn as it were to the purification of
human passion by divine aspiration, to the angelic interpenetration of sex symbolised by conjugal love.   The novel
may not be intelligible to all in its Swedenborgian rapture,
but it is the best corrective to the grotesque error of those
who say that the presiding genius of the *Human Comedy* is
the five-franc piece.   Balzac's style has never risen to such
heights as here, is never more serene than in the ascent
of the spiritual mount at the opening, whence the eye
wandered over Norway with " serrated edges like granite
lace," seldom more eloquent than in the closing vision of
the men of this world, clothed in the gold, silver, azure,
pearls, and jewels that they have torn from earth's bosom
or stolen from the sea, and for which humanity has toiled
so long in sweat and blasphemy.   " What do ye here, thus
ranked and motionless?" says the thrice accusing voice of
those who have beheld the mystic vision; " and with one
accord all opened their robes and showed their dried
bodies eaten by worms, a corrupt dust tortured by horrid
disease."   "You led nations to death," says the accusing
voice.   " You debauched the earth.   You turned speech
against nature, prostituted justice.   You cropped the pasture
and now you kill the sheep.   Think you to justify your-
selves by showing your sores?   I go to warn my brothers

who can still hear the Voice, that they may quench their thirst at the springs that you have hidden." It is in the light of words like these that we are to look at the corruptors and the corruption, at the sordidness and the vice of Balzac's *Human Comedy*.

CHAPTER VI

THE MATURITY OF BALZAC

THE years from 1836 to the death of Monsieur Hanski in 1842 are a period of arrested development in Balzac. They began with pecuniary embarrassment. His magazine, *The Chronicle of Paris*, suspended, leaving him under heavy obligations, and a lawsuit, in which he showed more sense of justice than wisdom, soon after deprived him of a steady source of income and of the sympathy of many useful men in the fraternity of authorship. Broken in health, harrassed by anxieties and disappointments, he sought refreshment in Touraine in June, and did not return to Paris till October, when he found himself obliged to give up many of those surroundings to which he looked for aid to his imagination. Yet this seemed to push him to new effort. "I am cast down, but not dismayed," he writes to Madame Hanska. He goes on to say that he has written the second part of *Catherine de' Medici* in a single night, *The Old Maid* (la Vieille fille) in three, and that last, most beautiful section of *The Accursed Child* (l'Enfant maudit) "in a few hours of moral and physical agony." Emendations for new editions cost this conscientious artist "more than many volumes." "I must surpass myself, since buyers are indifferent, and I must do it in the midst of protested notes, business annoyances, cruel financial straits, and the most utter solitude, deprived of every consolation." "Think of that when you read my work," he bids her, and we, too, should not be unmindful of it, though when he speaks of "the Augias' stable of my style" he certainly betrays an unnecessary and morbid anxiety. Toward the close of the year, however, he takes heart, having made a publishing contract that relieved him of pressing debts by mortgaging work to come and securing the mortgage by life insurance.

During this year letters show us that Balzac was working on *Lost Illusions, The Memoirs of Two Young Wives*, and *The Cabinet of Antiquities*. He practically finished *The Officials* (les Employés, 1837), and published also seven novels or tales composed in the main at this time. The list opens with the charming little *Atheist's Mass* (Messe de l'athée), a second tribute of Balzac to the good physician, with an ideal of brotherly love that should bridge all gulfs of station and of creed. The Auvergnat water-carrier who denies himself his humble ambition that a physician may not be disappointed of his lofty one, the sceptic doctor who buys for the soul's repose of his benefactor the masses for which he had longed, and himself devoutly attends them, both show the touch of nature that makes the world kin.

A somewhat higher place, however, belongs to *The Interdict* (l'Interdiction, Jan. – Feb. 1836), which exhibits in Madame d'Espard perhaps the most dangerous type of a society woman, a fashionable coquette of the Restoration, not vicious, but conscienceless, heartless, egoistic, a woman to whom magnanimity at her expense seems not only foolish but criminal. Her efforts to put her husband under guardianship reintroduce us to the purlieus of the law and to Balzac's righteous judge, Popinot, who would feel at home in the millennium. The whole story, though by no means without humour, is thoroughly romantic. Contrast is pushed to the utmost verge, both between opposing characters, as

the Marquis and Marchioness, and in single individuals, as
P.)pinot, who is a Saint Vincent de Paul in the morning
and a criminal judge in the afternoon. And then there is
a mysterious Byronic brother. Indeed all the personages
are forced. The appeal is to the heart rather than to the
head. It proceeds less from the mood of *The Marriage
Contract* than from that of *The Lily* and of *Séraphita*.

Facino Cane (March, 1836) also is romantic, a rather
insignificant fancy of a blind musician who had been a
Venetian prince. It is interesting chiefly for some interwoven reminiscences of Balzac's early struggles for literary
recognition. This was followed in June by the most noteworthy work of the year, *The Lily in the Valley* (le Lys dans
la vallée), a book written avowedly with the thought of
Madame Hanska ever present to the author, and having so
many admirable qualities that those to whom picturesque
and vivid description appeals, as well as those who delight
in sentiment *à outrance*, are apt to lose their critical balance in regard to it.

The Lily in the Valley has for heroine Madame de Mortsauf, a sort of ideal romantic Grisildis, who endeavours to
combine the corporeal duties of unappreciated wife and
mother with those of "the spouse of the soul" to Félix
Vandernesse, who has the incredible indelicacy to narrate
the tale to another lady, in whom he fatuously hopes to
find "a sister of charity," but who gives him only the good
advice to hunt up "some Madame Shandy." Henriette de
Mortsauf, however, even in her lifetime, by no means filled
Félix's heart. He was "the sport of two irreconcilable
passions, of which he felt the influence alternately." This
second flame, Arabella Dudley, shows Balzac's idea of the
phase passion would take in a Protestant environment.

Her love is supremely sensual, yet calculating and able to assume at any moment the mask of hypocritical indifference. The moral of this story, which contains little action and much " philosophy," is that love cannot live on alms, and that ideal passion overreaches itself. Henriette, a misunderstood wife of a hypochondriac husband, dies a pathetic victim to her jealous purity and her enterprise against common-sense, while Arabella discards Félix as she would an old glove, and we cannot feel that she lost much in losing him.

It is clear that in this novel Balzac intended a sort of projection into the ideal of his own aspirations and platonic relations toward Madame Hanska, but Henriette is also the romantic counterpart of the more soberly conceived Eugénie Grandet, and her romanticism exceeds at times the patience or the credulity of the reader. The novel contains, however, in its descriptions of the valley of the Indre, on which Balzac had dwelt fondly also in *The Woman of Thirty* and in *La Grenadière*, the most exquisite pages of their kind in all his fiction, and the oriental exuberance of his account of the harmonious chords of colour and the vertiginous gamuts of odour in the famous bouquets of Félix seem like the visions of a hashish eater. Altogether, then, though *The Lily in the Valley* cannot be called a great novel, it is unjust to call it, with Faguet, "the worst novel we know." No man in his generation but Balzac could have written it, and literature is the richer for the bankruptcy of Félix and Henriette in their effort to put asunder what God joined together, and to divorce the ideal from reality, the spirit from its corporeal symbol.

Of *The Accursed Child* (l'Enfant maudit), that followed in October, the larger part had been written and printed in

1831, but was now subjected to a revision that should, as Balzac said, " bring the rest to the height of the concluding part and make of the whole a sort of little poem of melancholy that should yield no place to criticism." It retains the sombre colouring of the tales of 1830 and early part of 1831, which accorded also with his present mood, and it shows besides, like other work of those former years, the typically romantic interest in the medieval past. Its tone, however, is wholly elegiac, and the sea is made a weirdly dominating symbol of the life of the hero, who seems hardly more human than the frail figure of his beloved, so delicate, so fragile, so sure to break rather than bend before the fierce will of the battle-scarred father. The exquisiteness of this story, especially of the concluding chapter, is almost mystic. One feels in it the spirit breath of the author of *Séraphita*.

Another exhibition of versatility like that which had associated *The Girl with the Golden Eyes* to *The Marriage Contract* binds in this October *The Accursed Child* to *The Old Maid* (la Vieille fille). *The Human Comedy* would not be complete without the autumn as well as the spring of maidenhood, and *The Curate of Tours* had been hardly sympathetic or just. Here in Mlle. Cormon we have a figure drawn at once with insight and sympathy, and placed against a background picturing with a Dutch minuteness the life of a provincial town in lower Normandy during the Restoration. The story is one of disillusion and sardonic humour, as might be expected from the circumstances of its composition. It is indeed a veritable " School for Scandal," thoroughly realistic, except perhaps for the grisette Susanne, in whom we may see one of the premonitory symptoms of *The Lady with the Camellias* and except also for Athanase Granson, a suicide suffering from the malady of the age, who, like Musset and Balzac's own Albert Savarus, perishes chiefly by his lack of will. Charming, however, is the sympathetic picture of Valois, a beau of the old régime, who cannot survive the abdication of Charles X. His rival, Bousquier, the Napoleonic liberal, is drawn with a pen perhaps less justly discriminating, but surely delightfully caustic. One feels throughout this novel that Balzac has passed into the second stage of his relation to Madame Hanska, out of the false and strained idealism of *The Lily* on toward the sober realities of *Lost Illusions* and *The Cabinet of Antiquities,* to be warmed toward the close by the sun of his love's complement reflected in *Cousin Pons.* The work of the year was closed with what is now the second part of *Catherine de' Medici, The Secret of the Ruggieri,* written, as he says, " in a single night," but as the introduction to it, *The Calvinist Martyr,* was not printed till 1841, both will be more fitly spoken of under that date.

The correspondence of 1837 is meagre, and the fiction shows some falling off in interest. The first part of *Lost Illusions,* published in February, was in good part composed earlier, and is best discussed, as is its continuation in 1839, in connection with its conclusion in 1843. This was followed in July by *The Officials* (les Employés), certainly to us one of the least interesting parts of the *Human Comedy,* for it is devoted in large measure to an attack on the organisation of the French administrative departments and on official nepotism. It is one of the less happy of Balzac's frequent expressions of his disgust with the Orleanist monarchy and all its works and ways. The central figure, Rabourdin, is a " little great man," a genius for civil-service reform, stifled by routine and intrigue, by pettiness and mediocrity, while his wife, who gave to the work its original title, *The Superior Woman*, painfully portrays the frequent struggle of refinement and ambition to gain the social recognition and fortune that are necessary to their healthy life. Such studies may be useful and true, but they are sure to be tedious, even when treated with the laborious art of Flaubert or the painstaking and keen analysis of Balzac.

Gambara, which followed in August, is little more than an application of *The Hidden Masterpiece* to music, another illustration of the cruel tragedy that attends the pursuit of the ideal in art. Here, however, the sombre tones are relieved by a background of comedy in Giardini, the cook " whose talents had ruined three restaurants," and there is intercalated in the story a very penetrating analysis of *Robert the Devil*. On *Gambara* followed the third Ten of the *Droll Stories* already noticed, and the year closes with *César Birotteau*.

This novel is closely connected in spirit with *The Officials* though superior to it in interest. We are taken here into the world of commerce. César, the brother of the unfortunate Curate of Tours, is a manufacturing perfumer, and his wife, a type of the simple, courageous helpmeet, with a commercial instinct sounder than her husband's commercial reason. There are some admirable pages of sympathetic delineation of the Parisian bourgeoisie, commonplace and jealous, but good and obliging, dupe of its own virtues and ridiculed for its faults by a society unworthy of it. Some of the minor figures are excellent, especially the smugly materialistic druggist Matifat and the dishonourably successful banker Tillet. But the story will be best remembered for its minute and perhaps partly autobiographic picture of the mental and moral tortures of commercial embarrassment and bankruptcy. In this novel, as in several others of this and the following years, the whole is by no means equal to the sum of its parts.

The year 1838 was marked by Balzac's journey to Sardinia on a fool's errand, seeking Fortunatus' purse in the scoria of Roman mines. Nothing was published until September brought *The Cabinet of Antiquities*, to be followed in October by the first part of the *Splendours and Miseries of Courtesans* and a conclusion to *The Officials*. Then November saw *The House of Nucingen*, and the new year found *A Daughter of Eve* in course of publication. No wonder that Balzac's letters show his mind always busy with what he calls "the moral campaigns of literary creation," "his forces and faculties at tension night and day to invent, write, render, paint, recollect." Already he conceives of his work as a co-ordinated whole and uses for the first time the words "Human Comedy" of "the grand edifice" of these "studies of manners." But he feels worn out, and tells Madame Hanska in January that he is sleeping fifteen or sixteen hours a day, "to recreate his brain," which indeed does not recover its usual fecundity till 1841.

The fiction of these comparatively lean years opens with *The Cabinet of Antiquities* (le Cabinet des antiques), a sort of continuation of *The Old Maid* (la Vieille fille), in which the opposition between the old and the new social ideals is transferred from the matrimonial to the political field. Bousquier, the dubious hero of the former novel, triumphs here in the person of his wealthy but plebeian niece, Mlle. Duval, over the aristocratic prejudices of Victurnien d'Estrignon, one of the younger specimens in this collection of fossils, where the old marquis and his sister represent with touching pathos those intransigeant nobles who neither learned nor forgot, and returned at the Restoration poor and out of touch with the new order.   Almost equally typical and pathetic is their old steward, now the lawyer Chesnel, who ruins himself to save the family honour, that the thoughtless prodigality of the spoiled child Victurnien has imperilled.   Thus the novel is an examination into the causes and the stages of the downfall of the old families, and its moral is summed up by the somewhat giddy Duchess of Montfrigneuse, who tells her effeminate lover : " There is no more nobility . . . there is only aristocracy. . . . You will be far more noble when you have money.   Marry whom you will.   She will be as much marchioness as I am duchess."   Whereon the old marquis comments sadly : " All is lost, even honour."

In *The House of Nucingen* (la Maison Nucingen) we leave the commercial side of Parisian life for that of the bankers and speculators who by their legalized trickery have come to take the place in literature of the Turcarets of a preceding century.   The fateful results, political and moral, of this dominance of the money power occupy also the early part of *Splendours and Miseries of Courtesans* (les Splendeurs et misères des courtisanes) written at this time, and indeed they reappear at nearly every later period of Balzac's work.   But for the moment he turned from this to study in *A Daughter of Eve* (une Fille d'Ève) " the type of a neglected wife between fifteen and twenty."   In this excursion into romance the colours are rather more toned down than in *The Interdict,* though Raoul Nathan, the poet, dramatist, critic, politician, and literary man-of-all-work, with genius o'erforming his rather ugly tenement of clay, is a conglomeration of qualities rather than a character, and Count Félix, after having become insufferable as a Grandison, surprises us at last by going to a masked ball, disguised as a woman, to flirt with his own rival. It is strange that Balzac should have fallen into such melodramatic vulgarity as this; but in these years he was beginning to feel the effect of prolonged platonic love. At first the relation with Madame Hanska was as stimulating to him as that with Frau von Stein had been to Goethe. Gradually, however, with them both, this attempt to divorce sentiment from sense produced a sterilizing effect, from which Goethe recovered through the Italian journey and Christiane, and Balzac through the revival of a normal relation between him and his beloved on the death of Monsieur Hanski in the winter of 1842. We may trace this effect in all the work published in the next four years.

During 1839 Balzac travelled in Northern Italy and went to Vienna to see Madame Hanska there. In the preceding year he had bought a little suburban estate where he built Les Jardies, the country house in which Gambetta met his death. Here he passed most of his time, with brief visits to Paris, until in 1843 he bought and fitted up with much elegance a city house in the present *rue* Balzac, in still deferred hope of a marriage with the now widowed Madame Hanska, that he was not to realise till a few months before his death. It was at Les Jardies that most of the literary work of 1839 and the following years was done, and the country life seems to lend a certain freshness to *The Village Curate*, published in three parts from January to August during this year, as well as to the first two parts of *Béatrix*, which was not completed till 1844.

In *The Village Curate*, as in the *Country Doctor*, we have a study of rural conditions, with many reflections on politics and social economy, and both books end with the death of a benefactor of the countryside. But here the point of the story is directed against the subdivision of estates, and peasant proprietorship, introduced at the Revolution, with results that Balzac thinks most injurious both to property and morals, to Church and State. Obvious traces may be seen here of the influence, if not actually of the hand, of Madame Hanska, but of far more real and artistic interest are some passages of truly exquisite Limousin landscape, and the character of the Curé Bonnet is a charming religious idyl. Less satisfactory is the heroine Veronique, the accomplice of a murder committed for love of her, but in whom religion gradually overcomes all earthly sentiments, until she dies a victim to her suicidal asceticism, after having satisfactorily demonstrated to the villagers the advantages of farming on a large scale. This death-bed scene is still famous, and in romantic days was thought to be highly edifying, but Veronique is quite too morbid to be satisfactory. Her parents, in whom natural acquisitiveness is gradually absorbed in parental love, are however, admirably conceived, as are also some of the minor figures.

Béatrix has a wholly different interest because of its quite obvious portraits of George Sand, of the Countess of Agout, of Gustave Planche, and of Listz, who appear as Camille Maupin, Béatrix, Claude Vignon, and Conti, but the story as a whole is unsatisfactory and unhomogeneous. It is true that the central character, Caliste, is equally contemptible as a youthful simpleton and as lover, husband, father, and partner in a " retrospective adultery ". with

Béatrix ; true too that his wife is always the patient Grisildis. But the really interesting characters, Camille and
Béatrix, seem hardly consistent with themselves, though
both represent phases of sexuality in which the heart has
no share and the senses very little. In these, and in the
thoroughly admirable Madame Schontz of the concluding
part, which belongs to the years of revival in Balzac's
genius after Monsieur Hanski's death had loosed its wings,
we have Balzac's contribution to the then much agitated
question of the " rehabilitation of the courtesan." He has
undertaken to show here that the most purely platonic
feminine affection, as well as the most egoistically cerebral
and the most impudently venal, have each certain common
traits in them of the average woman's instinct of social
conformity. The Béatrix of the second part shows an unselfish love struggling in the bonds of coquetry ; Camille
from her convent retreat confesses the folly of platonism ;
and Madame Schontz sacrifices instantly a wealthy and
genial companionship to a provincial ennui that brings with
it a regular and socially recognisable union. " On the
other hand," says Balzac, " women restrained by education,
rank, wealth, virtue, are attracted, secretly of course, toward
the tropical regions of love, so that these two feminine
natures have each back in their hearts, one a little desire of
virtue, the other that little curiosity about vice. In one it
is the last reflection of the divine ray not yet extinguished.
In the other it is the remnant of our primitive clay."
To illustrate this on its many sides is the not wholly realised aim of *Béatrix*. In its style the novel shows a labored
imitation of Gautier, from whose *Portraits* (1837) many
phrases and even sentences are incorporated, though not
in a way to affect the originality of the story.

Béatrix was succeeded in April by the second part of *Lost Illusions*, and this in August by *Massimilla Doni*, which, however, was not finished till December. This latter takes up the conception of the ideal in art, as it had been presented in *The Hidden Masterpiece* and in *Gambara*, and applies it to the passion of love. In the noble Emilio and in Genovese the singer, passion annihilates action. They are cured only by being trapped into the realisation of their desires by the worldly wisdom of a French doctor, before whose penetrating eyes the poetic ideals of old Venice flit to their limbo and leave behind four happy but quite unethereal lovers. The little tale contains a fine critical appreciation of Rossini's " Moïse " and closes with a bit of cynical irony worthy of the *Droll Stories*. Especial interest attaches to this story, for it is the nearest approach made by the author to the manner of Stendhal : almost no action, analysis by self-dissection in conversation, and a psychology so minute as to become almost painful. But the novel cannot be ranked among the more successful of Balzac.

Not altogether unlike this in its ethical bearing is the contemporaneous *Secret of the Princess of Cadignan*, which is really a sort of paraphrase of La Bruyère's remark that women " forget everything about their past lovers, even the favours that they have bestowed on them." Here this princess with a most varied past makes herself pass for a virgin martyr in the eyes of her poet-lover, Arthez, and possibly in her own also, so absorbed is she in the unquenched thirst of her present emotion. That little scene of human comedy is one of the most perfectly constructed in fiction, but the rest of the story is of very minor interest, though surely not so trivial as *Pierre Grassou*, a tale of

successful artist mediocrity, written in this year and published in the next, as was also *A Prince of Bohemia*, con-
sisting of some ill-natured satire on Sainte-Beuve, and the
rather tedious retailing of the café gossip of a certain
Lherminier at the Divan le Peletier, reproducing thus the
conditions of Diderot's *James the Fatalist*, though quite
without its verve and interest.

There is promise of better things, however, in *Pierrette*,
Z. Marcas, and *The Provincial Muse* (la Muse du département), and the fine *Second Study of Woman* (Autre
étude de femme) was written chiefly in this year also.
Pierrette has the same political bearing as *The Cabinet of
Antiquities*, but the shadow of this sombre period is upon it,
and it is one of the most gloomily sordid of all the scenes
of the *Human Comedy*. A sweet, simple child, killed with
refined cruelty, moral and physical, by the base calculations
of scheming relatives, " none of whom," as we are assured at
the close, "ever had the least remorse," is the central figure,
and the miscarriage of justice is so grotesquely horrible as
to justify the conclusion that " law would be a fine thing
for social scoundrelism if there were no God." But though
all this is very painful, the novel contains a curious study of
the " cryptogamous existences " of petty tradesmen, and in
Vinet a good type of the demagogues that were brought to
the surface in the scum of the political boiling of 1830.
Nowhere do Balzac's prejudices against the money-grub-
bing bourgeoisie of the Orleanist monarchy find a more
caustic expression than in this lawyer journalist and in his
Parisian fellow, Finot, in the second part of *Lost Illusions*,
with which *Pierrette* coincides in composition.

Pierrette was followed by portions of the *Petty Miseries of
Conjugal Life*, perhaps the most insignificant volume of all

the *Human Comedy*, and this in July by *Z. Marcas*, the
author's bitterest accusation against the bourgeois monarchy
for its suppression of the storm and stress of youth.
Marcas is the young Balzac, as he thought he was or might
have been, a titanic, but misunderstood political genius,
who needed only opportunity to move the world, but who
has fallen victim of the money power, and is crushed by
the ingratitude of the government he had served.   Nowhere does Balzac distil such concentrated contempt for
mediocracy with such mordant bitterness as here, and it is
curious to find also in *Z. Marcas* a prophecy of the second
and of the third republics.

The two stories of minor importance already mentioned,
A Prince of Bohemia and *Pierre Grassou*, with part of
Second Study of Woman and of *The Provincial Muse*, complete the work of this year, but in January, 1841, *A Mysterious Affair* (une Ténébreuse affaire) is ready for the
press, and something of his old fecundity enables him to
produce the first part of *Bachelor Housekeeping* in February, the conclusion of *Catherine de' Medeci* in March, addi-
tions to the *Village Curate* in May, *Ursule Mirouet* in
August, *The Memoirs of Two Young Wives* in November,
and *The False Mistress* in December.   The correspondence
for these years is scanty and somewhat pathetic.   In 1840
he writes to Madame Carraud that he is willing to make a
marriage for money, if only the girl be "witty and ambitious," for he is "exhausted physically and morally," still
overwhelmed by the necessity of rapid production to meet
advances from publishers and journals, too deep in debt to
present himself as candidate for the Academy, and even
breaking at last with the Society of Literary Men that he
had himself done much to found.

A Mysterious Affair (une Ténébreuse affaire) has the
merits of *The Chouans* in a more developed and chastened
form, but also the defect of that work, an intrigue that is so
complex as perpetually to escape all but the most attentive
readers. The secret police furnish here also the mainspring
of the story, and here as there history is interwoven with
fiction. Our interest, however, is less in this than in the
keen analysis of the various types of politician through
whom Napoleon was constrained to govern, but whom he
could never quite make up his mind to trust. Had he but
confided in Talleyrand, Masséna, and Fouché, says the novelist politician, "there would have been no more a Europe,
but a vast French empire."

Into the details of this story it is impossible to enter
briefly, and hardly necessary to our purpose to enter at all.
The date is 1804. The central figure, Malin de Gondre-
ville, is a trimmer, a miniature Talleyrand. His steward
Michu is an intransigeant royalist, masquerading as a jacobin the better to serve the interests of his exiled masters.
The heroine Laurence is just Scott's Diana Vernon, a
fanatic and fantastic royalist, who tricks the secret police
until their vengeance draws down the catastrophe. Michu
perishes and his masters are saved only by the intercession
of Laurence with the Emperor she has scorned. This interview on the eve of Jena is the crowning episode of the
whole book, which certainly deserves more attention than is
usually accorded to it.

The Calvinist Martyr, the first and last-written part of
Catherine de' Medici, is also the best, but the whole is interesting for its minute archæological reproduction both of
buildings and of manners, and also for its analysis of the
complex nature and policy of Catherine, whom Balzac

seems to have been one of the first to begin to apprehend. Excellent, too, are the portraits of Francis II. and of Charles IX., of Queen Mary of Scotland, and of Calvin. Less interesting is the extended study of the Rosicrucian Ruggieri, but the novel, as a whole, is sufficient to show that Balzac might have been as easily the first historical novelist of France as he is first in other fields of fiction.

Ursule Mirouet may be regarded as a sort of atonement for *Pierrette*. Here the simple and innocent girl triumphs over selfish and cynical schemers, but not without the intervention of spiritualistic visions and unaccountable conversions that give the work a place quite apart. Perhaps no story of Balzac is so uneven. The plot is far too involved, and the machinations of the expectant heirs grow wearisome. On the other hand, Dr. Minoret, "an atheist after the fashion of Rousseau's Wolmar" is almost always delightful, and the priest Chaperon is one of the best and wisest clerics in all the *Human Comedy*, while the holy innocence of Ursule sheds its fragrance over all, and makes her girlish love a true refreshment for the soul.

The Memoirs of Two Young Wives (les Mémoires de deux jeunes mariées), to which Gautier contributed two poems, is Balzac's first novel in letters, and attempts with much penetration and pathos to place thus in constant and effective contrast phases of the marriage of reason and convenience over against that of romantic love and passion. The letters of the young mother, Renée, recount some of the most charming scenes of private life in all literature, while the twice married Louise loses first her husband and then herself, both victims of the excess of their passion. The moral of this novel is that which Balzac selected for *The False Mistress* (la Fausse maîtresse), printed at the same time, that " friendship is richer than love, for it knows not the bankruptcies of sentiment and the failures of pleasure. After giving more than it has, love (such as that of Louise) ends by giving less than it receives." In *The False Mistress*, however, the situation is wholly different. The hero, Paz, is a trusted Joseph in Potiphar's household. He cannot leave his Potiphar, for he is necessary to the administration of his affairs. He loves Madame, and Madame loves him. But neither the coldness nor the faithlessness of this Potiphar can shake Joseph's fidelity, to which he sacrifices his reputation, and even the appearance of honour. This ultra-romantic tale deserves notice for the sureness and rapidity of its movement, and for the ingenious refinement of the trials to which the soul of Paz is subjected, but it is not a novel that lays hold on life.

Somewhat of the discouragement of the preceding years continues in 1842. In April he is thinking of abandoning literature altogether, and a reflection of this state of mind appears in *Albert Savarus*, published in May. This story has been often highly praised for its tragic force and for its plot, unduly so perhaps, for the intrigue depends on an improbable combination of accident and baseness, and the close is more fit to provoke moral revolt than tragic fear. Albert is the male counterpart of Camille in *Beatrix*. Himself an ambitious servant of love, he falls a victim to ruthless coquetry, to a truly romantic desire of self-utterance, that led him to write transparently autobiographical fiction, and to a pardonable lack of caution that led him not to post his love-letters himself, as Balzac later anxiously exhorts Madame Hanska to do. And these are by no means all the obviously weak points in a story that in spite of 90 pages is one of the least satisfactory in all the

Human Comedy. It is morbid, and so was Balzac when he wrote it.

Unsatisfactory also is *A Start in Life* (un Début dans la vie) that followed *Albert Savarus* in July. This is a sketch of commonplace Parisian and provincial bourgeoisie, in its way as minute as Flaubert's *Madame Bovary*, with more sordid realism, but with less psychological interest and practically no plot. The novel is largely in conversation, and such interest as it has is in the exhibition of types of bourgeois character. First there is Cardot, of the generation of 1795, as sensual as the Hulot of *Cousin Betty*, but shrewd where Hulot had been senile, a character not uncommon among the admirers of Jefferson two generations ago in America. Then there is Moreau to represent the rising into the bourgeoisie of a lower social stratum, and Madame Clapart, who spoils her son's career by unwise social ambitions. Others figure for us the romantic dandy and the typical middle-class man " in search of a social position." So, though *A Start in Life* is not interesting as a story, it has value as a social study, and the half-dozen pages on the character of Cardot, with his gradual discovery of what love costs old men, a preliminary sketch for the second part of the *Splendours and Miseries of Courtesans*, to follow in 1843, will be remembered and treasured by all judicious readers.

Passing over a small portion of *The Reverse of Contemporary History* (l'Envers de l'histoire contemporaine), printed in September, we come in October, 1842, to one of the great dates in Balzac's life, the first publication of the *Human Comedy* under that title, and with a preface in which he states the co-ordinating principles that make him an evolutionist, and his work unique in fiction.

This may justly be deferred till the examination of the novels shall be completed. We pass, therefore, to November and to *Second Study of Woman* and the finished *Bachelor Housekeeping*. The former is indeed less a novel than a conversation between some choice spirits at a *soirée* at Madame d'Espard's, one of the "high-fliers" of the *Human Comedy*. The talk turns on the position of women in modern society, and on the distinction between fidelity and constancy. Three little tales set off the discussion. Of these *The Great Bastion*, taken for the purpose from its original place in *The Message*, is the most famous, but that other story of the long-suffering captain who on the retreat from Moscow burns alive the faithless wife with her lover is a precious contribution to the "shiver in literature" and merits the remark of Marsay that "nothing is more terrible than sheepish rage."

Nothing can give us a more striking idea of the versatility of Balzac's genius than that he should be able to turn from such aristocratic company as that of the *Second Study* to the relentless sordidness of *Bachelor Housekeeping* (la Rabouilleuse, *or* un Ménage de garçon), one of the most vigorously drawn, intense, and fearful scenes of the *Human Comedy*. Here vice displays all its naked horror in the senile sensuality of the vulgar and timid voluptuary and imbecile, Rouget, in the soulless bestiality of Flore, in the fierce, satanic selfishness of Philippe Bridau, and the atrocious egoism of Maxence, both types of the officer of the Empire out of service. Against these, Philippe's mother and his brother Joseph, a study of the artist Delacroix, seem pitifully helpless and defencelessly childlike. It is curious to note, however, that parts of this story are very far beneath its average, and the pranks of the youth of Issudun are inexplicably silly. It is hard to resist the suspicion that Balzac was spinning copy here, as he had already done occasionally, and certainly did during the first half of 1843 in *Honorine* and *The Provincial Muse* (la Muse du département).

In the winter of 1842–1843 Monsieur Hanski had died and Madame Hanska, whom he had loved from afar for ten years, was now free, though bound to Russia by the interests of her children and of her estates. In August Balzac visited her at Saint Petersburg, and for the early part of the year he was restless in anticipation of this crisis, and working very unevenly. " I recognise," he writes, " the infinite depth of my passion by the immensity of the void that there is in my soul. Love for me is life, and to-day I feel it more than ever." In January, while in this state of mind, he wrote, and in March he published, *Honorine*, whose object, like that of *The Two Young Wives*, is to represent the bankruptcy of romantic marriage, and incidentally to discuss the social rehabilitation of the penitent adulteress, " a very rare and most monstrous exception," we are told, who dies in the endeavour to make her gratitude simulate love.

By June he had practically completed another study of adultery from a slightly different angle, *The Provincial Muse* (la Muse du département). This is the story of Dinah de la Boudraye, a woman who, after some years of unsympathetic marriage and of unquestioned pre-eminence in literature and wit in her provincial town, finds herself unable to resist the seductions of the witty and *blasé* Parisian journalist, Lousteau. The first three-fifths of the novel are occupied with this provincial scene. Then the stage shifts to Paris, whither Dinah follows Lousteau, and we have by far the strongest part of the story, a description of the petty miseries of adultery and of Bohemian journalism, that etches its moral with an acid as cutting as that of *Madame Bovary*. Admirably conceived is the cynical, dwarfish husband, who manages to turn his wife's fault to his own selfish ends and is in no haste to interrupt a relation that brings its own lingering punishment; " for in nature," says Balzac, " these extreme situations do not end as in books, by skilfully managed catastrophes; they end much less poetically, by disgust, by blighting all the flowers of the soul." In his more romantic period, in *The Woman of Thirty*, in *La Grenadière*, in *The Deserted Wife*, and elsewhere Balzac had shown the romance, the pathos, the tragedy of adultery. Here with a clearer realistic vision of life he was to show its petty vileness, and to preach from another text the same lesson of submission to social conventions and conservatism. There is more tragic fear in the momentary lapse of Dinah at the very close than in the tragic death of those earlier heroines, though the novel taken as a whole is almost as uneven in execution as *Ursule Mirouet*, much more so than *Bachelor Housekeeping*, and more than the fragments of the *Splendours and Miseries of Courtesans*, printed in May and July, or than *Lost Illusions*, whose publication, begun seven years before, was completed during the appearance of *The Provincial Muse*.

Lost Illusions (les Illusions perdues), begun in 1837 and finished in 1843, is the longest novel of Balzac and one of the most interesting. The " lost illusions " are those of David Sechard, a printer at Angoulême, and of his brother-in-law Lucien de Rubempré, a sport of fortune and finally a tool of the arch-knave Jacques Collin at Paris. The schemes and misfortunes of the inventor David were in part suggested by Balzac's own commercial experiences and are well told, though quite inferior in interest to the brilliant career and disgrace of the fair but weak-willed Lucien, a poet with aspirations to virtue and tendencies to vice. In this connection Balzac has found opportunity for another exposure of the scandals of French journalism, so true that even to-day it has not ceased to burn and smart. The French newspaper office was then what it often is now, "a shop where are kept on sale words of any colour to suit the public." It was this that gave the *Illusions* its immediate and sensational success. Now, by the number of its characters and their ramifications through almost all the Parisian scenes and many of the others, it has become one of the principal radiating points for all studies of the psychology of the *Human Comedy*, and an essential prelude to *The Splendours and Miseries of Courtesans*, the greatest triumph of Balzac's genius.

During Balzac's absence in Russia there had appeared a fragment of *The Reverse of Contemporary History* (l'Envers de l'histoire contemporaine), to be continued in the next year and completed in 1847. He returned more in love than ever with Madame Hanska, but it was not till 1846 that he could obtain any promise of marriage from her, and four years more before he could obtain its performance. One would not be unjust to the woman whom Balzac loved so long and faithfully, nor repeat the scandalous insinuation of the Goncourts' *Journal* (viii. 48 *sq.*), but it is impossible not to see from his correspondence that this uncertainty lamed his mind and perhaps injured his health. Madame Hanska had agreed to meet him in 1844. She did not, perhaps she could not, keep her promise, but he complains that her vacillation has made

him lose valuable time and business opportunities. Even
when she went to Dresden in 1845 she held him off and
again interrupted his writing. In the winter of 1845-6
he joined her on the way to Italy, returning in January
to go back to Rome in March, thus earning for himself
from Madame de Girardin the name *vetturino per amore*,
the "coachman for love." A little later at Strasburg
she pledged herself to him, and he visited her again
at Wiesbaden during that year. Such a life was not
favourable to literary production, and though love inspired
ambition, we can see from his letters that his health
was not bearing the strain. In February, 1844, he compares himself to Napoleon who "lived on the blood of
Europe," while " I shall have borne a complete society in
my brain." Soon he will have finished painting " Paris, that
great modern monster, under all its faces." He undertakes to work " with a fury more than French, Balzacian,"
and thinks, poor man, that he sees the end of his financial
troubles. Yet he tells Madame Hanska that without her
love he would write no more nor care for the world. He
reminds her how they have read his proofs together, how
she has helped him in the composition of *Modeste Mignon*
and *The Peasants* (les Paysans), as she had done also
perhaps, at least by suggestion, for *The Lily in the Valley*.
It is she who gives the title to *Cousin Pons ;* and yet he
feels and tells her that she " has no idea of what she is to
him " or she would not paralyse his mind by caprice and
suspense. And now let us consider the work of these years
of hope deferred.

In 1844 Balzac printed parts of the still incomplete
Reverse of Contemporary History, of *The Splendours and
Miseries of Courtesans*, of *The Peasants*, and of *The Uncon-*

scious Comedians (les Comédiens sans le savoir). He also practically completed the manuscript of *The Lower Middle-class* (les Petits bourgeois), which was not printed till four years after his death. Beside these there is the rather insignificant *Gaudissart II.*, an amusing description of the skill of a Parisian salesman in adapting himself to a customer's character and in selling him what he does not want, the concluding part of *Béatrix* (un Adultère rétrospectif), and the complete *Modeste Mignon*. This last, written as it was printed, from May to July, shows the new hope, before its deferring had made his heart sick. It is the most charming of the scenes of private life, being to *Père Goriot* what *As you like it* is to *Lear*. The satire here is lighter, the humour more playful than in any of the preceding scenes of private life, for Madame Hanska had smiled on it, and it was but justice that it should be dedicated to her. The subject is still that of *The Two Young Wives*, the question whether romantic love is the best guarantee of married happiness, but the lesson is taught here with an unwonted smile. Modeste's " cerebral love," that " worst vice of the French woman " in Balzac's eyes, is directed here to poetic genius and nursed by wide reading. She loves for his aspiring verses, Canalis, a " sacristan Dorat," whom she has never seen. In reality he is a Chateaubriand, with a little mixture of Lamartine, a *blasé*, dry nature, poetic only in its literary expression. Opposed to Canalis is Ernest, " an ordinary man, of positive virtues and safe morality, the sort that pleases parents," and toward the close an aristocratic suitor comes on the scene in the person of the amiable Duke of Herouville, the feeble scion of a decaying stock. Among these Modeste chooses, aided by the counsel of her father, the admirable Colonel Mignon, and by the unselfish love of the hunchback Bustcha. The novel has faults; the close is a variation, rather too long, on the old theme of a lover's ardour cooled by false news of poverty; and the resort to lying both by Modeste and Bustcha forfeits them somewhat of Anglo-Saxon sympathy; but the girlish shrewdness of the heroine is quite delightful and the literary satire will be enjoyed by all who know Chateaubriand and have discovered, what his own wife always knew, that he is not to be taken seriously. Lamartine too was a *poseur*, who liked to be pictured "with hair floating in the wind and David's harp leaning against his redingote," and Balzac put just enough of him in his Canalis to make the purpose clear. No doubt there is something of Madame Récamier in the Duchess of Chaulieu, who, however, plays but a slight part; and in Ernest, determined to be "the dupe of no one and of nothing," Balzac probably intended a little compliment to Stendhal. It is pleasant to find these scenes of private life after so many storms ending in such smiling sanity and peace.

The Lower Middle-class (les Petits bourgeois), on the other hand, carries us back to the environment of *César Birotteau*, but here we have the retired bourgeois with political ambition exploited by a heartless intrigue of a social struggle, Théodore de la Peyrade for the hand of Céleste Colleville, in which he is thwarted by the hidden hand of Vautrin's rival Corentin, while the girl is suffered to be happy with the man of her choice, Professor Félix Phellion. The novel has suffered undue neglect from the uncertainty as to the part in it of Charles Rabou, under whose care it was posthumously published, with *The Peasants* and *The Deputy of Arcis* (le Député d'Arcis), the latter with an avowed conclusion by this literary executor. But besides admirable types of the bourgeoisie, that "vital force of our corrupt society," with its acquisitive and administrative instincts exhibited in Brigitte Thullier, its old-time integrity in Phellion, and its baser side in that modern Tartuffe, La Peyrade, we find here a somewhat pale reflection of the detective romance that was to reach its height in the *Splendours*. Corentin reappears here as an impossible chief of police, employing public agents and funds in furtherance of private schemes, and selecting as his successor a man whose unfitness for any office of trust would be obvious to a child. Balzac rises, in this character, but little above the level of Ponson du Terrail's Racombole, but in Cérizet he has drawn an admirable figure of the petty usurer, and several of the poor victims of his favours leave ineffacable impressions on the imagination of the reader. While, then, *The Lower Middle-class* is by no means to be unreservedly commended, it is by no means to be neglected by any who are interested in observing the range of Balzac's genius.

The first part of *The Peasants* (les Paysans) appeared also during this December, 1844, and was all that was printed during Balzac's life. It lays bare with sternest realism the vices of peasant character. His references to this novel in the correspondence are constant, and he seems to have found it mentally impossible to concentrate his mind on it for long intervals of time, which shows plainly enough that his brain was calling for more repose than Madame Hanska, his creditors, and his publishers were giving him. "Is it written," he writes, "that to the end I shall be tormented like a school fag?"

Balzac's central interest here is the result on land tenure and on agriculture of the revolutions of 1789 and of 1830. He wishes to show how the land-hunger of the peasant,

which from a slave of the soil has made him its master, has
wrought the moral and economic injury of the nation, while
the financial gain has fallen, not to the cultivators, but to
their bourgeois exploiters in what Balzac calls the reign of
mediocracy. The scene is laid in Burgundy, where he
thinks the ideas of the Jacquerie have taken firmest root.
Montcornet, a general of the empire, is endeavouring to govern his large estate with generous firmness. His wife is an
angel of sentimental charity. They inspire in the peasants,
however, only hatred and contempt. The shrewd vicious-
ness and malicious bestiality of the innkeeper Tonsard, the
poacher Bonnebault, the vagabond boy Mouche, and best of
all his aged preceptor in vice, Fourchon, suggest even in details Zola's *Earth*, to which   *he Peasants* is, however, far
superior in breadth of vision. Shrewd as the peasants
are, they become the victims and the tools of the new
bourgeoisie, represented here by the unjust steward,
Gaubertin, and by the admirable figure of the country
usurer, Rigou, "the alpha and omega of democracy, deep
as a monk, silent as a studious Benedictine, shrewd as
a priest, tricky like all misers, always within the law.
In other times he might have been a Tiberius, a Richelieu, or a Fouché, but he was wise enough in his day
to be an unpretentious Lucullus and a miserly voluptuary."
With diabolical patience these men undermine the position of Montcornet and of all that aid him, the saintly Abbé
Brossetête, "a pariah on whom they spy like a common
enemy," and the soldierly guard, Michaud, whose murder they do not scruple to procure. So at last they acquire
what the peasants have won for them, and these last are
more helpless than ever in the clutch of a quasi-hereditary
bureaucracy and of usury. It is a gloomy outlook, and the

author seems to find, at the close, consolation only in the anticipated hour of the fruition of his love, implied in the marriage of the widow of Montcornet with Blondet, the literary spectator of the drama.

At the opening of 1845 we find these melancholy lines in a letter to Madame Carraud: "Pity me; I work sixteen hours a day, I still owe more than 100,000 francs, and I am forty-five." Too much of these sixteen hours, however, was spent in writing to Madame Hanska, for except for fragments of the *Petty Miseries* this year added to the *Human Comedy*, only a trifle in the style of *Gaudissart II.*, *A Man of Business* (un Homme d'affaires), which is a clever tale of a clever business trick, and the concluding parts of *The Unconscious Comedians* (les Comédiens sans le savoir), which was a mere device to report on the position in 1845 of various persons who had figured in the *Human Comedy* in former years. This, however, was not printed till April of 1846, and that year produced only parts or fragments of the truly petty *Petty Miseries*, of *The Reverse of Contemporary History*, and of those novels in which Balzac was to gather up all that was most brilliant in his genius, the *Splendours and Miseries of Courtesans* and *The Poor Relatives*. The latter was the first to be finished, *Cousin Betty* (la Cousine Bette) in December of this year, *Cousin Pons* and *The Splendours and Miseries* in May, 1847. In December of that year Balzac seems to have done his last work for the *Human Comedy* in completing *The Reverse of Contemporary History*, though he may have written further on *The Deputy of Arcis*, of which he had printed a part in May, 1847, and which he left unfinished.

This fragment, as its name implies, is a study of the French electoral machinery and its practical workings under the Orleanist monarchy, with which, as we know, Balzac had never been in sympathy. It is probable that of the two volumes under this title Balzac wrote only *The Election*, about half of the first, and that the three concluding parts are the sole creation of Charles Rabou, who suggests his model by occasional imitation and frequent unconscious parody. It is hardly just to Balzac to base any criticism on this novel. If it affords a just picture of the nominating machinery of the period, this would seem to have been clumsy, inefficient, and more subject to feminine influence than one would have supposed. Some of the scenes are vividly drawn, but there are very few of those master touches that had marked the preceding work of this year. It is as though his brain had not recovered from the strain of producing *Cousin Pons* when he set to work on *The Deputy*. But the correspondence throws no light on the matter. It shows him only wrestling with the remnant of his debts, of which it seems that he kept no systematic accounts, and emerging from these to enter on railway speculation and on a fantastic scheme for transporting lumber from Russia to France. That elasticity of mind and easy flow of genius of which Balzac speaks so exultingly to Madame Hanska in June of 1846 was gone forever, but it had sufficed to give us four great novels, running through almost the whole scale of Balzac's genius, like the brilliant finale of the spectacle before the curtain falls.

First, *The Splendours and Miseries of Courtesans*, begun in 1838, continued in 1843, in 1844, and in 1846, completed at last in December of that year, and printed in May, 1847. The interest throughout this long novel centres always in Jacques Collin, *alias* Vautrin, who had played a large part also in *Père Goriot* and in *Lost Illusions*. This man is the somewhat enigmatic incarnation of personal will pushed to the negation of all social obligations. His tools are the weak and fascinating Lucien de Rubempré and the courtesan Esther Gobseck, another of those virgins of the heart so frequent since Marion de Lorme. Through Lucien, Jacques Collin hopes to gain social recognition for his creature if not for himself, and through Esther he hopes to gain the means for it. Nucingen the banker is the intended victim. There are plots and counter-plots, and the intense suspense of the intrigue is ended at last only by the suicide of the heart-sick Esther. Thus far the novel of 1838–1844. In the continuation of 1846 we are told of the titanic struggle of Vautrin with the law, and of the truce between them by which the ex-convict becomes chief of police, when the suicide of Rubempré has taken from him the motive for his self-assertion. No novel of crime, in that lower kind, has ever surpassed this, but the *Splendours and Miseries* is much more than a criminal novel. Besides the battle of Vautrin and his band against the wiles of the shrewd detectives set on their track by Nucingen, is the touching though somewhat romantic struggle of Esther for purity of soul, and there are some firmly drawn types of the aristocracy, and an admirable picture of the courts, their personnel and procedure under the Restoration. The novel lacks the realistic intensity of *Eugénie Grandet*, of *Bachelor Housekeeping*, or of *Cousin Betty*, but as a romance and a novel of plot it is easily first in the *Human Comedy*.

In June, 1846, Balzac writes that the conclusion of *Splendours and Miseries* will give him the first money that will be really his, and will found his fortune. " The moment demands," he continues, " that I write two or three masterpieces . . . that shall prove that I am younger, fresher, more fruitful than ever." In *Pons*, he says, he will paint "the poor relative, overwhelmed with humiliations, insults, full of heart, pardoning all, and avenging himself only by his benefits. *Cousin Betty* is to show the poor relative overwhelmed by humiliations and insults, living in the intimacy of three or four families, and meditating there the vengeance of her injured self-esteem and her wounded vanity." The subject fascinated him. In July he writes: "I leave you to return to my Old Musician (Pons). I am well. My head is full of ideas. I work easily." He assures Madame Hanska repeatedly of the satisfaction that he has in it, greater even than in the great success of the *Splendours and Miseries*. It is "a work of excessive simplicity that contains all the human heart;" but *Cousin Betty* is to be "a terrible novel," and the thought of visiting Madame Hanska at its conclusion "gives his work an impulse such as he had never known."

This latter was the first printed of the two and had a sensational success, which indeed it deserved, for it showed Balzac's genius brightest at its setting, a guiding star for the whole naturalistic movement of the next generation. *Cousin Betty* is the most implacably naturalistic of all the scenes of the *Human Comedy*. In none do the characters brand themselves so indelibly on the mind as here those of Betty and Madame Marneffe, of Crevel and of Hulot, unless it be in *Cousin Pons* the figures of Pons and Schmucke, of Cibot and Remonencq. These stories, written in anticipation of his marriage, with mind almost free from financial anxieties, show his mental powers in their highest development, even while his physique was giving way under the tremendous strain to which for fifteen years he had subjected it.

It is not possible here to do more than suggest the kind
of strength that these novels exhibit.   In the former we are
shown the jealous intriguing poor relative, an old maid as
acrid and more perverse than the tormentor of Abbé
Birotteau.   Her cousin Hulot, an old general of the Empire,
is now the victim of a senile erethism, described with a
horrible minuteness that has been attempted but not attained in Zola's *Nana*.   These two compass the wretchedness and almost the moral ruin of Madame Hulot, and just
fail in attaining the same end with her daughter Hortense,
two figures of less interest.   But the strongest characters in
the book are Madame Marneffe and Crevel, the former a
Becky Sharp in her second or third incarnation, a demi-
mondaine, or "*demi-castor*," who has a dreamy look, a
candid face, and a strong-box for a heart ; the latter the
best type in literature of the materialistic, libertine, wealthy
bourgeois of the reign of Louis Philippe.   Interesting, too,
are the courtesans, the wandering black sheep of society,
Josepha and Jenny Cadine, in a numerous company, with
Madame Nourisson for their worthy shepherdess.   The hun-
dreds, possibly thousands of volumes that have since been
written on the various aspects of venal love have hardly
widened or deepened Balzac's analysis of this painful but
ever-present subject, and as a sombre study of human baseness *Cousin Betty* awaits its equal in fiction.

Cousin Pons, on the other hand, considers the poor relative in the light of a " nigh related guest " that outstays his
welcome while, and is made to quiver in all his sensitive
nature at his irksomeness.   Here, then, the tone is more
pathetic, elegiac.   We are bidden to watch the crushing of
unselfish simplicity under the relentless pressure of egoism.
But into episodes in the story Balzac has infused much of

his own spirit as an amateur collector, and it is said that more than one treasure from Pons' collection was in the author's. This gives the story a less intense unity than *Cousin Betty*, and there is also a regrettable abuse of dialect that threatens to change our admiration for Schmucke's virtues into irritation at his imbecility. On the whole *Cousin Pons* is most admirable for those pages in which it most resembles *Cousin Betty*. The concierge, La Cibot, whose negative virtue is transformed before our eyes into the basest unscrupulousness by social ambition, is a marvel of voluble hypocrisy, as terrible as Zola's Thérèse Raquin in her exhibition of the mastery of a fixed idea, which indeed appears also in the Auvergnat junk-dealer Romanencq, another character conceived with great power. The novel has scenes as strong, as touching and as unspeakably horrible as any that Balzac ever wrote, but as a whole it is inferior to *Cousin Betty*, if indeed it is just to speak of inferiority among works both so excellent and so far above even the usual high level of their author.

If, as Balzac has been at pains to show us in the whole series of his economic and political novels, materialism is the foundation of contemporary ethics, and mediocracy of contemporary politics, what remains for the representatives of the old creed and the old aristocracy who are not content to be Adullamites and who know that labour is prayer? This is the question that Balzac has asked himself in *The Reverse of Contemporary History* (l'Envers de l'histoire contemporaine), which crowns his work with an epic of charity and an elegy of pardon. A group of noble souls, to whose hearts and fortunes the revolutions have done despite, band themselves together into the Brotherhood of Consolation, with Madame de la Chanterie for their head, and Thomas à

Kempis for their guide. During one of the risings in the West against Napoleon, Madame de la Chanterie had been betrayed and her daughter guillotined by her son-in-law, the renegade noble and police-spy Contenson, abetted by an unscrupulous judge, Bourlac. This Bourlac, now reduced to the greatest misery, is saved from torture of mind, heart, and body by the unremitting and hidden charity of the woman he had imprisoned and whose daughter he had practically murdered. The theme, then, is Christian forgiveness, and the book, especially in its frequent ethical and philosophical digressions, takes the form of a pathetic plea for a faith that the author feels is passing away with the deadening of the spiritual life of his country. Madame de la Chanterie is perhaps the noblest female figure that Balzac has conceived, finer than Josephine Claës or Madame de Mortsauf, surely finer than Véronique Graslin. And so the *Human Comedy* rises *per angusta ad augusta*, from petty baseness to august nobility. It has its Inferno and its Purgatorio, but it ends with a beatific vision.

Balzac's last years were made unfruitful by illness. He spent the greater part of his time in Russia, whence shortly after his marriage with Madame Hanska he returned to Paris, to die there on the twelfth of August, 1850. At his funeral Hugo addressed those who had come to do honour to one who was to remain among the great glories of their literature. " Such coffins," said the poet, " proclaim immortality. We feel the divine destiny of that intellect that has traversed earth to suffer and be purified. So great a genius in this life cannot but be a great spirit hereafter."

CHAPTER VII.

IT remains to us, from that summit of Père Lachaise where Balzac lies buried, to survey his work as a whole, and to show, if it may be, wherein and why Balzac is the greatest novelist and one of the greatest seers of the human heart in all literature. Let us consider first what he tried to do, as he states it in the preface to his *Human Comedy*, as it may be read in the volume entitled *The Cat and the Racket* (la Maison du chat qui pelote).

He says here that the first thought of a Human Comedy came to him like a hazy dream or some impossible project that one caresses and then lets float away. Might it not be possible, he had thought, to do for human nature what Saint-Hilaire had done for the animal kingdom, to show that all society was bound together by a unity of composition which an evolution in varied environments had diversified, so that there were different species of men just as there were different zoölogical varieties? Might it not be as possible, though surely more difficult, to seize the differences that distinguish a soldier, a workman, a lawyer, a scholar, a statesman, a merchant, as those that differentiate the wolf, the lion, the ass, the raven, the shark, and the sheep? Might not Buffon's work for nature be repeated for society? But when he reached this point, he says he hesitated. To do this would require three thousand, perhaps four thousand characters, and he saw that even the genius of Scott had not been able to give unity to his creative fecundity. Then, after a time, as with a flash, the thought came to him: Let French society be the historian and myself its secretary. I will draw up the inventory of its vices and its virtues, gather the principal facts of its passions, compose types for it by uniting homogeneous natures into a composite character, and so perhaps I shall succeed in writing that history that so many historians have forgotten, the history of manners. And my point of view, the fulcrum from which my work shall move my readers, shall be that of the conservative Christian monarchist, who has lived under the Emperor, the Bourbons, and the Orleanist, knows through friends the Republic and the Old Régime, has an instinctive hate of mediocracy, and thinks government by universal suffrage "the only one where tyranny is boundless, and the only one that is irresponsible."

The novels, that are to be the minutes of this secretary of society, are to be ideal in their general conception, but real in their details. They must shrink neither from the painting of vice in its nakedness nor from the passion that melts and recasts our human nature, for without passion what place would remain for religion, history, fiction, or art? And here he pauses to defend himself from the strange charge that he is a sensualist, an absurd accusation that has been thrown up by moral moles against all his successors, — not unnaturally indeed, for the accusation is easy to make, it casts a sort of halo of self-righteousness about the accuser, and is almost impossible to disprove or to efface from minds soft enough to receive the impression. He claims boldly and truly that he has succeeded in the difficult literary problem of making virtue interesting. There are many noble souls in the *Human Comedy*. How

fresh in the mind of every reader is the fragrant memory of
Pierette Lorain, of Ursule Mirouet, of Constance Birotteau,
of Eugénie Grandet, of Marguerite Claës, of Ève Chardon,
of Renée de Maucombe, Madame Firmiani, and, above
them all, the angelic Madame de la Chanteraie ; and who
shall say that manly virtue is not lovable in Joseph Lebas,
in Genestas, in Dr. Benassis and Dr. Mirouet, in the
curates Birotteau, Bonnet, and Chaperon, in the righteous
judge Popinot, and the printer David Sechard? while Balzac has crowned his defence of human nature in the characters of Schmucke and his friend Pons.   There is no need
to continue the list.   All that he need ask is that his work
be read as a whole, for as a whole it must be pronounced
serious in purpose, high and edifying in tone.

We speak of reading it as a whole, yet we know it is
incomplete.   But what remains is cyclopean.   It was, as
he said, no small task to conceive and paint the living portrait of two thousand of the striking figures of an epoch,
and in their mimic life to formulate not only individuals
but the chief events of social life, those situations that are
reproduced in all existences, and then to give to his scenes
such a variety of setting that his work should have its geography as well as its genealogy.   The immensity of such a
plan, that embraced at once the history and the criticism of
the society of half a century, the analysis of its ills, and the
investigation of its fundamental principles, could alone
authorize the title, ambitious and yet just, " The Comedy
of Human Life."

This Comedy he divided, adopting in part previously
chosen collective titles, into Scenes of private life, of provincial and Parisian life, of agricultural and village life (*vie
de campagne*), of politics and war, and to these he added a

series of philosophic studies. There are those who extol
the analytic acumen displayed in this arrangement, but it
is to be feared that they are the dupes of a scheme more
convenient to the publisher than valuable to the reader.
For Balzac frequently transferred tales and novels from one
series to another to suit the publisher's convenience or
his own changed fancy; and it is time wasted to insist on a
classification that places *A Passion in the Desert* among
military scenes, and *Adieu* among philosophic studies, with
Sarrasine hovering between philosophy and Paris, and *Père
Goriot* between Parisian and private life. The only "philosophic" way to study Balzac's work is to study it first as
it grew in the author's mind, and then as it presents itself
in its entirety. The former we have already endeavoured.
The latter we will now essay. But first a word in regard
to the attitude of criticism toward Balzac in the last fifty
years.

He died at the height of his fame, widely mourned, and yet
hardly appreciated by the critics or by the public; else how
could Sainte-Beuve, in his thoughtful Essay ("Causeries,"
ii. 443) have compared Balzac, as like in kind, to Dumas
père or to Eugène Sue? How could he have spoken with
a certain condescending regret of the talent that had passed
away, while he ignored the genius, or have wished for the
novelist of the future "a calmer life, inspirations more
subtle, but gentler, healthier, more serene?" It is true
that old wounds may have rankled in Sainte-Beuve's breast,
and yet very few at that time measured at all the height
of that splendid and sovereign intelligence which, as Hugo
said at Balzac's grave, " disclosed in sudden revelations the
most sombre and tragic ideals, . . . dug into and sounded
the depths of the abyss that is in every man, and could

rise from those terrible studies that had made Molière melancholy and Rousseau a misanthrope, still smiling in serene calm."

Even during the next decade few discerned the supreme place that is now accorded everywhere, always, and by all to Balzac in fiction. George Sand, writing with complacent garrulity in 1857, sees indeed that he is "the first of novelists" and "pre-eminently the critic of human life." The novel was to him, she says, "a frame and pretext for an almost universal examination of the ideas, sentiments, customs, habits, legislation, art, trades, costumes, localities, — in short, of all that constituted the lives of his contemporaries." She saw that "this great anatomist of life" was essentially moral in his life and works. But she thought he lacked the power to idealise sentiment, that his style was laboured, his taste false, and his composition bad, though these great faults were, she admitted, redeemed by great merits.

In 1859 Gautier followed with his friendly "portrait," which, like everything that Gautier's pen touched, is charming, but it is surely not criticism in any serious sense, nor meant to be. Then followed the really epoch-making study of Taine in 1865. Since then the lamp of Balzac's fame has burned ever steadier and brighter. Taine first saw the monumental, classic character of Balzac's novels, that element that made him not of an age but for all time. And ever since there has been gathering around Balzac a literature that has revealed to us more and more of the depth and breadth of his social vision, and has established his place as one of the world's great creators in the realm of imaginative literature.

The dominant trait in Balzac, whether we consider his

style, his imagination, or his thought, is exuberant virility. He seemed, said Champfleury, "like a wild boar at play." His life is always intense, both in his work and in his recreation. No labor is so irksome to him as idleness, no feat of the imagination so difficult to him as its repose. His animal nature is as ebullient as his intellectual. Probably chaste in life, he delights in debauches of cerebral sensuality, which he drapes in a piquantly diaphanous medieval veil, for he is a complete man and extreme in every manifestation of his nature. We shall see this intemperance in his style, in his thought, in his imagination, in his composition. It is this that makes him a romantic realist, the incarnation of the natural and sane reaction from a generation that had nursed a sentimental morbidity on René and Obermann. Romantic by the vigour of his imagination, he was realist by the nature of his mind. As one of his critics has said, he united the temperament of an artist to the spirit of a commercial traveller, — an epigrammatic way of saying that he observed quickly and accurately all about him in its practical aspects like a man of business, who trusts he is disabused of the illusions of the ideal, who understands quite well that money is the mainspring of the new democratic society, for better- or worse, as it had been of all his own adult life. For, as Taine excellently says, Balzac was not only a busy man and a man of business, he was so with a Parisian intensity. "In this black ant-heap of Paris democratic institutions and centralised government have gathered all the ambitious and inflamed all ambitions. . . . To succeed, that word unknown a century ago, is the sovereign master of all lives ; " and it is this that gives to Balzac his titanic energy, that wishes to be all-embracing even at the cost of haste and incompleteness. " Hoping to build a monument

that shall endure rather by its mass and by the heaping up
of its materials than by the beauty of the edifice, I am
obliged," he writes to Madame Hanska, "to touch on
everything, that I be not accused of impotence."   Thus
Balzac, as well as his *Human Comedy*, reflects the spirit of
his time, the spirit of intense labour and desperate struggle
with an ever-widening sea of things to be known, of forces
to be conquered, of complex interests to be reconciled.
He shrinks from the conception of the world in which he
labours, " that great cloudy cancer spread out over both
banks of the Seine."   Yet no one that had been less of his
age, no one who had been less typical of its struggle for
life, could have rendered that state of soul in its grand and
terrible manifestations and in its little unconscious betray-
als in garment and gesture, could have seen it with a
judicial eye, seen through it with analytic insight, and beyond it with a seer's vision.   He was so wholly of his
world, and yet he so wholly dominated it.   Nothing human
was foreign to him, neither grossness, nor sensuality, nor
luxury, nor the passion of the artist and the collector, nor
the unbridled curiosity that for a new experience is ready,
with the aid of hashish or opium, —

> "To plunge to the gulf's bottom, heaven or hell, what reck we ?
> To the bottom of the unknown to find the new."

And yet with, may we not say *because* of, this intensity of
physical and material life, he was haunted with the questions of political sociology and moral economy, and capable
of rising on the wings of an inspired fancy to the mystic
union of the soul with the sources of its spiritual being.
For shall not he who has a perfect knowledge of the muddy
vesture of decay that wraps the soul have glimpses of the

soul? Shall he who knows the chrysalis be ignorant of the butterfly?

No person less broadly human than Balzac could have written *Séraphita*. No person less gifted with spiritual vision than the author of *Séraphita* may write without fear or reproach *Cousin Betty* and the *Droll Stories*. Such a brain was necessary, says Taine, in a passage that itself conveys somewhat of the vertiginous quality that we feel in Balzac, " a brain with its surroundings and its mode of existence, to vivify that enormous forest of ideas to empurple the flowers in it with that sombre metallic lustre, to fill its fruits with that mordant and too intense sap. . . . The style is embarrassed, overloaded. The ideas jostle and stifle one another. Complicated intrigues seize the mind with their iron pincers; piled up passions blaze and roar as in a furnace. And under that wild light stand out in sharp relief a multitude of figures with set, tormented faces, more expressive, powerful, living than the real themselves; among them a vile vermin of human insects, crawling caterpillars, hideous lizards, venomous spiders born in festering decay, fierce to burrow, to tear, to accumulate and to bite; and over all are dazzling fairy spectacles and dolorous nightmares big with all the dreams that gold, science, art, glory, and power can inspire." If such power seem more than human, let us remember that we cannot measure genius with the yardstick of the commonplace. If we cannot comprehend Balzac nor find the universal formula that shall correlate the multitudinous phases of his protean genius, it is at least something that we should know wherein and why it eludes our comprehension.

In the endeavour to approximate to this correlation, of whose inadequacy no one will be more conscious than is the author, it will be well to consider first Balzac's style, then his manner of constructing his stories, to pass thence to his view of society as represented in his characters, and finally to consider his philosophy of life.

If Balzac's style is sometimes heavy, it is not for lack of care. He himself, while saying that there were but three men in Paris who knew French, Gautier, Hugo, and himself, which in a sense was true, was, as we have seen, constantly tormented by artistic scruples, correcting and recorrecting his proofs, thinking that his reputation depended on third and fourth revisions, and making alterations that equalled and often far exceeded the original cost of composition; but it may be doubted if the last state of his copy was not often worse than the first. His error is not carelessness but over-elaboration. The sentence is apt to drag its coils around the idea, to constrict it instead of transfixing it. And then he is embarrassed by his wealth of words. Nothing so admirable as the descriptive power of his epithets; few things so exasperating as the familiar thought veiled under technical terms. You are teased with the hope of some flash light of genius, and are irritated to find that the bizarre language masks only a respectable commonplace. He is not conscious of this. The words are not bizarre to him. He "knows the language." But, as he said, there were only two others in Paris who did so, and Taine is not wrong when he observes that the reader of Balzac will have to endure sometimes what will seem to him "scientific jargon, philosophic clap-trap, and grandiloquence." But Taine exaggerates this fault, and notes justly that the feeling is intensified by the modes of thought and culture inherited from the French eighteenth century. It is there, however, and it is a fault, but it has its compensations.

Here, as so often, the style is the man.   It is the natural mold for the ore that flows from this seven times heated furnace of imagination.   Balzac's course could never have shackled itself to the mincing steps of eighteenth-century classicism.   If he studied, as he said, for seven years before comprehending the French language, it was that he might make it his instrument, fashioned to his pen, suited to his mind.   And, for him, language was not primarily to convey thoughts in logical sequence, but to evoke images in picturesque and suggestive succession.   This new end could not be attained by the old laws of rhetoric and eloquence, for he was concerned with evoking new images, not with the kaleidoscopic redistribution of old thoughts. The mind is strangely stimulated by these images, drawn from all the multiplicity of its experience, so that the whole range of our sense-perceptions is brought into correlation ;   "chemistry explains love, cookery has its bearing on politics, music and the grocery business are related to philosophy," and the whole of our knowledge is woven together into a network where each is connected with all.

A style so interpenetrated with creative imagination has in its intenser passages an element of poetry that is singularly fascinating to many minds.   The pages swarm with implied or real metaphors, the brain seems in a constant travail of creation, an endless ebullition of images.   Read the description of the bouquet in *The Lily in the Valley*. There is nothing to exceed it in its kind outside of the verse of Hugo, and it is approached but seldom by Zola. There is but one adjective to define it, an adjective that recurs so often to him who would write of the genius or the labour or the style of Balzac, — it is vertiginous.   Your head swims as you read of those perfumes that communi-

cate to all beings the intoxication of fecundation, so that
your thoughts renew their green. Inexhaustible exhala-
tions stir at the bottom of your heart the budding roses
that modesty represses there. There are leaves that seem
the vague image of longed-for forms, supplely bending
like those of some submissive slave. Above them stretch
out flowers prostrate and humble, as suppliant as prayers.
Others above these seem like those deep violet hopes
with which first dreams are crowned, and others with their
twining stalks like vague desires twisted in the recesses of
the soul. "And from the bosom of this rushing, overflowing torrent of love there darts a magnificent double red
poppy spreading the flame tongues of its fire above starred
jasmines and dominating the incessant rain of pollen, that
sparkles like a beautiful cloud in the air, reflecting the
light from its thousand dazzling particles. What woman,
intoxicated by the odour of love hidden in vernal grass,
will not comprehend the luxuriousness of that yielding, that
tender whiteness, troubled by movements uncontrolled, and
then — that red desire. . . . All that we offer to God was
it not offered to love in that poem of luminous flowers that
sang incessantly their low melodies to the heart, caressing
there its hidden joys, its unavowed hopes, its illusions that
blush into life and die away like the virgin cobwebs of a
summer night?" This paraphrase is but a fragment of the
passage, but it will illustrate my meaning better than any
words of mine, for the only way to describe Balzac's style in
its glory is to let him speak for himself.

But no man's best is his average. It is obvious that
what has been said can apply in its entirety to but few of
the ninety-two titles that make up the *Human Comedy*.
Much of any novelist's work is straightforward narration,

much is dialogue through which the author reveals character, explains its evolution, or advances the action.   When
the narrative does not call for epic breadth or dramatic
intensity Balzac is apt to hurry on from picturesque description to psychological reflection or dialogue, and here his
style is often simply the style of everybody, and calls for no
comment.   Where action is to be narrated he prefers to
put his description of it into the mouths of his characters,
and in this kind he gives us such masterpieces as the story
of Napoleon in the *Country Doctor*, or of the passage of
the Beresina in *Adieu*.   This suggests what may be a fault
in his dialogue.   His characters are apt to speak at length,
to indulge in tirades.   There is little sparkle in his conversation, little repartee and fencing of wit, and what there is
is not always of the best.   He is more successful with the
lower than with the higher social spheres, better with
intense or eccentric characters than with his men and
women of the world, but he occasionally over-charges his
effects, notably in the stammering of Grandet and the
jargon of Nucingen and Schmucke, in which he is said to
have found delight, and in which his readers surely find
weariness.

Both in description and in the longer speeches his
periods are apt to be over long and involved, the result,
it may seem, of his method of composition.   Taine pitilessly collected a number of the most glaring instances of
this fault, and it has since been usual to say that Balzac's
style is bad ; but such passages are not very numerous, and
they are the defects of really great and unique qualities
which show their promise on almost every page, and attain
not infrequently a great achievement.   And in almost
every novel both good and bad coexist with a great mass

of what is simply ordinary, for with all his care Balzac never attained the sustained polish of Mérimée, Flaubert, or Maupassant, and probably never aspired to the persistent dithyrambic of Hugo's prose.

In the construction of the novels regarded as stories there is a noteworthy lack of proportion, but if we regard them as studies of character they will be seen to have a greater, sometimes an entire unity. The best constructed of the novels are, doubtless, *Eugénie Grandet* and *The Poor Relatives*, but even here the narrative is interrupted by digressions that seem like little essays, and by descriptions of quite unnecessary minuteness. Every reader of Balzac will have noticed with what detail he fixes the scene of his story, the city, the street, the house, the room. We can almost count the fly-specks on the walls of the Vauquer boarding-house, and the number of steps in Grandet's stairway. From house we pass to furniture, from furniture to clothes, and the bodily externals of manner, and face, and hands. Then we learn of the man's previous life, of his antecedents, his friends, his bank account. All this makes the story slow in getting under way, but once started it has the greater momentum. You see his figures and live their life, as happens with few other novelists, but it must be admitted that Flaubert attains the same effect with better-hidden art. As Taine puts it, "There was in Balzac an archeologist, an architect, an upholsterer, a tailor, an old-clothes-dealer, an appraiser, a physiologist, and a notary." One by one these came and read to him their detailed reports. Only then did the fire of composition begin. This is a fault, and would have been serious had it not been that his age and ours find almost as much pleasure in science as in art, with a delight in reality for its own sake, a tendency that has found its fullest expression in Zola.   Many of Balzac's descriptions are minutely photographic rather than broadly picturesque.   We see the room or the landscape rather than feel their psychic influence.   And yet Balzac's interest is never in description for its own sake, but always in its effect on character, which through the very multiplicity of these prolix details insinuates itself more completely into the mind, so that those philosophers who see in character the sum of environing influences will naturally most admire both his method and its results.

Taine "dares to say that Balzac has risen to the level of Shakspere."   We should perhaps say that he has produced the same effects, though less often and less deftly, because he was a slightly inferior genius and a much inferior artist. His characters live in the mind long after his plots have faded from them.   They are often too complex.   If one reads Balzac for the story, Cerfbeer's Balzacian Dictionary (*Répertoire*) is almost as essential to enjoyment as the novel itself, and if one is studying character it is a necessity.   No ordinary brain can carry this complex diversity and grasp at once the detail and its place in the general composition.   And yet this last is most essential to any just comprehension of Balzac, for he wished his work to be a philosophy of human life.   He saw each in its relation to all.   His steadfast aim was to give what Taine calls "an abridged history of the nineteenth century," which should be at the same time "the eternal history of the heart." Therefore it is that he is preëminently systematic, that his work must be judged as a whole to be judged at all.   Let us consider now the parts of his system, the successive strata of his society.

At the bottom are the narrow money-grubbers, provincials often and usually tradespeople, always commonplace, yet immensely varied, for Balzac comprehends and enters into their dreary materialism as it shows itself in attitude, word, and gesture, more fully than any other French novelist, unless it be Flaubert. Of these men the five-franc piece is indeed the mainspring, and it would seem that they interest him most. At least he leaves them almost all rich and with a satisfied ambition. Nucingen has his thirty millions, Rastignac is a minister, Tillet satisfies every lust and vengeance; even Rigou of *The Peasants* has his way. An iron will, pursuing purely material ends, would be the strongest force known to the *Human Comedy*, " unless," as Balzac himself says, " there were a God."

Over against these we may naturally set off the young people, in whom experience has not yet killed the power of romantic devotion. Such are apt to become their passion's fool, as Caliste de Guenic and Lucien de Rubempré, or incarnations of worldliness like Rastignac. Rare exceedingly is the final balance of power between sentiment and wisdom as we see it in Félix de Vandenesse. It might seem that Balzac saw what Musset, Stendhal, and so many others regretted, that the young men of that day lacked moral force, and were suffering from a weariness of the will that sank from high ideals to those lower ambitions that had their last blossoming in such men as Maxime de Trailles and his fellow dandies of the boulevards, — a race that could be as confidently predicted in the generation that should follow Waterloo as it would be out of place in the generation that followed Sedan.

Besides these realistically studied normal money-grubbers and money-spenders, there are symbolic exaggerations of these types that we may note later. And then there are the grotesques of virtue, men whom Balzac means to be admirable, but who, too often, are exasperating. Such are Popinot, the righteous judge and somewhat imbecile dispenser of charity ; such the Marquis d'Espard with his truly fantastic notions of honour and of honesty ; such too is the notary Chesnel in his dogged devotion to the family of the Estrignon.

We may dismiss quite briefly the personages who exist only as *raisonneurs*, mouthpieces like Bixiou or Marsay. The wit of these last is sometimes fiercely cynical, though never descending to the satanic depths of Vautrin, but more often it is coarse, rollicking, blunt, full of strange metaphors and caricatures, a medley of Rabelais and Abraham a Sancta-Clara, not unlike Balzac's own conversation if we may trust report, the flint-sparks of a heart repelled by reality and disillusioned of its ideals. These characters are bitter, misanthropic, even brutal. They are Mephistophelian pessimists, sneering like Schopenhauer at pleasures even while they pursue them, terrible commentaries as well as commentators on the tendencies of social mediocracy.

Balzac's *Woman of Thirty* was such an immediate success, and met so obviously a long-felt want among feminine readers, that it must have had more elements of truth for that romantic generation than it has for ours. With his young girls he is, as a rule, less successful, a little fearful perhaps of seeming dupe of their virtue. Even Eugénie Grandet is not always quite herself, and Taine is quite right to say of a certain letter of hers to Charles that she would have worn out her inkstand before discovering the first phrase, and broken it before writing the last. Here, more perhaps than anywhere else in the *Human Comedy*, the author shows through the character, and we see him, too, behind the saintly wives, Henriette de Mortsauf, Véronique Graslin, and their like. His virtuous women perorate and weary. One feels more sympathy, more affection even, for the animal fidelity of Big Nanon, or for the plaintive virginity of Mlle. Cormon, the "old maid." One is far more affected even by that other old maid, Sophie Gamard, or by the diabolical Sylvie Rogron. And so, too, with the married women, and those who should have been. As a physician feels at home in a hospital, so Balzac is more at ease with the morally sick, maimed, or deformed, whether the disease be mild and infantile as in Modeste Mignon, or cancerous and mortal as in Madame Cibot, or distorting and half ridiculous as in Madame Soudry and Madame Camus, or ravenously wolfish as in Madame Évangelista. These women have bartered themselves more or less successfully for social position and money, and they will barter their daughters for the same and think they are doing them a good service. Then there are the forerunners of the new woman, Madame de la Baudraye, Madame de Bargeton, or the more frankly unconventional Duchess of Maufrigneuse and Duchess of Langeais. But possibly most successful of all are the courtesans, masked or open, Aquilina, Josépha, Esther, and the admirable Madame Schontz. Balzac's intense imagination dwells with almost equal pleasure on the intellectual debauch of the blue-stocking *Précieuse* and the orgies of overflowing physical life, and he is at home, too, with the parasites of social disease, such as Madame Nourisson or Jaqueline Collin.

But beyond all these, in the depth of the impression that they make on the mind, are a few personages that may be regarded less as types of existing characters than as symbols of social tendencies, of the forces that move the modern

world.   There is the paternal instinct rising to a pitch of
sublime absurdity in Goriot; there is the triumph of brute
force over all tender emotion and all moral restraint in
Philippe Bridau, the soldier let loose on society; and in
Jacques Collin there is a similar triumph of will at battle with
the world for the flesh and the devil.   Then there is intellectual absorption dulling the moral nature in Balthazar Claës,
and there is avarice eating away mind and soul in Grandet,
as the sexual instinct does in the senile Baron Hulot.   All
these are fascinating creations of a power that is at once
poetic and moral.   And we have but begun the list.   There
is Madame Marneffe, of whom it might be said, perhaps
more truly than of any other in the *Human Comedy*, that
her feet lay hold on hell; there is Cousin Betty, the incarnation of jealousy; and we shall find a similar mental deviation bordering on monomania in many minor figures also,
especially in the *Philosophic Studies*, where, as Taine observes, the little story of *Massimilla Doni*, if we include its
natural preface *Gambara*, counts no less than seven of
them.   With such symbolic characters should be ranked
also the mystics, Louis Lambert and Séraphita.   It is perhaps their deviation from normal nature that makes them
interesting, and surely they nurse and widen the scope of
the imagination, as it is given only to the greatest creative
writers to do, to Homer, Dante, Goethe, Shakspere.   " You
see less quickly, less easily, less brilliantly " in Balzac than
in them, " but you see the same things, as remote and as
deep."

But what then were Balzac's views of life and of human
destiny?   What was his philosophy?   To ask such a question of his contemporaries in fiction, of Hugo, Gautier,
Dumas, would be labor lost, but it is not so with him.

Indeed, it may be urged rather that there is an excess of synthesis in his novels, that the individual work suffers from the obtrusion of general ideas, from the constant endeavour to link the special to the universal. Almost all his personages reason about themselves, and what they do not reveal the author is at pains to explain. Flaubert will give you all the materials for judgment and let you divine the character. Balzac gives you the materials and a commentary as well.

The strongest motives for action in the world as he sees it, possibly the only motives, save for exceptional cases, and as it were by the grace of God, are the passions, chief among them sexuality, avarice, and gluttony. People disguise these passions to themselves by their incapacity for right reason ; they disguise them from others by hypocrisy and by the mutual covenants of social life. But selfishness is at the bottom of all, and the democratization of society has tended to make this selfishness more base and more contemptible. With society thus organized the material victory will be to the strong and the shrewd. "The virtuous," says Balzac in *The Poor Relatives*, "have almost always slight suspicions of their situation. They feel that they are the dupes in the great market-place of life ; " which is as true now as it was in St. Paul's day, though there has been doubtless a noticeable development of rudimentary altruism and an amelioration of morals. But in this Balzac sees no reason to hope that society left to itself will become altruistic or virtuous.

From this follows necessarily his profound aversion for what he calls mediocracy, beneath which he sees a lower depth of democracy. He is quite sure that the world will go wrong if the moral aristocracy do not set it right.

Therefore he believes in large estates, a landed squirarchy, monarchy by divine right, and the established church. But his tendency seems rather toward what the Germans call State Socialism than toward feudality, though it is not difficult to find a chain of phrases that would indicate in him an extreme reactionary who regards absolute government as the only one under which the laws will cease to be " spider's-webs through which the great flies break and in which the little ones remain," the only one that can control "the poison shops" of the press, and the only one where " arbitrariness will save the people by coming to the aid of justice," and education by religious orders shall crown the edifice ; for it is his conviction that " thought, the source of woes and blessings, can be prepared, governed, and directed only by religion."

For political philosophy, Balzac lacked historical perspective. There were epochs of history that he knew extremely well in their detail and in their spirit, but he knew them as a romancer, not as a politician. And so, in his political economy he is, as he was in his psychology, a seer rather than an observer, with the prophet's confidence which sometimes surely was a self-deceived credulity. One may become a demagogue by intuition, but not a statesman. So when Balzac reasons from his experience of men he is a materialist, as in *Cousin Pons ;* when he lets his fancy roam in a new heaven and earth, political, social, and moral, he creates a new man for the new environment, as in *The Reverse of Contemporary History, Louis Lambert,* or *Séraphita,* with a little touch of materialism still, for his imagination, like that of Gautier, is of the type that seeks to body its fancies in magnetism, Mesmerism, and " ethereal fluids."

Thus it happens, and not unnaturally, as Taine ingen-

iously shows, that Balzac was at once a materialist and a
mystic, with a mind that could not dissociate itself from
matter and an imagination that could not fetter itself with
the patience of scientific deduction.   Cabanis had taught
that all mental acts have a physical substratum, and led by
this truth, that was to him an *ignis fatuus*, when Balzac
abandoned observation he became sometimes a Swedenborgian mystic, sometimes a physio-psychologist, sometimes
an intuitive reasoner "who acts, sees, and feels from
within."   Many such mystics there have been, but none
who had in anything approaching Balzac's degree the
power of seeing and picturing the real; and none who had
like him the novelist's power of self-projection, so that he
could give to these ideas objective literary form.   It is true
that in doing this he strained the novelistic *genre*, as
Hugo, in the same period, was straining that of the drama.
He tried to make it serve ends and carry ideas extraneous
to it.   "Oppressed," says Taine, "by an exuberance of
theories, Balzac put into his novels politics, psychology,
metaphysics, and all the legitimate or spurious children of
philosophy.   Many are fatigued by it, and reject *Séraphita*
and *Louis Lambert;* but they should observe that these
works terminate the whole, just as the flower terminates
the plant, that the genius of the artist finds here its complete expression and final evolution; that all the rest pre-
pares for them, explains them, presupposes them, justifies
them."

   Thus in a single, though the most important, sphere of
metaphysical speculation, Balzac's idea of the Will, as symbolized in *The Ass's Skin* and discussed in *Louis Lambert*,
with its hypnotic divagations in *Ursule Mirouet* and in
Séraphita, finds its material, realistic expression in the rela-

tion of Jacques Collin to Lucien de Rubempré, whom he dominates, and to Rastignac whom he inspires; and so in Balzac's conception of social love, as we see it in *The Two Young Wives*, there is the actual counterpart of the symbol contained in Séraphitus-Séraphita.

But though surely we are not dupes of our own ingenuity in speaking of the "philosophy" of the *Human Comedy*, it is clear that Balzac's system is neither complete nor consistent with itself. He sought his philosophy of life by intuition, and gave us such glimpses of it as he received. The result is hardly more unsatisfactory than the systems that have been elaborated by other methods. None has yet correlated our intuitions and our perceptions, perhaps none ever will. The interest that this matter has here is not in the success, but in the effort. Here was a novelist who at least tried to see life steadily and see it whole, — who tried to correlate all the material and moral and spiritual factors of social life. And when a man's life is given to such an effort, shall it be called a failure, can it be called anything but an inspiring success when the greatest critic of France in the last half-century can say of him : "With Shakspere and Saint-Simon, Balzac is the greatest storehouse of documents that we have on human nature"?

CHAPTER VIII.

PROSPER MÉRIMÉE is a novelist whose place in the evolution of fiction it is difficult to fix, and therefore peculiarly interesting to study. It is customary, and not unjust, to regard him as the successor of Stendhal; but he had in him elements of closer relation to George Sand and others that suggest Balzac, while perhaps, after all, he will be found more closely allied to Flaubert than to any of his early contemporaries. He became intimate with Stendhal in his youth, about 1823, and they shared in many sympathies and antipathies, especially in a contempt for the ethics of the bourgeoisie, which Mérimée expressed with an irony keener than Stendhal's and lighter than Flaubert's. The three were alike in their objectivity, and all excelled, though in different ways, in psychologic analysis. But in their romantic pessimism Mérimée and Flaubert part company with Stendhal, who never wholly threw off the rationalistic optimism of the eighteenth century, while Mérimée's cruel irony is more impassively indifferent than Flaubert's, having, as Lanson observes, little trace of the eighteenth century save in the audacious crudity and dry scepticism of his thought. With George Sand he shares the power of picturesque description, but he is too cynical to share her buoyancy. He has the sombreness of Balzac, unrelieved by the latter's idealism; and he has Stendhal's morbid dread of being the dupe of his emotions, which in him showed itself in what none of these other four possessed, — a high-bred, aristocratic, polished impassivity in his social bearing, and a corresponding pellucid but cold correctness in his style, where art hides art even more effectively than in Flaubert. His indifference goes so far as to suppress studiously all appearance of interest in his own work. He represents the most highly wrought of his novels as the accidental result of some experience of travel, and in one case, *The Chronicle of Charles IX.*, anticipates the author of *The Lady or the Viger*, with the suggestion that the reader shall choose whichever denouement may suit his fancy. Until the rise of Flaubert he was the best, almost the only, representative in France of the strictly objective school in fiction. It is here that his peculiar service lies.

Mérimée was a Parisian, born in 1803, and living just long enough to witness the bloody setting of the imperial sun, which had lighted the last two decades of his life with a sympathy that was both political and personal. Of his early life we know little more than that his family was well-to-do, and had on his mother's side a strain of English blood, to which his countrymen were wont to attribute a certain austerity in his manners. He was educated for the bar, and entered the civil service, but was sufficiently in touch with the literary currents of his time to be among the first to achieve notoriety in the romantic manner with a pretended translation from the Spanish, — *The Dramas of Clara Gazul*, published in 1825, and *The Guzla*, a volume of pretended translations from the Illyrian, in 1827. Neither of these belong directly to our subject, yet both are characteristic of the man. He understood the creed of romanticism perfectly; he could say its shibboleth with

faultless correctness, but he was very sceptical of the value
of his accomplishment. As he tells us in a witty preface to
The Guzla, written in 1840, the creed of his fellow-roman-
ticists of 1827 was "no salvation without local colour. We
meant by 'local colour' what they called *manners* in the
seventeenth century, but we were very proud of our word,
and we thought we had imagined both the name and the
thing." He would have liked to visit some strange
country with his friend Ampère, and as they had no
money, the idea came to them to write their travels in
advance, and use the money to see whether they had made
any mistakes. Mérimée was to take the literary side. He
read a volume of travels, another of statistics, learned a
few words of Slavonic, and wrote in a fortnight a collection
of ballads, — alleged translations that deceived the scholars
of England, Germany, and Russia. "I could boast," he
concludes, "that I had attained 'local colour;'" but the
process was so simple, so easy, that I began to doubt the
merit of it."

The year following *The Guzla* saw Mérimée's first work
in dramatic fiction, *The Jacquerie* (1828), interesting
chiefly because it showed at the outset all the qualities,
except polish of diction, that were to mark his work to the
close. These were, an astonishing command of language, a
remarkable power of conveying to the reader the spirit of a
distant age and foreign scene, — in this case the medieval
France of the peasant war (1358), — a predilection for
scenes of terror and blood, and the peculiarly cruel vein of
irony already noticed.

But in the next year *The Jacquerie* was surpassed in all
its qualities by *The Chronicle of the Reign of Charles IX.*,
(le Chronique du règne de Charles IX., 1829), whose

central scene is the massacre of St. Bartholomew, which to
him seems to illustrate the observation that all morality is
relative, and suggests that "the decadence of energetic
passion has been to the gain of tranquillity and, perhaps, of
happiness." The story is told with great verve, and is full
of adventure, of murder and blood; but there is shrewd
historical analysis also, with picturesque scenes of bygone
manners. The irony that runs through all Mérimée's fiction
concentrates here its brightest flashes in the sermon of
Père Lubin, and its most mordant bitterness in the spiritual
brawl of priest and parson over the bed of the dying Vol-
tairean Mergy, while the novel ends nonchalantly with a
request to the reader to finish the story as best suits his
fancy. As a whole, *The Chronicle* is a well-told story, but
it lacks the stylistic finish and the intensity of the short
stories of this same year. In the evolution of fiction its
place is with *The Jacquerie* in the brief and brilliant series
of French historical novels, inspired by Walter Scott, inaugurated by Vigny's *Cinq Mars*, and drowned in the
flood of Dumas' fiction.

Mérimée now began to write short stories for the *Revue
de Paris* and the *Revue des deux mondes*, and continued the
latter relation for twelve years. The stories of 1829 and
1830, with two exceptions first published after his death,
were gathered in 1833 in *Mosaic* (Mosaïque) ; in the
same year appeared also a longer story, *The Double Misunderstanding* (la Double méprise). Several volumes of
history and travel followed, and Mérimée's next contribution to fiction was *Colomba* (1840), which was followed
by *Carmen* in 1847, and by another collection of tales in
1852. The posthumously printed *Last Tales* (Dernières
nouvelles) complete his work in this field.

The close of 1830 showed Mérimée in possession of all his powers as a writer of fiction. In the preceding year he had written *Federigo* (1829), a Neapolitan legend, that would be utterly blasphemous if it were not so naïvely childish and so curious in its intermingling of classic mythology with the teaching of the Roman Church. He had also written *The Taking of the Redoubt* (l'Enlèvement de la redoute, 1829), a story from Napoleon's Russian campaign, that takes us in ten pages close up to the cannon's mouth, with a restrained concision that makes it almost a perfect model of the short story. And if here his style reaches the climax of his powers, in *Mateo Falcone* (1829), his irony reaches the utmost pitch of its cruelty. Here is a man who has murdered his rival in love and yet has so Corsican a feeling of honour that he kills his son, a boy of ten, for failing in hospitality to a criminal; leaving the reader to conclude that, when civilisation is stripped off, all moral action is the result of prejudice and of fatality. And yet one hesitates to accord *Mateo Falcone* the supreme touch of pessimistic irony when one reads *Tamango* (1829), the ghastly story of a slave-selling negro chief, and of the slaver captain Ledoux, who insisted that on his ship, the "Hope," "one must show humanity and leave a negro at least five feet by two to enjoy himself during a six weeks' passage, for after all the blacks are men like the whites." This genial trader who varnished his fetters is massacred with his crew by the kidnapped Tamango ; and the negroes, masters of a craft that they can neither sail nor steer, die the cannibal victims of drink, of one another, and of starvation, — all but their chief, whom irony reserves to work for the English Government on the fortifications of Jamaica till fever releases him from this "liberty at six cents a day."

Perhaps more bestial horror has never been crowded into so little room or recounted with such cold precision as in this story.

The work of 1829 was completed by the less significant semi-historical *Vision of Charles XI.*, and by a little imitation from the Spanish in rhythmic prose, *The Pearl of Toledo* (la Perle de Tolède). Then 1830, that *annus mirabilis* of French literature, brought *The Etruscan Vase* and *The game of Tric-Trac.* To this year belongs also the *Spanish Witches*, where the superstitious shrewdness of the Valencian peasantry is most cleverly and romantically shown, though it is perhaps hardly equal in art to the other work of 1830.

In *The Etruscan Vase*, a story less well constructed than is usual with Mérimée, love and then jealousy seize on the else calm and clear mind of Saint-Clair and lead him with an inexorable fatality to destruction. In his proud nature, inclined to retrospect, ambitious, distraught, opinionated, and reserved, there seem many traits of Mérimée's self. The same fatalism of crime impels the gambler to fraud in *The game of Tric Trac*. "When I swindled that Dutchman I thought only of winning twenty-five napoleons. I did not think of Gabrielle. That is why I despise myself," says Lieutenant Roger, who was else, we are told, loyal and brave. And so, generally, in the stories that make up *Mosaic* we have tragic terror, but not tragic pity, the freest development of passion, such as Stendhal had sought, with an even greater affectation of indifference and moral negation.

Always to some extent an enemy of the conventional, Mérimée was perhaps least so in *The Double Misunderstanding* (1833), which seems rather in the manner of Bourget or of Prévost, a bit of pathologic psychology. It

is the story of the unhappy marriage of Julie and the Marquis of Chaverny, whose coarse humour grates on the nerves
of his wife, as appears in several admirable domestic scenes.
Châteaufort, a young officer, tries to profit by her humour,
but she feels no affinity for him.   Then her love's complement appears, Darcy, in whom it is said Mérimée sought to
paint himself, with a little vanity of vice, as he had done
perhaps also in the Saint-Clair of *The Etruscan Vase.*   To
him her soul is drawn like a boat sucked into a whirlpool.
In vain does he reveal himself in unfavourable lights, as in
the cleverly interposed episode of a rescued Turkish slave.
She yields, she hardly knows how or why, to his cynical and
cold fascination, and then in her moral revulsion works
herself into a fever of which she dies.   " Write to him,"
she bids her nurse as she lapses from consciousness, " write
to him that he does not know me ; that I do not know
him."   That is the " double misunderstanding."   And yet,
concludes the author, " These two hearts that misunderstood were perhaps made for one another."

The Souls in Purgatory (les Âmes du purgatoire, 1834)
is a development of the legend of Don Juan de Maraña,
the incarnation of materialistic will trampling for his lusts
on the honour of women, the lives of men, and the love of
God, and then converted by a terrifying vision and turning
his strong will toward furious penitence, as unspiritual at
the last as at the first.   And beside him is the enigmatic
figure of Dona Theresa, who loves her father's murderer,
and though herself professed a nun, consents, as though
compelled by some mysterious force, to escape with her
lover, and dies of disappointment as she would have died
of the realisation of her hope.   Here, too, love is a tragic
fatality, respecting neither law nor life.

A more exquisite work of art is *The Venus of Ille* (la Vénus d'Ille, 1837), drawn from a medieval Latin legend contained in the chronicle of Herman Corner. This Venus is an ancient statue of *Venus Turbulenta*, in which the artist has impersonated malicious absence of all sympathy and the irony of cruel disdain. On her bronze finger a youth on his marriage day places in sport his betrothal ring, and at night she comes to claim his body and soul, to press him to death in her metal arms, herself a symbol of imperious passion. The story is old in its outline, but in the beauty of its setting and in the skill with which from an opening of gross and even humourous commonplace it evolves and maintains an atmosphere of terror it is unsurpassed. First the scene, the weird slopes of the Pyrenees and the plain of Toulouse below, with its relics of an irrepressible paganism contrasting with the sordid materialism or the bourgeois comfort of its inhabitants; then the old goddess exhumed to be witness of the new feast, the insult to her divinity, her anger, her vengeance, and the strange veil of mystery that the author has thrown over the whole — give to the supernatural the illusion of reality.

Colomba followed *The Venus of Ille* in 1840. Since 1835 Mérimée had been much occupied with notes of archeological travel, in the course of which he had spent two months in Corsica, and had published a volume of his impressions. Corsica is also the scene of *Colomba*, in whose two hundred pages there is probably more exotic life than in any work of the French language, unless it be *Rarahu*. The book is still, what it was from the beginning, by far the most popular work of its author, and, whether true or false in its local colour, it certainly produces the illusion of reality. To the strange life, material and

moral, of the Corsican *maquis* we are introduced by an
artistic prelude that brings to the island Col. Nevil and his
daughter Lydia, an Englishman and an English girl, treated
conventionally but with ironic humour, and possibly with
more justice than English critics have liked to admit; for
Mérimée knew England, and his English are never grotesque caricatures of *l'anglais waterproof et mackintosh,* like
the jumping-jacks of Gautier's fancy.   On the boat with the
Nevils is Orso, an officer, Corsican by birth but now apparently wholly French in spirit, in whom Lydia shows a frank
and quite English interest.   The party reach Ajaccio, and
we get the external local colour while still moving in the
conventional world of social ideas.   But presently this
exotic calm is disturbed by the advent of Orso's sister
Colomba, a true Corsican nature strangely mixed of charm
and savagery.   She is beautiful, graceful, cunning, unscrupulous, devoted, morbidly revengeful, and winsomely loving.
The psychic purpose of the story is to show how this native
ferment will plant itself in Orso's heart and permeate his
blood, transforming him, to his own surprise, into the hero
of a vendetta ; for Colomba thinks that the Barricini have
wronged her father, who is dead, and with that fierce family
pride that is the dominant passion of the Corsican, she
looks to her brother for vengeance and nurses with almost
diabolical malignity the old spirit.   The psychologic
touches here are so firm, the graduation in the notes so
perfect, that we find ourselves accepting as natural the life
and modes of thought of the bandit Brandolaccio, or the
feuds that divide communities in fiercest hate and intrude
themselves even into the chants improvised at the burials
of the dead.   "I must have the hand that fired, the eye
that aimed, and the mind that conceived the deed," she

sang, and did not rest till the sons were dead, and the father a senile idiot, shrinking in terror from her reminder of her triumphant vengeance. When Orso has killed the brothers who had fired on him from ambush, it seems to us as natural for a bandit to ask pardon for regretting the victims of so fine a shot as it is for the colonel to desire a coroner's inquest; as natural for the little bandit girl to announce their deaths by the sign of the cross as for the Englishman, first, with his sense of law to have wished the double-barrelled gun he had given Orso at the bottom of the sea, and then with his own viking blood stirred to add, " Brave fellow ! I 'm glad he had it." Indeed, when the tale is over and Orso is taking leave of the freebooters to return to civilisation with his English bride, Castriconi seems half right when he says : " Believe me, Mr. Orso, nothing 's comparable to a bandit's life . . . if only one is better armed and more sensible than Don Quixote."

Sainte-Beuve compares Colomba to Electra urging Orestes to avenge the death of Agamemnon. Her joy in conquering her brother's mind to serve her passion seems to him classic in a truer sense than Electra's. Yet the story is the most cheerful, indeed, the only cheerful book of Mérimée. We pass through murder, but we come to marriage-bells, and the irony is less persistently sardonic. His pessimistic fancy habitually seeks escape from present conditions by creating a world of fiercer primordial passions, but he has never treated conventional society with such genial persiflage as in *Colomba*.

This gentler tone characterises also Mérimée's next story, *Arsène Guillot* (1844), a bit of tender pathos standing quite alone in his fiction. The central figure here is a frail girl who, on her mother's death and the desertion of lovers, attempts suicide and dies after an illness, of the shock and of consumption. During her illness she is cared for by the pious Madame de Piennes, who had become interested in her through a meeting at a church whither she had gone to burn a candle before the image of St. Roch; for her mother had told her that this celestial patron, if placated, would surely provide her with a human one. Both women have formerly enjoyed the affection, platonic or material, of Max, who meets Madame de Piennes by Arsène's bedside, and is, as it were, united to her by Arsène's dying words. Thinking her dead, the pitying Max exclaimed: "What happiness had she in this world?" All at once, as though reanimated at his voice, she opened her eyes and murmured, "I have loved;" and while of course, as the author remarks, he has said nothing to authorise rash judgments, he has said that on Arsène's tombstone might be traced in a lady's hand the words: "Poor Arsène, pray for us." This conclusion is certainly pathetic, and Mr. Pater regards it as "ethically acceptable."

The irony with which this tale is interpenetrated is directed partly against the tendency to think ill or even cruelly of the socially or morally unfortunate, and partly against the unnecessary torture of the feelings inflicted by well-intentioned but canting piety. The little story is full of lines that cling like barbed arrows. At the opening we read of the aristocratic who "buy the permission to pray to God apart from the rest of the faithful." The cynicism of the doctor is untranslatable, but among the motives of Madame de Piennes' interest we are expressly told to reckon "that sentiment of curiosity that many virtuous women feel to make the acquaintance of a woman of another sort." To say that hell is paved with good intentions or with women's tongues comes with Mérimée to the same thing, "for women, I think, always mean well." Such passages, with the candle of St. Roch and the denouement, will suggest an ethical tone that seems perhaps less commendable than that of *Colomba* or of *Carmen*, while in its art the story yields to neither.

The reader feels more at ease with Mérimée's morality, and more disposed to enjoy his art, when the scene is foreign to our time or mode of thought; and as, to speak of masterpieces only, *Colomba* is more satisfactory than *The Venus of Ille*, so *Carmen* (1845) is a more unalloyed literary feast than *Arsène Guillot*. The posthumously published *Viccolo di Madama Lucrezia*, of 1846, also does well to place in a foreign country its tragic intensity of passion and spice of diablerie, though here the author, affecting an indifference that suggests Stendhal, has shown us too much of the machinery of his method to preserve the artistic illusion.

In *Carmen* there is something of the same affectation. The story is introduced by the way, as an incident in the researches of an antiquarian; and when it is over, the author goes on as though there were no climax, with some erudite remarks on the gipsies and their language. This tale, thus indifferently offered is, however, the capital presentment of Mérimée's determinist morality. It is, as Sainte-Beuve has ingeniously remarked, the *Manon Lescaut* of our century. The satanic power of love, the fatality that drags a generous man from folly to vice, from vice to crime, from crime to murder and execution, has seldom received so concise and terrible a presentation. As in *Colomba*, we are introduced gradually to a life and morality so strange that it might else remain unreal, and even with this precau-

tion, while José Navarro, the soldier, smuggler, highwayman, and murderer, is made acceptable to our imagination,
there is more of the inexplicably demoniacal in Carmencita,
the fascinating and savage Delilah, gipsy cigar-girl and
smugglers' spy, than there was in the Corsican maid. Once
under her spell, he obeys because he must. His struggles
to free himself involve him the more. At last, made frantic
by her alternations of tender affection and faithlessness,
swayed perhaps in his weakened will by her grim prophecy,
" I first, then you," and hoping to the last that she will beg
for mercy, he kills her and surrenders himself to certain
execution, still doubting in his prison cell whether she was
a poor misguided child or a demon, but knowing that she
has destroyed him, body and soul.

Of that dainty bit of irony *Abbé Aubain* (1846), Mérimée's only story in letters, it may suffice to state the situation. A lady living in the country to restore her fortune
by economy grows intimate with a young abbé, and finds
him so sympathetic that she imagines him in love with her,
and so secures him a promotion that implies a removal,
which he shrewdly or naïvely attributes to her conscious or
unconscious love for him. Much of the interest of the story
lies in the food for psychological speculation that its incompleteness affords. This, too, is a phase of literary affectation, but one that is easily pardoned.

It was apparently about the time of *Abbé Aubain* that
Mérimée became interested in the Russian novelists Pushkin
and Gogol. On the latter he wrote an article (1851), with
translations of scenes from two stories ; and from the former
he rendered four tales, which, though they bear the stamp
of Mérimée's individuality, interest us here only from the
fact of his choice. The first, *The Queen of Spades* (la Dame

de pique, 1849), is a weird bit of ghostly diablerie and gambling, culminating in insanity. *The Bohemians* (1852) is a tale of savage love and jealous murder, recalling *Carmen*. *The Hussar* (1852) is a phantasmagoria of witchcraft in four pages. And finally *The Pistol Shot* (le Coup de pistolet, 1856) shows the intense passions of a semi-civilisation in which admiration for skill and courage overcomes the deadliest hate. It seems then that, as was natural, Mérimée was attracted in others by the qualities that he himself possessed, — by the intense, the exotic, and the exceptional.

Of original stories Mérimée wrote but three after the publication of the stories collected in 1852. These are : *The Blue Room* (la Chambre bleue), written in 1866; *Lokis*, printed in 1869; and perhaps the posthumously published *Djoumane*, though internal evidence would lead one to place this wild Algerian dream in the earlier and more romantic period, for while it opens with a clean-cut, realistic description of gipsy snake-charmers, it soon passes over into a weird, fantastic vision of serpent caverns, oriental voluptuousness, and inhuman horrors, much more in the spirit of 1830 than of the second empire. *The Blue Room*, a mediocre piece of rather gruesome fooling in the manner of the last century, with more snickering in the irony than is usual in Mérimée, seems to reflect the influence of the imperial court and the evenings at Compiègne, but *Lokis* carries us once more to the weird lands of crime and passion, interweaving the vampire and werwolf superstitions of the past with modern theories of heredity. Here a son, whose mother before his birth had lost her reason in a bear's embrace, couples the nature of his noble ancestors with brute ferocity. The bears have an instinct that he

shares their nature, and ghastly presentiments prepare us
from the outset for the denouement where, in excess of
love, he sucks the life-blood of his bride and escapes to
the beasts of the forest. The tale is treated with admirable restraint. There is the same artistic preparation here
as in *Carmen* and *Colomba*, gradually leading up to the
foreboding presage of the soothsaying snake-charmer in
the Lithuanian forest morass that hurries the story to its
dreadful close.

But though the imagination be romantic, the style here
and always is thoroughly realistic, and it is by this art that
he succeeds in making *Lokis*, *Carmen*, or *Colomba* seem to
us as natural to their environment as gloves and evening
dress to our own. Thus he fascinates us by the extraordinary at the same time that he evokes our sympathy by
the appearance of reality. This tends to give a certain
malignity to his ironical scepticism. It has been said that
he "despised" men too much to have faith in their
progress. We shall not look for moral inspiration to one
who could say of a drama, "The piece appears wearisome,
although immoral;" nor can we look for intellectual inspiration to one who poses as a dilettante and is sure that
to excel in any art "one must be a little *bête*." No doubt
Mérimée toyed with morality, and no doubt his fiction contributed to the weakening of the will that characterised his
generation. But as an artist his work has a refined distinction that is the more charming for its seeming lack of
effort, hiding the most consummate art of limpid harmony.
His work appeals only to a refined taste, and to that it will
appeal always for its restrained and delicate sense of proportion, so singularly lacking in his naturalistic successors.
He is in the novel what Gautier is in poetry, the represen-

tative of art for art's sake.   His style has been compared to a sheet of glass, through which all that he wishes to show appears clear and distinct, while the medium itself leaves at the first reading no sensation.   Yet if the critic concentrate his attention on this style, he will find that all in it has been subordinated to an esthetic purpose that produced its full effect of aristocratic daintiness and elegance, even while unrecognised.   Among all French novelists Mérimée is pre-eminently the artist.

CHAPTER IX

THEOPHILE GAUTIER holds an important place
among the critics of France and among her poets,
but he is surely most widely and perhaps most deservedly
known for his work in fiction. An epigrammatic critic has
said that he is the only successful writer who gave his
whole life to writing without ideas, feeling, or imagination,
and yet with no love of commonplace. Like most epigrams
this is but a half-truth. Whether we consider Gautier's
brilliant books of travel, his volumes of criticism, his poems,
or his novels, we shall not find in any of them a philosophic
view of history or of morals. In his novels psychologic
analysis is either absent or laboriously futile. He has not
even strong imagination, but he has an admirable fancy, and
above all a power of picturesque description that is unrivalled in our century. In his literary esthetics he stands
apart from his fellows of the romantic school. Where they
were seeking a Gothic intensity of purpose, he sought, so
far as the stress of his life gave him time, a Greek perfection
of form. The romanticists had felt strongly drawn to the
middle ages. For him the centuries between Titus and
Louis XIII. were a blank. The romanticists had sought to
make of environment and of description in general a
symbol of the ideal and of character. Gautier professed
and showed for this the most supreme indifference. He

described for the joy of the spiritual eye.   His place among the novelists is that of a sincere and true painter in prose.

Gautier was born at Tarbes, an ancient city in the department of Hautes Pyrénées, in 1811.   But he came very young to Paris and was educated there.   It is characteristic of all his literary life that in these earliest years, though a regular and close student, he showed more interest in archaic and decadent Latin than in the classics.   He was attracted less by the normal than by the primitive or the over-refined.   It is difficult to account for this predilection, but easy to see that he shares it with many of the creatures of his fancy, especially with the Albert of his *Mlle. de Maupin.*   His first effort in composition was an attempt to imitate Musæus, his second to reproduce Coluthus' *Rape of Helen.*   Already, however, the authors of the French renascence began to interest him.   He revelled in Brantôme and Rabelais, and, thinking that he discerned in himself a taste for painting, he embraced that profession with romantic enthusiasm and contempt of commonplace.

It was now, at the age of eighteen, that he met Hugo and was presently received into the *Cénacle* of the romanticists.   Gradually he abandoned painting and became the centre of a group of " flamboyants," ultra-romanticists, who, more in sport than earnest, delighted to bait in countless ways the bears of academic classicism.   He tells us himself, in his half-comic *History of Romanticism*, how with flowing hair and scarlet waistcoat he led the fight for dramatic emancipation in many Parisian theatres, and especially in the famous " battle of *Hernani.*"   This early period was marked by the publication of two volumes of verse, *Poems* (Poésies, 1830) and *Albertus* (1832), which showed a very highly developed technic and a power of description strangely weird and minutely realistic. But the most characteristic work of Gautier's youth is his first volume of collected stories, *Young France* (les Jeunes-France, 1833), with which are now bound eight tales alleged to be "humour-ous" that call for no comment.

Young France is a book easily misunderstood, and many have mistaken its irony for earnest. Here, with the non-chalance of youth, he mocks with delicious persiflage both the romantic liberties that he claimed and the classic restraints that he scorned. In *The Bowl of Punch* he shows young men "the danger of putting modern fiction into action," parodying by turns Janin, Sue, Hugo, and even Balzac. Romantic medievalism is satirised in *Wildman-stadius*, its penchant for vice in *Under the Table*, its taste for the weird in the nightmare life-in-death of *Onuphrius*, with a little of the author's own mind, as we shall see, its bourgeois imitation in *Daniel Jovard*, and the real banality of its passion in *She or She* (Celle-ci ou celle-là), the longest, the wittiest, the most libertine, and the most thought-ful of them all, for its apparent licentiousness masks a strong plea for sanity and realism. And lest the whole be misunderstood he adds to it all a preface of most admirable fooling. In short, *Young France* is genius laughing at its own joy of life. But its moderation of style deceived many into taking it seriously as the programme of the ultra-roman-ticists. This restraint, even in satire, was no affectation, it was part of his literary character. It showed itself in dis-dain for politics during these years of intense excitement, and in the disengaged poise that characterised his whole literary life, in which the only events were his books and his travels to Italy, Spain, Russia, Algeria, and the East, while for his support he depended to the last almost wholly on journalistic criticism.

Gautier's next novel, *Mlle. de Maupin*, was the frankest expression of his hedonistic creed and also a curious attempt at self-analysis. Gautier's Albert is René in the last phase of his disease, a precociously corrupt enthusiast of beauty, whose pursuit of a fleeing ideal persuades him that the dream is not only more precious than the reality, but also more true. And *Fortunio*, two years later, is on the same verge of confident but ever-deceived hedonism, naturally joyous and wholly pagan. These two characters stand ethically quite apart in Gautier's work, partly, no doubt, that he might not offend a public on whom he depended, partly too because life had brought experience. Even in the fiction of the forties, a sort of moral resignation, though not a moral reconciliation, succeeded to the hedonism of youth.

Mlle. de Maupin is an exquisite work of art, but it spurns the conventions of received morality with a contempt that was to close the Academy to Gautier forever. With a springboard of fact in the seventeenth century to start from, he conceives a wealthy and energetic girl of twenty, freed from domestic restraints and resolved to acquire, by mingling as man among men, more knowledge of the other sex than the conventions of social intercourse would admit. He transfers the adventures from the real world to a sort of forest of Arden, where the Rosalind of Shakspere might meet a Watteau shepherdess and a melancholy Jacques. Thus he helps us over the instinctive repulsion that we feel for the situation, and gives a purely artistic interest to the self-revelation that comes to his heroine and to Albert from their prolonged association. Various forms of love reaching out for an unattainable ideal occupy the body of the book, and when once the actors learn to know themselves and each other Gautier parts them forever. In its ethics the book is opposed to the professed morality of nearly all, and doubtless to the real morality of most, but as Sainte-Beuve said of it: " Every physician of the soul, every moralist, should have it on some back shelf of his library," and those who, like Mithridates, no longer react to such poisons will find in *Mlle. de Maupin* much food for the purest literary enjoyment.

Gautier calls *Fortunio* (1837) " a hymn to wealth, beauty, and happiness, the only three divinities that we recognise." Ethically this book is open to the same criticism as *Mlle. de Maupin*, but artistically it merits higher praise, because it transplants us frankly to wonderland, and having set us down there makes no attempt at psychological analysis or justification. Fortunio has boundless wealth and has been educated in Oriental luxury. No material wish or whimsey has been left ungratified. He comes to Paris, where lavished fortunes enable him to guard his seraglio in Eastern seclusion. He has also a pavilion at Neuilly for his whimsicalities and for his pet lion and tiger. He is the masculine ideal of a sensualist fancy, a composite of Apollo and Bacchus, and if he mingles in Parisian society it is only in that undiscovered corner of it where everybody is rich and fair and young.

The social and personal ethics of Fortunio are of course false, but the well-worn theme of the purification of the courtesan by love is treated with a sentimental nonchalance that disarms criticism. It is surely a venial sin if disgust at canting hypocrisy betray the joy of youth too far in its generous protest. There is no mortal poison here. Satiety stands too obviously behind the curtain. But the art of the tale is as perennial a joy as that of *Aladdin* or *The Forty Thieves*.

Fortunio, says Gautier, " is the last work in which I have freely expressed my true thought." But during all his life he found in short stories a means of partial self-projection, of fixing those dreams that he regarded as " the most enduring of the goods of this world." There is something of himself in all his heroes. It is clear, too, that the demands of conventionality galled him more at first than later. His next volume of fiction, the *Trio of Novels* (Trio de romans, 1850), is distinctly his worst. It were difficult to imagine a story that should unite in higher degree the improbable and the commonplace than *The Innocent Roués* (les Roués innocents, 1846). *Militona* (1847) contains some bits of brilliant description of Spanish life, but its humour is grotesque exaggeration, and its fabulation belongs to the childhood of the *feuilleton*. Indeed the story is chiefly interesting for a sort of sub-acid irony of protest against its own banality. But the restive Pegasus feels the editor's hand on the bridle and checks his natural instinct of artistic liberty. " They have made me a kennel," he writes in a poem of this time, " where I watch, pressed down in the *feuilleton* of a newspaper, like a crouching dog." And one feels the same restraint in the last of this Trio, *John and Jenny* (Jean et Jeanette, 1850), where social emancipation is danced to a minuet when we feel he would have preferred the Carmagnole. The date of the story gives it its chief interest. Beneath the conventions of the *feuilleton* we catch the spirit of Sue's socialistic novels, and of the second manner of George Sand, with something of the emancipatory spirit of 1848 and something of that joy in luxury that marks the coming of the Second Empire.

The volume of short stories, published in 1845 and again in 1858 and containing eight tales besides a republication of *Fortunio*, is of a different tone and a much higher artistic value. The stories are of various dates, but the key-note is struck by *Fortunio* and the emancipated inspiration of romanticism is far more apparent. One of the tales, *The Nightingale's Nest* (le Nid des rossignols), dates from 1833, and *The Dead Leman* (la Morte amoureuse), probably the best, from 1836; but as they were revised at the time of their collected publication, there is no reason for insisting on their chronological order. Enough that taken together they represent the frankest expression of Gautier's ideas during fifteen years of enforced literary toil. It is said that he put most of himself into the hero of the first of them as they are now arranged, *The Golden Fleece* (la Toison d'or, 1839), and certainly its hero, Tiburce, is a curious character, whose singularity, as Gautier says, " had the advantage of not being affected." Many things that are said of him seem to accord remarkably with the impressions of the friends of the author. Like Gautier, Tiburce had been a painter. Like Tiburce also, Gautier " would stay for whole days on his divan supported by two piles of cushions, without saying a word, his eyes shut and his hands hanging " and " troubling himself as little about the affairs of the time as of the news from the moon, preferring to do nothing than to work, wholly detached from all human things, and so reasonable that he seemed crazy." Much psychological self-insight is shown in the analysis of the artistic nature of the poet-painter. His search for physical beauty had made him sceptical of moral beauty, and, as physical dissimulation

was more difficult than psychic, he clung to material perfection. "Art had taken possession of him too young and
had corrupted him and falsified him," so that he had become "bold in thought, timid in action," loving fiercely,
but loving a chimera of his fancy that, like a captive bird,
was ever seeking some opening through which to soar into
the blue of heaven.

Now the psychic result of such a state of mind, as Balzac
well shows in *The Hidden Masterpiece* (le Chef-d'œuvre
inconnu), and Zola in *The Work* (l'Œuvre), is to place the
ideal so far beyond the power of material execution or
attainment as to paralyse effort. Thus here Tiburce so
loses himself in the beauty of Rubens' Magdalen in the
"Descent from the Cross" at Antwerp that her living
counterpart serves only to suggest the picture, until Gret-
chen dissipates this phantom barrier to their marriage by
inducing him to give external artistic form to his ideal, and
thus wins him back from cerebral to natural love.

The stretching out of loving arms toward a figment of the
brain that found an artistic expression in *The Golden Fleece*
pursued Gautier as phantom love through his whole literary
career, for one finds it in his youthful poem *Albertus*, and
it persists to the last both in his tales and his novels. In
Omphale (1834) it is the piquant eighteenth-century marchioness who descends from the picture in the rococo pavilion of the rococo garden to bring visions of the regency
to the young bachelor, until the prosaic uncle rolls up the
canvas and sends it to the garret. In *The Dead Leman*,
(1836) it is the courtesan seen at his ordination that haunts
the country priest and makes his life at first a desperate
struggle and then a weird double existence of which he
hardly knows which half is real and which a fantasy. The

artistic structure of this tale, the gradual initiation of the
reader into the realm of uncanny spirits, is above praise.
The wild night-ride that brings the priest to the bed where
Clarimonde lies dead, the watch where prayer yields to
passion, and the dead lips and arms respond to the kiss that
gives her ghost the right to visit him, until, nursed vampire-
like upon his blood, she turns into dust when touched by
holy water, and leaves her priestly lover in horror-struck
regret — all this is treated with a restraint, yet with a power,
that make *The Dead Leman* one of the great ghost-stories
of the literature of the world.

Again we find Gautier seeking a phantom love in the
grandiose life of ancient Egypt or Lydia or Greece, enjoying, as he says, "the high contemplation of a human soul
whose least desire translates itself in vast actions, enormi-
ties of granite or bronze," for in our time "man no longer
finds scope for his imperial fantasy."

Such a dream is *The Golden Chain* (1837), that tells us
of the love of Ctesias for the Athenian Plangon, who would
recover in his affection her virginity of soul. *A Night with
Cleopatra* (1838) is a similar dream of the hero of low
degree, Meiamoun, made worthy by his love to buy with
his life the ephemeral favour of Egypt's queen of beauty, a
dream suggested, no doubt, by the "Sleeper Awakened" of
the *Arabian Nights*, or by Shakspere's Christopher Sly. Very
closely allied to this, though with a happier ending, is *King
Candaule* (1844), where Gautier has lavished all the resources of rhetorical harmony to evoke soft Lydian airs, and
all the colours of his literary palette to paint the grandiose
luxury of the last of the Heraclidæ. On the story itself
there is no reason to dwell, for it is taken, even in its details, from the first book of Herodotus ; but the splendour of

the descriptions stands out in sharper outlines and clearer colours here under the Lydian sky and there beneath the sun of Egypt than in any work that had preceded. Here, as in the more trivial *Nightingale's Nest* and *The Marchioness's Pet Dog* one seems to see the author giving himself over, like his own Tiburce, to an unbridled fancy, heedless alike of the demands and of the limitations of reality, but with a most exquisite feeling for beauty in nature and in man, with senses most delicately responsive to every stimulus, and with a power to convey sensation in words that is most rare.

A second collection of stories, ten in number, followed in 1863, though the greater part of the volume had been already published before the close of 1852. Here the weird and uncanny element that was observable in the best work of the earlier collection gets decidedly the upper hand, and shows a preoccupation, so common in the sceptics of hedonism, with occult philosophy and spiritism. Thus *Avatar* (1856), the first story in the series, busies itself with the curious though quite futile question of what situation would be created by a transfusion of souls so that the spiritual nature of one man should be combined with the body and mental aptitudes of another.

Less attractive, because less frankly unreal, is *Jettatura* (1856), a story of Naples and of the evil eye. That Neapolitan porters should shrink from the cross-eyed aristocrat Paul is probable enough, that Count Altavilla should do so is possible ; but that this should worry a Parisian gentleman such as d'Aspremont into a vague terror in which he thinks himself responsible for the obviously hereditary consumption of his fiancée Alicia, is what would require greater skill in morbid psychology than Gautier possessed

to make other than incredible, unless indeed one is prepared
to agree with him that "dreams are as real as reality."

There is in *Jettatura* a fine duel fought in the ruins of
Pompeï, and this is also the scene of *Arria Marcella* (1852),
— a remarkable story of retrospective passion, and the
most vivid of all Gautier's resuscitations of antiquity.
Phantom love is again the subject, and again we feel that,
in the hero Octavien, Gautier has painted a phase of his
own nature. Octavien is a young artist who lives so in the
realm of the beautiful that he loves its ideals beyond all
reality. He "could love only outside of time and space,"
and "had composed for himself an ideal seraglio with
Semiramis, Aspasia, Cleopatra, Diana of Poictiers, and Jane
of Aragon." He had loved statues too, and now the lava
print of a woman's form found in the house of Arrius
Diomedes at Pompeï has filled him with a longing to trans-
port his soul to the century of Titus. In this mood he has
a vision of restored Pompeï as he sleeps amid its ruins.
He converses with a courteous citizen, who escorts him to
a play of Plautus. Among the spectators is Arria. She
takes him to her home, for, as she explains to him, "the
flame of your thought has darted to me; my soul felt it in
that world where I float invisible to gross eyes. Belief
creates the god, and love the woman. . . . Your desire has
restored me to life." But her Christian father enters to
trouble joy, and under his exorcism Marcella crumbles back
to dust.

Somewhat similar, though less highly wrought, is *The
Mummy's Foot* (le Pied de momie, 1840). The little story
opens with a dazzlingly minute description of the shop of a
collector of antiquities, where the author in his search for
a· paper-weight chances on the foot of Hermonthis, a

Pharaoh's daughter, and dreams that night that the princess comes to seek it, talks with her severed member, receives it kindly as his gift, invites him to visit her father, and takes him through marvels of more than Egyptian grandeur, where, " holding him by the hand, she saluted graciously the mummies of her acquaintance." In return for her foot he begs her hand, but her father declines because of the disparity in age, and at that moment he awakes.

Again, in *The Opium Pipe* (la Pipe d'opium, 1838), it is a dead or sleeping beauty that revives in answer to his love, and here as there, and as also in *The Hashish Club* (le Club des hachichiens, 1846), the mode of the story is a dream. In the same group may be placed also the feebly fantastic tale of peri-love, *The Thousand and Second Night* (la Mille et deuxième nuit, 1842), of which the author says in mock penitence that it caused the death of the sultana who ventured to narrate it to the critical Schahriar. The other stories in this volume call for no notice.

During the twenty-five years between the writing of *Fortunio* and the publication of the last of these short stories Gautier had written three novels. The first, *The Mummy's Tale* (le Roman de la momie, 1857), works to a rather dangerous length the antiquarian vein of some of the best of the short stories; the second, *Captain Fracasse* (le Capitaine Fracasse, 1861–3), is described by the author himself as " a bill drawn in my youth and redeemed in middle life," and is a uniquely fascinating romantic fancy; while the third, *Spirite* (1865), is the author's last dream of phantom love, with an appeal to sceptical credulity more successful, though not more artistic, than that of *Jettatura*. With this novel Gautier fittingly closed his literary career.

The Mummy's Tale elaborates into a novel one of those

vivid glimpses of the past that were rendered so wonderfully in *The Mummy's Foot* and in *Arria Marcella*. But for this fuller treatment Gautier lacked, as perhaps the science of his day lacked, adequate preparation and direct knowledge of the country; yet, in spite of this, he was able to produce a book that satisfied the antiquarians perhaps better than it could the literary critics. The style is indeed marvellously polished, and in some of the descriptions of landscape and architecture he has written with an art that he himself has hardly rivalled. But all this masks a psychic unreality that is truly exasperating, and the story, for all its elaboration, produces far less effect of illusion than those shorter evocations of a mysterious and ghostly antiquity.

Captain Fracasse had been announced in 1836. It began to appear in December, 1861, and it would seem from the preface that the first chapter was not written till 1855. Gautier had already shown his interest in the period of Louis XIII., and had proved his minute knowledge of it in *The Grotesques* (1844), a volume of literary studies. Here he has treated the same epoch in the spirit of 1830, and has given us what Sainte-Beuve calls "the classic of romanticism." The novel, however, falls into two parts of nearly equal length, but very different in character and very unequal in literary value. The former and better part resembles superficially Scarron's *Comic Novel* (le Roman comique, 1651), for both tell of the adventures of a band of strolling players in the days when Molière was of their number, and in both a beautiful maid, of birth above her station, is made the centre of intrigue and of romantic interest. It was wholly characteristic of Gautier's artistic temperament that he should prefer to study life in comedy, than, like Balzac, to note comedy in life. His personages stand out with wonderful precision, not as characters but as picturesque figures. Gautier says that he would have the reader feel "as though he were turning over etchings by Callot or engravings by Abraham Bosse," and this is much the effect of these harmonious and well-ordered pages, where we see men, animals, ruined castles, palaces of princes, and dens of thieves as vividly as in a dream, and yet penetrate as little beneath the surface to the spirit of the individual or the society.   Every freak of fancy is punctuated with a realistic detail.   This first half of *Captain Fracasse* is the most complete expression of Gautier's genius as a painter in prose, and yet the death and burial of Matamore is the only touch of true pathos in it all.

Wholly different is the second part, a phantasmagoria of freakish adventures that might have sprung from the brain, though it could never have flowed from the pen, of Alexandre Dumas.   French critics are agreed that the second part of *Captain Fracasse* "does not exist for those of delicate taste."   But in the former Gautier has caught the spirit of Scarron's *Comic Novel* so completely, and yet given to it, as Sainte-Beuve says, such a bath of youth and art in the Castilian spring of his style, that he has, as it were, encrusted this modern book in the literature of a long past age, and his novel is in its way an even more astonishing evocation of a vanished society than Hugo's *Notre-Dame*. It is a picture, not of an epoch alone, but also of a romantic ideal that had slowly matured in Gautier's mind during the three decades that separate it from *Young France*.

The second part, however, is by no means devoid of interest.   Indeed, individual chapters are equal, if not superior, to anything that went before.   He has made the

Paris of Richelieu live, and his Pont-Neuf is almost as real
to us as that of our own day. It is only when he abandons
description for action that his work ceases to be unique
and threatens at times to grow commonplace. Most admirable, too, are the scenes of criminal life in that den of
thieves, the *Radis couronnée*. The whole is instinct with
the nonchalant gaiety and bizarre joy of sense and colour
that characterised the "grotesques" of this curious reign,
Cyrano, Scarron, Saint-Amant, and that poor martyr to his
wit, Théophile de Viau, not in vain the namesake of "Our
Théo."

It is difficult to conceive a stronger novelistic contrast
than that between this picturesque evocation of the past
and the nebulous, mystic spiritism of Gautier's last novel,
Spirite (1865), in which he returns to that phantom love
that so often haunted the short stories. Here he has not
recourse to a dream, as in *The Mummy's Foot* or in *Arria
Marcella*, nor yet to the Oriental hocus-pocus of *Avatar*.
He bases his story, as Balzac had done *Séraphita* on the
Swedenborgian teaching of angels and of celestial marriage.
In this conception of the spirit world that "has its infatua-
tions as well as ours," there is a suggestion of Dante's
Beatrice, but we know that this love "enkindled by the
impossible" and gradually passing into an hallucinated "cer-
tainty of future happiness," where, in the climax of passion,
"art itself is forgotten in love," is a favourite situation with
Gautier. Still, for those who do not sympathise with this
doctrine the idea has found more artistic expression, and
such readers will remember *Spirite* most pleasantly for its
beautiful descriptions of the Acropolis and of the Parthe-
non. As a whole, the book is an appeal to the sceptical
credulity of a generation in search of a new faith. It struck

the popular fancy, but gained the author more immediate fame than lasting reputation.

Indeed, if we consider Gautier's fiction as a whole, we may say of it all, as of *Spirite*, that its supreme excellence lies in the dazzling brilliancy of its descriptions and in the rippling harmony of its diction.   Gautier lacks insight into character and the touch of natural sympathy that belongs to the highest genius.   His vision is fascinating, but it is not inspiring.   Let us recognise frankly his limitations, and then let us surrender ourselves on fit occasion to the delight of his plastic art, by which this artist of language builds the soulless fabrics of his vision with a vocabulary of unmatched resource and a perception of the delicate nuances in words that is as exquisite as it is unrivalled.   Like Shelley he seems capable of creating from the shapes that haunt thought's wildernesses, from lake-reflected suns and yellow bees in the ivy bloom, pictures so clear, so clean cut, so exquisitely finished, that they have become things of beauty and joys forever to those whose eyes are trained to see them.   His work can never be very popular, but it will remain for generations far from the limits of a vulgar fate.   In epic imagination he is inferior to Hugo, possibly even to Vigny. In humour and charm he is inferior to Musset.   And yet to those who love his form of literary art his fiction gives the more enduring delight.

CHAPTER X.

GEORGE SAND.

THE most fertile of the contemporaries of Balzac, if we except the dubious fecundity of Dumas, and surely the most facile of women writers in all time, is she who was Lucile-Aurore Dupin by birth, Madame Dudevant by marriage, and by choice and fame George Sand. To those who are fascinated by the problems of heredity, few men of genius offer a more interesting study. On her father's side she was descended from an old and wealthy bourgeois family. No one more eminently respectable than her paternal grandfather Dupin de Franceuil, the tax-contractor (*fermier général*) and friend of Rousseau, who had married in middle life, a daughter of Maurice de Saxe, the famous general and son of the otherwise famous Countess de Königsmark and the also notorious King of Poland, Augustus the Strong. Her grandmother had been previously married to Count Horn, a natural son of Louis XV., and thus she could claim a sort of connection with the royal family of France, while her mother was a plebeian of the plebeians, the daughter of a certain Delaborde, a bird-trainer and dealer in Paris, herself by profession a dressmaker, quite without all accomplishments but those of a native charm that she had been somewhat negligent in guarding.

It was this that attracted the notice of the gay young officer, Maurice Dupin, who, much against the will of his aristocratic mother, married her in 1803, and having fulfilled his mission by giving to the world this child in 1804, was killed by a fall from his horse four years later. The young Aurore had the curious fortune to be " born among roses, to the sound of music." She inherited from father and paternal grandfather a dashing temperament and democratic sympathies, and from her mother she acquired her taste for an adventurous life, while both influences were much modified by the aristocratic training of her father's mother, under whose care she remained till she was thirteen. But Aurore continued to visit, love, and admire her mother, and so was brought in contact with conflicting affections, whose double-twisted thread can be traced throughout her life and her works.

Her childhood was passed at the ancestral homestead at Nohant in Berry. Here she was formally instructed after the rigid precepts of old-school pedantry, and, with a democratic independence, proceeded to supplement this instruction in two ways : first, by the sentimental novels then in vogue, especially the *New Héloïse, Paul and Virginia, Atala*, and *Corinne ;* secondly and most, by contact with nature in this French Arcadia, brooding in sombre valleys over the memories of her childhood and the faint echoes of the Napoleonic tragedy, or chasing butterflies by the Indre and learning to know the beauty of nature as none of her contemporaries knew it, because she loved it more than they.

Thus she came to know the life of an artificial society, of sentimental fiction, and of peasant reality, and already as a child she was putting all this material to use with the creative instinct of the born romancer. Encouraged by her mother she began, like Goethe, to tell stories before she could read or write, continuing them, just as she was to do in later years, until her fancy wearied of the situation and the characters she had conceived, and then dropping the thread for another. Thus she entertained the peasant children at Nohant, where also she invented and acted little plays with her sister and Ursule, a child companion. But when she was thirteen her grandmother seems to have thought that a little Parisian polish would add to her chances of marriage, and she was sent in 1817 to the fashionable convent school of the English Ladies, where, curiously enough, both her mother and her grandmother had been imprisoned during the Revolution. Now the effect of this convent life on the future novelist was to give her a deeper idealism and a comprehension at least of religious feeling, to which till then she had been wholly a stranger. She had come here proficient in shooting, fencing, and dancing, but ignorant of the sign of the cross. She took at first a natural place at the head of the rebels to discipline, and went by the name of the Tomboy. But presently she underwent a psycho-physiological change. She had periods of sadness, waves of undefined longing, until one evening, alone in the convent chapel, her spirit was touched, as she thought, by the spirit of God and she was converted. This change was sentimental, not rational. Her ardent imagination had fed on the rich food of Roman ritual and she had cradled herself into a religious dream. So the practices of piety which at first she embraced with ardour were soon abandoned, but she never ceased to feel and to respond to the religious sentiment, and a thread of mystic idealism can be traced through the greater part of her volumes.

At sixteen she was withdrawn from this hot-bed of artificial emotions to the deathbed of her grandmother and to

nature and freedom. Again she walked or rode by the
Indre and mingled familiarly with the peasantry. She
began to read more widely, and indeed with more zeal than
comprehension, letting Chateaubriand think for her now,
as she had let Rousseau feel for her before, and as in later
years she was inclined to take ideas ready-made from
socialistic friends without quite understanding their impli-
cations. A natural result of this was mental dyspepsia.
She had gloomy moods, meditated suicide or the cloister,
but was withdrawn from these vagaries by legal complications attending her grandmother's estate, and while visiting
with her mother met a burly country squire, Casimir Dudevant, whom in 1822 she was overpersuaded to marry.

George Sand was no woman to be content with a marriage of convention, and of all men a realistic philistine
must have been most uncongenial to this free-minded and
warm-hearted girl. He managed her dower of five hundred
thousand francs most admirably, but he neglected her heart.
Still they lived together, " suffering each other's foibles for
accord," for eight years, interrupted by travel and a brief
stay at her old convent, and they had two children, to whom
she was always a devoted mother, the need of loving being
one of the most marked traits in her character. But almost
as prominent was her independence. She could not brook
the subjection to a Bœotian squire. In 1829 she claimed
and obtained the right to live for considerable intervals at
Paris on a monthly allowance of 250 francs that he made
her from her large fortune, and she endeavoured to eke out
this pittance by decorative painting and kindred feminine
arts. At last in 1831 a partial separation was agreed upon,
and this was made final in 1836. It is important to dwell
on this unfortunate marriage, for its humiliations and reve-

lations completed the outfit of the novelist for the first period of her development. It was the ferment of blighted hope, of discontent with the society that made such marriages as hers natural, that penetrated like a yeast this talent composed of intimate knowledge of aristocratic life, inherited democratic sympathies, close contact with nature and its children, and the ideal aspirations kindled by religious sentiment. All these things were necessary that George Sand should write even her first novel, *Indiana*.

Almost every one has hidden in his life the possibility of one novel, but George Sand did not immediately discover this, and her articles printed in the Figaro attracted little notice. She had already written a story, but with the self-criticism of which she was always capable decided that it was unworthy of publication. At the office of the Figaro she met Jules Sandeau, a young lawyer and afterward a novelist of some note, and together they wrote *Rose and Blanche* and signed it Jules Sand. This book had merit enough to attract publishers, and in 1832 she published her first independent novel, under the name George Sand.

Indiana achieved a great success, and if we seek the causes of this in the criticism of the time it will appear that it was because men felt that the story was naturalistic, imperfect perhaps in execution but broadly human in conception. Here was no romantic medievalism, but the persons and manners of her own day, living a familiar life, talking a familiar language, and feeling as strongly as was still possible in an age of social restraint. It is well to stress this point here at the outset, because George Sand is as much the mother of " naturalism " as Flaubert is its father, though it must be confessed that her child has often the defects of her qualities. To this matter there will be frequent occa-

sion to recur.   As for *Indiana* itself, the opening, as usual
with George Sand, is better than the close.   There she was
on familiar ground.   She could find in her own heart the
blighting ennuis of the ill-mated heroine, her expectations
of a fairy land of sentiment, and her discovery of a desert
of sordid domesticity.   She had known, too, how under
these conditions the pent-up fire of passion might break
a way for itself if it felt the attraction of a kindred sympathy, and she knew also, perhaps, that most men who lend
themselves to satisfy such feelings are petty and contemptible.   Her Indiana is a nobler Emma Bovary.   Her lover
Raymon, the most interesting character, is even more contemptibly seductive than Flaubert's Rodolphe, because he
has perverted a nobler nature.   Clearly in 1832 this was
a new note in fiction.   Could the note be held and the success maintained?

That question was answered, almost before the critics
had asked it, by *Valentine* (1832), written during a visit to
Nohant, whence it drew much of its picturesque inspiration.
Yes, George Sand had not merely the power to look within
and tell what she saw there.   She had a perennial spring of
creative imagination, that in the course of the next forty-
three years was to pour out in a constant stream eighty-four
volumes of novels, ten of correspondence, eight of memoirs,
five of dramas, and leave many more for the gleaner in this
abundant harvest.   It is impossible here to speak of all the
novels in detail, or to speak of some of them at all.   Nor is
this necessary to the present purpose.   All of them in her
first period, from *Valentine* (1832) to *Mauprat* (1837),
have the same inspiration and the same general characteristics.   All represent projections of various phases of her
own experience and re-assertions of an intense individualism.

They are types of the domestic novel, the lyric cry of the misunderstood wife. They are transpositions into narrative prose, sometimes so rhetorical and warm as to be almost rhythmic, of the romantic dramas of Hugo and the romantic odes of Musset. Their intense assertion of independent personality is of their time, and finds in that time a passionate echo and a revolt as passionate. To some she was in these years "the true priestess, . . . an inspired bacchante who leads in our century the choir of intelligences." To others she seemed profoundly immoral, antisocial. The battle over *Valentine*, where also the beginning is good and the end weak, reached its height on the appearance of *Lélia* in 1833, a story produced under conditions public and personal that tended to make it a gloomy cry of despairing genius, beating its wings against the confining bars of social law and custom. In the political world the revolution of 1830 had aroused more hopes than it had justified; the cholera of 1832, the failure of the *émeutes* of 1833, and the Polish massacres of that year had caused a deep discouragement among liberals everywhere; Saint-Simon and Fourier had shown to women a bright horizon that had roused a general restlessness among them both in France and Germany; and meantime her own domestic life had brought her many disillusions. "She was at this time," says Sainte-Beuve, "in a vein of bitterness and social misanthropy, on the eve of breaking an old tie, in a true moral isolation," seeking for some heart worthy to receive the outpourings of her overflowing affection, and presently to find it, as she thought, in the poet Musset. For the moment, however, she had lost faith not only in marriage but in love itself, and the waters of bitterness gush with geyser energy in the sombre periods of this eloquent poem in prose, the

revolt of passion bruised by masculine egoism, nauseated
by masculine fatuousness, despairing of finding any object
worthy of its devotion, and bursting at times in its enforced
sterility of heart into imprecations of society and of creation
itself.

Lélia marks a climax in this Byronic, dithyrambic declamatory vein, from which *Jacques* (1834) and *Leone Leoni*
(1835) afford a descent to earth. The former is a sort of
gospel of free love. The husband here is no longer the
unsympathetic boor of *Indiana* nor the unsympathetic gentleman of *Valentine*. He is a hero of magnanimity, who
makes way for the lover by considerately killing himself.
The lover, too, who in *Indiana* had been so ingrained a hypo-
crite as to be hardly conscious of his hypocrisy, and in *Valentine* had become an attractive and not altogether ignoble
gentleman, is in *Jacques* a hero as capable of passion as
Madame Dudevant, who is throughout the heroine.

This wild assertion of the divine right of passion was the
herald of a long line of similar novels in France and Germany, that continued to remind the author of her youthful
aberrations long after she had herself outgrown them. For
already *Leone Leoni* (1835) though it may place passion
above reason shows an attempt at serious psychic analysis,
while her work during 1834 had been made, as she says, to
sell rather than to read. This change had been wrought in
her by Musset, with whom she had made a journey to Italy
in the winter of 1833–4 that has been the subject of numerous books and of acrimonious controversy. We are concerned with it here only as it affected her novelistic talent.
It gave her her first passionate love, and her first realisation
of the inadequacy of passion as a rule of life. " I am
deadly sad," she writes to Sainte-Beuve on her return to

Paris; "I do not know if I shall survive this terrible crisis of
the thirtieth year." Both she and Musset were racked with
like pains, but they poisoned his nature while they greatly
deepened hers. In *She and He* (Elle et lui, 1859), the
novelistic precipitate of this journey, she says: " God makes
some men of genius to wander in the tempest and to create
pain. I studied you in your light and in your darkness, and
know that you are not to be weighed in balances like other
men." And so she presently recovered her self-poise.
New friends began to gather about her, Balzac, Liszt, Delacroix, and the philosophic priest Lamennais. But though
calmed she felt morally exhausted. In February of 1835
she sought refuge at Nohant and in the next year she
arranged a final separation from her husband that left her a
woman of independent fortune.

Such conditions were most unfavourable to literary production, but the effect appears less in the quantity than the
quality. Greater depth and tenderness come with 1835,
the former in *Leone Leoni*, the latter in *André*, which is the
idyllic prelude to *Devil's Pool* (1846) and *Little Fadette*
(1849). Then in 1836 the result of separation from her
husband appears in the more balanced art and firmer drawing of character of *Mauprat*, in which this first individualistic period of her genius reaches its full development; for
The Last Aldini (la Dernière Aldini, 1838), *The Master
Mosaists* (les Maîtres mosaïstes, 1838) and *The Companion
of the Tour de France* (le Compagnon de la Tour de France,
1840) show the arrested development that marks a coming
transformation in her thought and fiction.

Individualism, says Brunetière, culminates always in a
negation of order and social justice. In George Sand
prosperity, fame, travel modified the generous enthusiasms

of youth. The mother's point of view is not that of the bride. As early as 1836 she tells her son that ambition should not be for self, but for society. The sentimental socialism of Lamennais, Barbès, and others begins to attract her enthusiastic assent. There is some timid socialistic kite-flying in *The Companion of the Tour de France*, and in *Spiridion* (1840) there is a brief and futile effort to seek the solution of society's troubles in mystic interpenetration of politics and religion. Then the new sympathies fire completely her genius, and for eight years she dazzles the world with brilliant pleas for the ideals of the revolution of 1848.

Life at Nohant, with the stimulus of frequent visits to Paris, proved very favourable to steady and rapid production. Between 1841 and 1848 she issued forty-four volumes, all more or less tinged with this general warmth of universal sympathy, where aristocratic dames marry artisans, and mechanics refuse the proffered hand of wealth and nobility. The best of these novels are *Consuelo* (1843) and *The Countess of Rudolstadt* (1844) ; the most radical are *Mr. Antony's Fault* (le Péché de M. Antoine, 1847) and *The Miller of Angibault* (le Meunier d'Angibault, 1845). None of them can be read with satisfaction to-day. In them all the heart is right, but the head is wrong. They are declamatory and exceedingly uneven. But they seem very attractive to those minds, numerous after every political convulsion, whose thirst for truth is not satisfied by philosophy or religion, and who are as sure as Hamlet that the world is out of joint, and as powerless to set it right. And these novels are also very significant in the evolution of fiction both at home and abroad. George Sand was among the first to see that a sympathetic study of the lower classes would give new life to romanticism, which was in its nature democratic and even, as she said, "revolutionary." And so these studies of artisan and peasant life, beginning in 1840, and thus preceding Balzac's *Peasants*, or Sue's *Mysteries of Paris*, or Hugo's *Misérables*, are an essential prelude to the topsy-turvy naturalism of Zola. That is the historical significance of novels that widened their author's heart and chastened her sympathies for the more artistic and wholly delightful work of her third period, when the revolution of 1848 and its collapse had given to her socialistic dream a rude awakening.

In February of that year she had been drawn into active journalistic life, but the obvious incapacity of the people for self-government soon cooled her enthusiasm, and after the accession of Napoleon she withdrew once more to her country estate at Nohant in Berry, where she resided almost continuously until her death in June, 1876. During all this time her pen was ceaselessly busy, and the complete bibliography of her writing, from 1849 to her death, counts one hundred and thirty-five volumes, some of them of course smaller than those in which her works are published to-day.

Her later manner shows itself first in studies of the peasantry of Berry, of which the spirit and manner had been anticipated in the preceding period by *Jeanne* (1844) and by *The Devil's Pool* (la Mare au diable, 1846), while in *Teverino* (1846) she seems to have sought relief from her socialistic friends by a flight into fairyland. Of the country idyls, the most noteworthy beside the ever exquisite *Devil's Pool* are *François le Champi* (1849), *Little Fadette* (la Petite Fadette, 1849), and *The Bell Ringers* (les Maîtres sonneurs, 1853). It is difficult to speak too strongly of the idyllic charm and gentle sympathy with the children of nature that pervades these books and makes them redolent with the scent of wild thyme and sage. Love had pulsed in her first novels, the passion for humanity in the socialistic tales. Here was the third element, foreshadowed since *Valentine*, the sentiment of nature, that led her to observe with loving care the material details and the revelations of soul in life among the lowly. If she still moralised as in the socialistic novels, it was now as an optimistic realist, admitting, as she says, " the right of the literary artist to sound and exhibit the plague spots of society," as Balzac had done, but feeling that fear increases rather than heals egoism, and believing that the mission of her art was " a mission of sentiment and of love."   More and more from year to year this habit of thought built up in her a more objective esthetic mind, until in 1867 we find her writing that " the whole secret of the beautiful, the only truth, love, art, enthusiasm, and faith " is in loving persons for what they are in themselves, and not for any reflection of one's self that one finds in them.   But that is to assert the impersonality of art in its noblest form.

In an introduction to *The Devil's Pool* the author says she is a realistic optimist, but the tale has in it nothing of Utopia.   It is a delicious idyl of a ride by day and night, and of an often interrupted conversation in which Marie reveals her simple, loving heart to the honest Germain, and reaps the fruit of quickly ripening seed sown quite unconsciously.   It is a trifle and yet a masterpiece of rustic poetry, a work of perfect nature.

Again before 1848 she struck the same note in *François le Champi* (printed in 1849).   Here as in *The Devil's Pool* it is a little boy that brings his elders to a realisation of their love, and the whole is treated with a most dainty charm, as though she truly loved the peasants of whom she wrote. Then the collapse of socialism in 1849 gave her back wholly to her art. She sees that " direct allusions to present ills, the appeal to fermenting passions, is not the road to salvation. Better a gentle song, a rustic pipe, a tale to lull little children without fear or pain, than the spectacle of real woes reinforced and darkened by the colours of fiction." Thus *Little Fadette* becomes, as Caro says, the first pledge of the reconciliation of Madame Sand with her genius. We can see that she has been reading to good effect her Virgil in the depths of Berry. As in *The Devil's Pool* she had endeavoured to render the charm of the prattle of childhood, so here she goes a step further in an endeavour to convey the flavour of rustic language, putting her story into the mouth of a countryman, but modifying his words so that she might seem, as she put it, " to speak clearly for a Parisian, simply for a peasant." Our modern dialect writers have more courage, but few have attained such a happy result in what is at best an artificial rather than an artistic excellence. The psychology of childhood, both in the twins Sylvanet and Landry and in the shrewd little Fanchon Fadet, poor yet proud, who passes for ugly till metamorphosed by her love, is admirably seized and developed with precision and yet with sympathetic pathos, and we find the same traits also in *The Bell Ringers* (les Maîtres sonneurs, 1853).

But this bucolic genre, however charming, could not long afford scope for her genius. She could not let slumber in her those stronger and more intense feelings that had found expression in her earlier novels. But now these qualities were to show themselves no longer obscured by the smoke of passion, but burning clear and bright in the serener air of the rich experiences of half a century. She turned first from the pastoral to the drama, whither we will not follow her, and then in the novel, which was to her the more natural genre, she took all society for her theme, and wrote a number of stories excellently told and quite free from social or political preoccupations. She tried historical novels also, returned to the working classes in *The Black City* (la Ville noire, 1861), and in the same year gave us her best novel of aristocratic life in *The Marquis of Villemer*, having in the preceding year published her most curious psychological novel, *Jean de la Roche*.

On the whole it is perhaps these last with *Mlle. la Quintinie* (1863) that best unite the various elements that make up her literary genius. The subject of *Jean de la Roche* is that studied with such marvellous acuteness in Zola's *Page of Love*, the morbid jealousy of a child, in this case a brother, in Zola's a daughter, that bars the course of normal love. This morbid passion and its physical accompaniments are acutely dissected, and in their gradations serve as the mainspring of an action by which two noble hearts are tempered and strengthened. The whole work breathes a tender and hopeful magnanimity, and the close is more deftly managed and more artistically satisfying than is usual with George Sand.

The *Marquis of Villemer* has for its heroine Caroline de Saint-Geneix, lady-companion to the Marchioness of Villemer, one of the most delightful aristocratic figures in fiction. She has been described as "a complicated character, marred by the abuse of social relations, incapable of living alone, incapable even of thinking when alone, but charmingly witty when brought into touch with the wit of others, whose sole joy in this world is conversation which does her the service of stirring her ideas, of drawing her from herself." Here as in *Jean de la Roche* the real theme is love discovering itself and overcoming some barrier not lightly to be despised or put aside. This is indeed the nature of all love stories. But in this last and most genial period of George Sand's genius the note is never forced, the situation never reaches the tension of tragedy. So again in *Mlle. la Quintinie* (1863) the obstacle is religious difference in two nobly minded lovers where the indignation that George Sand felt at Feuillet's *Sibylle* (1862) never alters the self-restrained delicacy with which she portrays the various attitudes of the French mind toward Catholicism. In all these stories and in the others also we feel that the obstacle that separates the magnanimous youth and the tender maid is very largely a figment of their imagination, to be dispelled by some mutual confidence that their love impels, or perhaps by some chance. The psychology is shallow perhaps, but it is not false. You are not shown the abysses of the human heart, but you are pleased to watch the moonbeams playing on its rippling surface. George Sand seldom asks you to think. She is content to win your sympathetic interest. Indeed it is doubtful if she herself thought clearly. Her best characters are those of women, energetic and resourceful and of artistic temperament, which is only to say that, here at the last as at the first, she unconsciously introduced herself into the creatures of her imagination ; but, as her sympathy kept her ever young, her young girls, so timidly romantic, so modestly coquettish, were almost always charming. These are the special characteristics of the works of her last years, from 1860 to her death, work very uneven, often prolix, but on the whole the most broadly human of all, and including those novels which with *The Devil's Pool* are likely to have the widest and most enduring popularity.

George Sand, says Faguet, was one of the best balanced organisations that ever lived. Her mind was clear but not wide, admirable for superficial observation whether of manners or of men, fond of ideas yet not fully apprehending them, with the instincts of a thinker and without his power, much more calm herself than the creations into which she poured what had begun to ferment in her mind, and so freed herself of its possession. But if her thought is not deep it is quick, and so is her feeling, which is always generous, and her imagination, which is always alert. Therefore she begins by being romantic, and she remains more or less romantic to the close, though she has described with singular felicity in *Mlle. la Quintinie* and *Mlle. Merquem* (1868) the transition from the romantic spirit of the reign of Louis Philippe to the materialistic, positive spirit of the Second Empire, a transition of which it has been said that it left fathers more youthful in feeling than their own sons.

To George Sand, whether as individual or as novelist, love is the mainspring of life. "Nothing is strong in me but the necessity of loving," she writes. It is love alone, sexual, parental, or altruistic, that gives meaning and value to existence or meaning and charm to nature. It is love alone, and in the greater part of her novels, sexual love, that is the motive of all effort, the inspiration of all struggle. If one can love without effort and without struggle, if there is no obstacle, the rest of paradise has begun on earth, there is nothing more for the lovers to do but to exist and love. Of course this is most marked in the novels of the first period, where it reaches at times an exaggeration that is

almost comic. The altruistic element is most marked in
the second period, and later we find a fusion of both.
There is in her attitude a touch of mysticism. " Love,"
she tells us, in *Valentine*, " is superior to all other sentiments
because it has a divine origin."

In *Jacques* we are told that Providence presides even
over inconstancy, an idea developed with eloquent ingenuity
in *Lucrezia Floriani* (1847), and even as late as 1857, in
Daniella love is presented as an initiation into a fuller
comprehension of Deity. " There is no crime where there
is sincere love," says Jacques. Society is responsible. Of
course when George Sand writes thus she means by love
what Goethe means by his Eternal Womanly, "the holy
aspiration of the most ethereal part of our soul toward the
unknown," as she makes Lélia say. But this mystic Platonism has never far to seek for its sensuous symbol, and we
do not need to go outside her own novels to find a mocking commentary on what Caro calls " the hallucinations of
cynical chastity."

Out of this theory of her first period, that love is a divine
thing that brooks no contradiction, springs naturally the
view of her second period, that it abolishes social distinc-
tions of wealth or caste. By this she appealed to the instinct of sacrifice that characterises romantic love, and she
won the sympathy of many who, it is to be hoped, did not
try to practise her preaching. For love does not level
ranks, though it is to this thought that we owe the generous
and gracious inspiration that created some of her most
charming young women, the Marie of *The Devil's Pool*, the
Caroline of *Marquis de Villemer*, Geneviève, Edmée, and
Consuelo.

But to one who has this conception of the sacred rights

of passion, submission to the conventions, moral and social, becomes a fault, if not an impossibility. There is in her work no Christian resignation. The pride of passion quivers through it all. Hence the declamatory element in her second period. Hence, too, those strikes for moral freedom and appeals for social liberty, those prophetic visions of conjugal utopias in the work of the first period, though she says herself, in response to some criticisms of Nisard, that her nature is that of a poet rather than of a legislator, and that she may well have said in her haste "social laws" when she meant "social prejudices," abuses, or vices.

Her attacks, first on marriage, and then on social conventions generally, on what she called "the infamous decrepitude of the world," being based on sentiment and instinct rather than on coherent reason, on the inspiration of ambient socialism rather than on original thought, naturally yielded to the experience of life. *Valvèdre* (1861) contradicts *Jacques* (1834). The most that can be said for the socialistic novels is that they are more readable than any of the works that inspired them, and that they are the aberrations of a good heart as well as of a great genius. But what if we bring this heart and this genius back to nature? Let country scenes soothe the disappointed political reformer, and let their mysterious charm calm her perturbed spirit. For her poet nature this will be the most favourable of all environments, not merely for the development of her powers of artistic description, but for healthy ethical growth. No one has watched nature with such sympathetic closeness as she who says that she has "always found it infinitely more beautiful than she expected," and never gloomy save in the hours when she saw it with gloomy eyes. So, to her, nature was both a consolation and a recreation,

for as she says again : "The creations of art speak to the
mind alone, but the spectacle of nature speaks to all
faculties. It penetrates us through all pores as through all
ideas. To the purely intellectual sentiment of admiration
the sight of the countryside adds a sensual pleasure. The
freshness of the brooks, the perfumes of the plants, the
harmonies of the winds circulate in the blood and the
nerves at the same time that the splendour of their colours
and the beauty of their forms insinuate themselves into the
imagination."

If one sees nature with such eyes one will not describe it
objectively. It will always be a response to human feeling
or a symbol of human thought. The smell of sage clinging
to the hand from some now distant mountain plant will suggest "how precious a thing is perfume, which taking nothing from the plant whence it emanates clings to the hand of
a friend and follows him on his journey to charm him, and
to recall to him long the beauty of the flower that he
loves. The perfume of the soul is memory." Passages
like this are found in her work from the outset. Almost
always the psychic situation stands in relation to landscape,
and therefore almost all her stories are of country life, of
men in touch with nature, responding and corresponding to
their environment, which in its turn seems to sympathise
with them. It was fitting that her last thought should have
been of her garden, and her last words, "Don't destroy the
green."

George Sand was of no literary school and answered to
no shibboleth. No novelist ever had in greater measure
the story-telling instinct, the perennial flow of imagination.
No sooner had she written the last word of one story than
she was ready to begin another. She knew no anxious

elaboration. She never took, as Balzac tells us he did, ten days to think out a story before putting pen to paper, much less the laborious years of Flaubert's literary gestation. Her mind was full of interesting situations. She selected what struck her fancy and "let her pen trot." When the situation ceased to interest her she drew her work to a close, preferring to give literary life to another of the crowding children of her brain. Naturally and inevitably, then, her work lacks design and ordered composition. Quickly conceived it passed almost as quickly from her mind, until presently she could hardly recall the characters or situations of former creations of her fancy. She could never have knit her volumes into the unity of the *Human Comedy*. Her characters are not real to her, as Balzac's were to him. For while the details of her work are observed with minute realism she is apt to combine these into "superior beings" and romantic adventures, even when she proposes to write a book "wholly of analysis and meditation," such as the half-autobiographic *Lucrezia Floriani* (1847). But even here there is more realism than we at first perceive, for the romantic generation had a mode of expressing passion that was all its own, and George Sand did not escape the spirit of her time any more than Balzac escaped it.

As romanticism began to wane she became conscious of this tendency to exaggeration. So in a preface to *Lucrezia Floriani* she tells us that she "loves romantic events, the unforeseen, intrigue, action," and yet "does all she can to keep the literature of her time in a practicable path between the peaceful lake and the torrent." Her instinct would urge her to the abyss, but with calmer reason she sees that the torrent of imagination has pushed before it acts of un-

reason, or of crude improbability, and "a retrograde movement forces her back toward the smooth and monotonous
lake of analysis," and as she does not recompose her story
the reader has to make all these transitions with the author,
and the novel loses in art what it gains in freshness of conception. It is only occasionally that the inspiration remains with her to the end, and then the excellence that she
attains is rather the gift of genius than the conquest of talent and will. In this she forms the most striking contrast
possible to the novelists of the scientific generation who followed, or even to her early contemporary Balzac. From the
point of view of the originators of fiction, no book would
be a good novel that was not a good story. Many of our
modern novelists might well shrink from the application of
this canon. None could bear it with more equanimity than
George Sand, in spite of her lack of delicate reserve and
concise sobriety.

If now from her general conception of the novelist's art
we pass to her style in the narrower sense of diction, it
would seem that she had almost from the very first the
qualities that distinguished her to the last. Her style was
like herself, full, rounded, supple, mobile, almost always
easy, often fiery, sometimes too high-pitched and over-em-
phatic, and sometimes passionately eloquent. She seemed
to possess, instinctively, all the resources of the language,
writing well as naturally as most write ill, and so falling
sometimes into the fault of her talent, into that facile prolixity that leaves no scope for revery, and mars at times the
work of all natural stylists, such as Hugo, and rarely that of
the conscious artists, such as Flaubert. A worse fault than
prolixity is the occasional false emphasis, the author being

carried by a stream of words beyond the depth of her ideas. And then, sometimes, she plays with her talent, giving free bridle to fancy in long conversations that doubtless amused her, and may amuse us, but do not advance the story. And finally the books date themselves as of the romantic school by an excess of sentiment and of false notes in its expression. But all this need not, and should not, blind us to a merit and charm that no change in popular taste can take away, though George Sand's fame will, no doubt, seem to rise and fall as the literary pendulum sways between realism and idealism. It surely reached its lowest point in the decade that followed her death (1876), and now tends to wax with the waning of pseudo-scientific fiction. But whether she be widely read or generally forgotten, it is but justice to say, as has been said, that there is hardly a woman anywhere to-day whose life she has not affected, for her influence has been felt in every changed idea in the relation of the sexes in our generation. And more, in French literature her influence has been steadily tonic. For there pulsed through her a splendid confidence in the power of the human will; she was as fundamentally and naturally optimistic as Madame de Staël. If she protested against marriage it was only in the name of purity. All her excesses grew from her greatness of soul. As Matthew Arnold has well said, "though others in the literature of our century may have been greater, wiser, purer, more poetic, the most varied and attractive influence is hers." Her passions and errors will be forgotten, while "the immense vibration of her voice will not soon pass away. There will remain of her the sense of benefit and of stimulus from the passage upon earth of that large and frank nature, that large and pure utterance — the utterance of the early gods. There will remain an admiring and ever widening report of that great soul, simple, affectionate, without vanity, without pedantry, human, equitable, patient, kind. . . . In her case we shall not err if we adopt the poet's faith, —

'And feel that she is greater than we know.'"

16

DURING the first half of the nineteenth century the two French writers of most commanding genius are surely Hugo and Balzac, Hugo for imagination and form, for language and style, Balzac for the breadth of his conceptions, for his scientific spirit and psychologic insight. And now at the opening of the second half-century comes one who seeks to unite the minute realistic vision of Balzac with the highest rhetorical skill, and we have the few precious masterpieces of Gustave Flaubert; only five volumes as against Balzac's fifty, but five volumes that can perish only with the extinction of literary art. For his labour was as intense, as indefatigable, as that which piled up the half-hundred volumes of the *Human Comedy*, and it was more prolonged. There are few, if any, men of letters whose life has been a more enduring martyrdom to an endeavour to realise what was perhaps an unattainable ideal. If it be true to say, with Bourget, that French prose is unique among all languages of the world for its capabilities of polished precision, if France possesses the kingdom of the Written Phrase, surely Gustave Flaubert is a king in this realm, who, though dead, has as yet no successor.

But the importance of these five volumes is not only in their faultless style, but also in the precision with which they enunciate a view of the art of fiction that was to exercise a dominating influence on the succeeding generation.

It seemed, says Zola, as though with the appearance of *Madame Bovary*, in 1857, the code of the new art, "the formula of the modern novel, scattered through the colossal work of Balzac had been deduced and clearly enunciated in these four hundred pages." It became a type, a definite model. "Not one of the beginners of that day who has come to anything that will not recognise at the least an initiator in Gustave Flaubert."

He was born in 1821. His father, Dr. Achille Flaubert, was chief surgeon at the hospital at Rouen, where his virtues have remained legendary, and he bequeathed many of them to his son, in whom he would have desired to see his successor. Gustave Flaubert had always a certain unerring power of psychic dissection. His interest in truth conquered, or at least he strove to make it conquer, any manifestations of personal sympathy, and this gave to his writing the appearance of hardness. But for medicine he had no aptitude. Indeed, it is rare that any vocation is more strongly or earlier marked than his for literature. The first letter of his correspondence, written at the age of nine to a schoolfellow, proposes a literary partnership in which he should write the comedies, and to the end he welcomed no diversion from his art. In this aspiration he found, however, no sympathy at home. But the family were wealthy, he was able to travel on leaving school, and since he showed no aptitude for medicine he began in 1840 to study law and literature in Paris, returning, however, for considerable periods to Rouen, and already blighted with the knowledge that he was an epileptic. The influences, both at Paris, and previously at school, were strongly romantic. At fourteen he had conceived a violent love for a lady whom he has pictured as Madame Arneux in *Sentimental Educa-*

tion, and from 1846 to 1854 he carried on a tender correspondence with Madame Colet, a literary lady of some distinction in Paris. His first sympathies were wholly with the
men of the thirties. " I do not know," he writes, in a notice prefixed to the poems of a schoolmate, Louis Bouilhet,
" what may be the dreams of schoolboys now-a-days, but
ours were superbly extravagant. Inspired by the remote
echoes of romanticism . . . those gifted with enthusiastic
hearts sighed for dramatic scenes of love with the obligatory
gondolas, masks, and ladies swooning in post-chaises on
Calabrian hills ; sterner minds aspired to the conspirator's
sword. . . . And we were not only troubadours, revolution-
ists, and orientalists ; above all we were artists. We ruined
our eyes reading novels in the dormitory, we carried dag-
gers in our pockets like Antony. . . . We merited little
praise, but then how we hated everything mean, how passionate was our craving for greatness, . . . how we wor-
shipped Victor Hugo."

Meantime the young enthusiast of beauty was growing up
in the most prosaic of all recent French régimes. He
found himself therefore with a nature and an education out
of touch with his surroundings, and it is such natures as
that, in various environments, that he has chosen for the
special object of his study. Having no sympathy with the
materialistic trend of a democratic society, and wishing also
to hide an infirmity of which the dread was never absent
from his mind, he became more and more a recluse. With
the exception of two journeys to the East and to Carthage,
both undertaken for literary ends, he spent his life between
his suburban house at Rouen and occasional visits to Paris.
At times he would remain cloistered for months together,
and after his mother's death there was little of luxury or

even of comfort in surroundings where everything spoke of
the unremitting study in which he sought consolation for
the domestic life that his disease forced him to forego.
This had a controlling influence on his artistic point of
view. "All the occurrences of life appeared to me," he
says, "as material for description. Nothing, even my own
existence, has to me any other significance." That is to
say, literature was to him an end in itself. He was the
type of the artist for art's sake, and naturally so, because it
was in art that he sought diversion from the pain of self-
contemplation, from his epileptic's fear of life. If literature was to be his consolation it could be so only by being
rigidly, uncompromisingly objective. He defends this
view of the novelist's art with passionate iteration in the
whole series of his ten years' correspondence with George
Sand.

It was under these circumstances and with these aims,
personal and literary, that he wrote *Madame Bovary*,
which was first published in the *Revue de Paris*, during
the last quarter of 1856. Precisely how long he had had
it in hand is not clear, possibly since 1852, for though he
worked intently and incessantly, " eighteen hours out of the
twenty-four," it is said, his interest was in the labour, not in
its completion. " I have in my mind," he writes, " a certain method of writing, a certain fitness of style that I seek
to attain. . . . When the time comes and I think I have
plucked the apricot I may be willing to sell it and let
people applaud if they find it good. But if by that time it
is too late, if nobody cares for it any more, never mind."
" I seek something better than success, I seek to please
myself."

Once before the public *Madame Bovary* attracted

immediate and wide attention, stimulated at first no doubt by the astounding fatuity of the government, who saw fit to prosecute its author and publisher for immorality, and that in the heyday of the Second Empire. The prosecuting attorney's speech is such a monument to human imbecility as almost to make Flaubert's *Bouvard and Pecuchet* superfluous, and the acquittal was accompanied with " considerations " that one would have expected rather under the Long Parliament in England than in the France of Louis Napoleon. The ultimate result was to make the author famous in spite of himself, and to make of his first novel a starting-point of a new school in fiction, as *The Lady with the Camellias* four years before had been in the drama.

Madame Bovary is not only not romantic, it is the bitterest satire on romanticism. Its scene is the world of commonplace and the lesson of it is that in that world sentiment leads to shipwreck, and self-sufficient mediocrity to success. And in this, as Sainte-Beuve observed at the time, it marks the new epoch, the epoch of science, minute observation, maturity, and contempt or dread of sentimental sympathy. Holding his pen in the same spirit that his father had held the dissecting knife, he lays bare for us here first the weary banality of provincial life, and then the hopelessness of the romantic revolt against banality. There is of course another solution of the difficulty and a brighter side to the picture, but that it is not his present purpose to see. Throughout the book we shall not find a person to imitate or an act to admire.

The first of the personages to be introduced to us and one of the most interesting characters of the book is Charles Bovary, a doctor mediocre and almost contemptible even in his goodness, as true to nature and as common in real life as he is fatuous and banal. We see him first at school, the typical dull pupil, then struggling through his medical examinations and bundled by his parents into a marriage that was not expected to bring him sympathy, and did not actually bring him money. Then he is attracted to the daughter of a well-to-do farmer, Emma, the chief figure of the novel, whom after his first wife's death he awkwardly courts and presently marries, himself apparently the more innocent of the two ; for Emma's education had been that of religious sentiment spiced by Lamartine's poetry, English *Keepsakes* and romantic novels, a deliberate perversion of soul, the results of which it is the purpose of this novel to show.

Charles was happy in his marriage. " He went about ruminating his bliss like those who savour still after dinner the taste of the truffles they are digesting." Emma meantime was still " seeking to discover just what in life people meant by the words ' felicity,' ' passion,' ' intoxication,' that had seemed to her so beautiful in books." Clearly her husband was not one of those gentlemen " brave as lions, gentle as lambs, virtuous as men never are, always well dressed, and who wept like water jars," of whom she had read at fifteen in novels from the circulating library. His conversation was " flat as a street sidewalk." She grew weary of his monotonous caresses, and presently an event came into her life that acted as a transforming yeast in her moral nature. She was invited to an aristocratic ball.

From the moment that she had come in contact with this new social sphere there began to grow in her a ferment that did not cease till it had destroyed her, body and soul. In her desire she confounded the sensualities of luxury with the joys of the heart, elegance of manners with delicacy of sentiment. "She desired at the same instant to die, and to live in Paris." Her husband, watching her lassitude with stupid affection, thought a change of environment would help her, sacrificed his growing practice to her incipient infidelity, and was doubtless despised the more for his affection.

Their new home was still in Normandy, at Yonville near Rouen. Here the passive incubation of Emma's moral disease reaches a critical stage. She meets Léon, a law student who shares her romantic sympathies, but he is too timid and she not yet sufficiently corrupt that their relations should pass beyond the platonic, and he leaves Yonville to pursue legal studies and lose somewhat of his naïveté in Paris.

At this point we are introduced to M. Homais, a character as typical as any in the novel, and so finely drawn as to have become almost from the first a byword. He is the incarnation of commonplace, "one of our first citizens, pompous, a self-made man, and believing in his maker," but a shrewd intriguer, knowing how to use the press and to manufacture and guide public opinion, with his mouth always full of half-masticated science, the bright peony-flower of mediocracy, just the man to impose himself on the masses, and on those whom they naturally choose to govern them, and to be crowned with honour and decorated with the Cross at the story's close, — the true type of "triumphant democracy." Set off against Homais is the curate Bournisien, he too hopelessly commonplace and unable to comprehend, much less to guide, poor Emma's aspirations toward a higher social life, and to teach her to bear ennui, to create for herself worthy aims, or at least innocent distractions. A number of minor characters also make their appearance, — the sacristan Lestiboudois, the notary Guillaumin, the money-lending merchant Lheureux, — all admirably individualised, but none of them essential to our present purpose save only the burly country gentleman Rodolphe, to whose vulgarity, masked under a veneer of sentiment that is the ironical echo of her own, Emma falls victim after having tried to get sentimental consolation in religion, and finding it, when so approached, as stale and as commonplace as her domestic relations.

The courtship of Rodolphe is a scene of admirable irony. The mocking parody of romantic sentiment is relentlessly bitter as he whispers his temptation to her at a country fair, between the pauses of a politician's speech in which fatuous demagogy reaches its artistic climax and ultimate expression. The fatal step once taken, "the summits of sentiment seemed to be sparkling beneath her, thought and ordinary existence appeared only far away, below, in shadow between the intervals of these heights." But from this pinnacle she is drawn irresistibly down to the commonplace, and below it to the base, the sensuous, — yes, there are moments when we see, as by a flash, that she would not shrink from the criminal, from murder itself. In vain she beats her poor wings to rise to the heights of sentiment, and strains language to make it say what she can no longer feel. "Their great love seemed to diminish beneath her like the water of a river that had been absorbed into its bed, of which she saw now the muddy bottom." The eternal monotony of passion wearied her lover also, and when in utter desperation of thwarted romanticism she suggests flight together, he writes her a letter, over which he sprinkles water with his fingers to simulate tears, and elects to travel alone.

The shock was terrible.   Again she sought refuge in the
religious sentiment, "addressing to the Lord the same
tender words that once she had murmured to her lover,"
and comparing herself, in the pride of her devotion, to
La Vallière.   To distract her, Charles takes her to the
opera at Rouen, and we have a good pendant scene to
Fielding's Partridge at the theatre.   The sentiment of
Italian opera is poison to her, and when now she meets
Léon once more she is so charmed with the situation, and
with the necessity of defending herself, that she neglects
the defence.   Admirable is the account of the mental and
moral disintegration of Emma under this new relation.
She comes to feel a cowardly docility toward her husband,
and at the same time plunges into debt and reckless false-
hood; but, since "she was more charming for her husband
than ever, made him pistache-cream-cakes, and played
waltzes after dinner," he thought himself the happiest of
mortals.

We need not follow her in the last steps of this corruption,
"almost immaterial, it was so deep and so dissimulated."
Here as before it is a desperate and a vain struggle to satisfy false sentiment, culminating in the revelation that the
second idol of her romantic fancy was a sensual coward as
the first had been a sensual Don Juan.   Here, then, is her
final shipwreck.   Abandoned with a base subterfuge by
Léon, once more rejected "with that natural pusillanimity
that characterises the strong sex" by Rodolphe, without
once suspecting, so distorted had her moral sense become,
the depth of such abasement, the only refuge that remained
to her from the bitter dregs of sentiment deceived and
mocked was poison.   Her education had made it impossible for her to adapt herself to the actual world.   Her ideals

of religion were as unreal to her as her ideals of domestic or
of social life.   Flaubert would have us regard her as a
typical victim of romanticism, somewhat overcharged, as all
types are apt to be, and yet essentially true.   She is the
tragic reduction to the absurd of romantic love, and with
all her faults more sinned against than sinning.

Admirable in its unflinching realism is the description of
her last hours, to which the mortal banality of the funeral is
a most artistic foil.   To the last and even beyond the grave
she held the love of the poor simple Charles, whose vulgar
head, as Sainte-Beuve says, needs but a single touch of the
sculptor's thumb to become nobly pathetic.   Even when
he discovers her faults he blames himself rather than her or
her lovers, feeling perhaps, in his dim way, that she too was
of those who love not wisely but too well, a victim of her
environment.

Such is the story and such the social and ethical bearing
of *Madame Bovary*, but no summary can do justice to the
many passages of vivid narration or of exquisite description, whose studied euphony appears first when they are
read aloud, as Flaubert himself was wont to read repeatedly
every paragraph that he wrote.   Only when we subject them
to such tests do we realise how some of his pages stand,
as he himself said, " by the sheer power of their style,
balanced like the earth without support in the heavens,"
now with the serenity of a Grecian marble, now with the
finished detail of a Dutch master, now with the subtle
harmony of Lydian airs or with the sinuous grace of a
Tennysonian song ; quite lost on the majority of readers, but
an enduring delight to the few, as surely they were to their
author.   And then there are scattered up and down through
the book a multitude of happily turned phrases, usually

of irony, where we seem to see the author poising on his needle-point the acid drop and placing it with slow, delicate precision upon the quivering nerve.

The danger of romantic imagination — such had been the subject of *Madame Bovary*, and such continued to be the subject of *Salammbô* seven years later, but with a radical difference; for while in *Madame Bovary*, he had used the realistic method on his own Normandy, he undertook here to apply it to an age and land of which his ideas were inevitably the products of trained imagination, the Carthage of 240 to 237 B. C., during the revolt of the mercenaries that followed the first Punic War. He called this "epic realism." The result is an interesting literary feat, more interesting, perhaps, than Chateaubriand's *Martyrs*, with which it is natural to compare it, but the book is not so popular, and surely it is not so significant as *Madame Bovary*. It does not live as a whole. Its characters may be true or not for their country and time, but they are not true for us. We do not sympathise with them, because we do not understand them, and therefore their fate rouses a languid interest beside Emma's shipwreck and Homais' success. There seems to be, as an acute critic has said, a disproportion between the subject and the means used in treating it. To recount the story is quite unnecessary to our purpose, but it contains passages, and they are not a few, which in picturesque brilliancy surpass anything attempted in the former novel.

One of these is at the very opening, an orgiac feast granted by the timorous Carthaginians to their mercenaries returned from the long war with Rome. The confusion of peoples, customs, and languages, the varied profusion of meats and drinks, the gradations of drunken recklessness, the apparition of Salammbô in mystic splendour chanting her rhythmic liturgies, — all this is done with great skill ; and an African sunrise in this chapter is perhaps the finest half-page that Flaubert ever penned. But the story is ill-articulated. Its construction is defective not merely artistically, but logically. The style may be always restrained, but the subjects, crucified lions, immolations to Moloch, and the like, are intentionally bizarre. Flaubert may tell us nothing that is not suggested by his scanty authorities, but he does not treat them in a critical spirit. All that could be observed by the attentive traveller is handled as well, possibly better here than in *Madame Bovary*, but what could not be observed, the psychology, is at least fanciful and illusory. It attains the exotic only by ceasing to be broadly human. Salammbô, as the author shows her here and as she appears throughout, is too " different," in Stendhal's sense, from any type of mind that we know, to be interesting or even intelligible to us. Though passing her life in virgin adoration of the feminine principle of fecundity, Tanit, to which Moloch is the corresponding male principle, it is as a Venus Urania that she worships her, and her days are passed in an unaroused innocence of mystic revery. She is, in fact, as Sainte-Beuve says, a sort of sentimental Elvire, as unreal as that figment of Lamartine's romantic dreams, and suggesting also the Velléda of Chateaubriand's *Martyrs*, as romantic, though of course from her environment more artificial than she. It may be that the modes of thought and feeling in ancient Carthage were radically different from ours. If they were, then that time and country are not good subjects for historical fiction, for you can restore antiquity, but you cannot resuscitate it.

Taken as a whole, then, *Salammbô* must be regarded as a

failure, but it was a failure such as only a great, indefatigable, and high-souled artist could have made.   Here
more than in any other of his novels we feel the struggle
between the old romanticism and the new scientific spirit.
The book arouses wonder rather than sympathy.   It will be
admired, it will not be enjoyed.   In a natural reaction
against the milk-and-water antiquity of Fénelon and the
Young Anarcharsis it describes cruelly a cruel civilisation,
but we feel, rather than know, — for who knows? — that the
impression is at least incomplete.   Then, after this supping
full of the horrors of Moloch, the author invites us to break-
fast with the jackals and "the eaters of unclean things."
There is a too constant evocation of the ghastly and weird,
and the superb descriptions, magnified and irradiated by
the sun of Africa, do not suffice to relieve the monotony.

Seven years after the world had been perplexed by
Salammbô it was perplexed once more by *Sentimental
Education* (l'Éducation sentimentale, 1869), which fell
on evil days for literature, for it appeared just as all France
was intent on the life and death struggle of the Second
Empire.   Thus it failed to attract the critical attention that
might otherwise have fallen to it, and since the novel needed
criticism to be understood, it quite failed to be enjoyed.
Indeed even to-day fewer critics discuss the question whether
it is good than why it is bad.   As the title may suggest, the
novel is a pendant to *Madame Bovary*.   That was to show
the effect of sentimental education on a provincial woman ;
this should show it in a Parisian, Frédéric Moreau, with the
revolution of 1848 and its preludes for a background.   The
story is of the slightest, slighter even than that of *Salammbô*.
The book is the picture of a generation and of its political
and moral bankruptcy culminating in the Second Empire.

If it be urged that the novel lacks unity, Flaubert would reply that life lacks it, and that this is an advance in realistic art; and as such the school of the Goncourts regarded it, with considerable temporary effect on the development of fiction. Thus to Zola it seems "the only truly historical novel that I know, the sole true, exact, complete one, in which the resurrection of dead hours is absolute, with no trace of the novelist's trade."

Such an attempt may show praiseworthy daring, and to it Flaubert gave the most minute and intense study, but it was inevitable that the result of this painful gestation should lack interest, because it lacked unity. We do not seek in a novel the reproduction of life, but the impression of life. And then the tendency that we noted in *Madame Bovary* to present only characters of a contemptible mediocrity, whether of vice or virtue, is pushed here beyond reasonable limits. It might be as true as the multiplication table, but it would not be interesting. But is it true? Is not Flaubert the dupe of his own limitations? He liked to boast that he was implacable to humanity, but he forgot that he had himself said that disillusion is of the nature of weak minds. "Distrust the disgusted. They are almost always the impotent." One cannot but feel that *Sentimental Education* marks a growing sterility in Flaubert's genius. "Withered Fruits" was the book's original title, and the novel itself may seem to be one of them, though the book is one of considerable interest and power, and contains some very brilliant episodes.

Flaubert is not merely "implacable" to humanity, he is unjust. In *Madame Bovary* there was a corner left for true sentiment and honest pathos. Here there is nothing of this. Nobody is magnanimous, frank, or noble; all is petty,

vulgar, contemptible. Flaubert's irony itself has no generous fire, and the strongest sentiment that we feel in finish-
ing the novel is pity for the man who has such an outlook
on the world. We may call it "a magnificent marble
temple erected to impotence," and speak of "epic platitude," but, as Brunetière finely asks in connection with this
novel, "Of what use is it to love art if one does not love
mankind?"

Throughout this long panorama of social disillusion and
political incompetence the style is curbed, held rigidly
down to the mediocrity of the subject. One cannot help
feeling that it must have cost almost as much effort to the
author as it does to the reader, though there are occasional
flashes of irony that reveal the depths of human nature.
Nor should the episodic scenes in the novel be forgotten,
the boat trip on the Seine at the opening, the ball in the
demi-monde contrasted with the cold banality of the
banker's reception, and a death-bed ghastly in its egoism.
Still better is the charming idyl of love at Fontainebleau,
with the sad tale of the youth of Rosanette, who had found
it a misfortune to have a mother. Excellent, too, are the
historical scenes, the joyous sacking of the Tuileries and
the brutal desperation of the mobs of June, with their yet
more brutal suppression. While, then, no one would claim
that *Sentimental Education* is a good novel, it may be
read with profit and even with pleasure as the imaginative
projection of a close study of the national mind of France
in a critical period of its evolution.

Again there was a pause of years in Flaubert's productivity, and in 1874 he published *The Temptation of Saint
Antony* (la Tentation de Saint Antoine), the shortest of his
novels, if indeed that name can be stretched to cover this

unique production, on which we are told he had laboured for twenty years. It was a strange and paradoxical thing, this effort to convince the thoughtful of the futility of thought. In the nature of things the book could be interesting and even intelligible only to those of wide and recondite learning, for under the veil of the old legend of the temptation of Saint Antony in the Thebaid, a frequent subject of medieval art, he has undertaken to exhibit to us, no longer the folly of provincial mediocrity as in *Madame Bovary*, or of the desires and ambitions of Parisian youth as in *Sentimental Education*, or of a sordid commercial state and an ancient faith as in *Salammbô*, but it is the folly and futility of thought itself and of the whole sentient world of which he has tried to put the quintessence in these three hundred pages of the most polished prose of our half-century. Externally the book has much the appearance of a drama, the speakers being indicated, and all description, whether of scene or action, relegated to smaller type, but yet in a style as studied and rhythmic as that of the speeches themselves.

The book is nihilistic to the core, but its pessimism is romantic. Flaubert's heart is the victim of his mind. He suffers, like Antony and Salammbô and Frédéric and Emma, from the pale cast of a thought that is ever bruising itself against reality. They all are projections of the world-pain of his generation, that undercurrent of materialistic sentiment that tells us in advance that all our ideals are dissolving views. So Flaubert says life seemed to him, even when a boy, "like the smell of a nauseating kitchen escaping through a ventilating hole. One had no need to taste to know that it was sickening," no need to study to learn that knowledge would but increase unsatisfied desire. Of this feeling the *Temptation* is the supreme expression in

17

fiction. The ethics in such a case are a matter of temperament, or perhaps with Flaubert, of pathology. The art must be a subject of universal admiration. The book cannot appeal, however, to any but literary artists, and it has hindered rather than aided the appreciation of his genius, though Mr. Saintsbury has pronounced it the best example of dream literature in the world.

The Temptation of Saint Antony was followed three years later (1877) by three tales which represent in miniature the two sides of Flaubert's literary nature : the disgust at the sordidness of modern life, and the revels of imagination in the reconstitution of a grandiose past. The first of the tales, *A Simple Heart* (un Cœur simple), has for its central figure a servant, taken as a young girl into the family of an average woman, leading an average life, suffering its usual deceptions, and dying unemancipated from its usual illusions. The story is told with a simplicity and restraint that is the height of art and pathos, so that it may be both read with pleasure and studied with advantage.

Equal praise in another kind may be given to *Julian the Hospitaller* (Julian l'hospitalier), the medieval patron saint of hosts and hospitality. Flaubert finds the legend of this saint "in a series of glass paintings in a church in my country" and undertakes to tell with medieval naïveté this story of the feudal noble, hunter, parricide, and penitent. The whole has something of the dim religious light of these ancient stained windows, something of their quaintness, of their sudden transitions, and of their atmosphere of miracle. It is as though the author would repay himself by this feat of the imagination for the restraint of the former story, and found in the feat such delight that, *St. Julian* finished, he turned to *Herodias* and the death of John Baptist.

Here there is more historic realism. The local colour is studied in detail, though not without an element of the grandiosely romantic, but the wild discord of jarring factions, the intensity of religious feeling in the seething brains of these Galileans, the haughty indifference of the materialised Romans, the morbid satiety of Antipas, the satanic passions of Herodias, the heartless, soulless grace of Salome, the fierce conviction of the prophet voicing itself in unbridled denunciation, all this is as wine to Flaubert's genius, and it seems at moments as though the sun of Palestine had touched his brain also, so that the effect of the whole may be described as dazzling; yet whether the climax is in the scene of the dungeon or in that of the dance, it might be hard to determine, so masterly are they, though so different. It is here and in *Madame Bovary* that Flaubert shows the least effort and attains the greatest success. But by a strange and sad perversity of a great mind already verging on mania he returned with saturnine humour to the harder and longer task, and in *Bouvard and Pécuchet* erected a monument to human stupidity, " the book of his revenge " he called it, with all the faults of the *Sentimental Education*, and with none of the redeeming elements that might overcome the unpleasant nervous impression and persuade us to listen to his doleful lesson.

Flaubert marks in fiction what Taine marks in criticism, the passage from idealism to realism, from the romantic to the naturalistic. He belongs to neither school and unites both, neither forgetting his youthful admiration for Hugo and Chateaubriand nor sanctioning Maupassant and Zola, who called him master. It was because he was romantic that he was a pessimist, and that not from reason but from sentiment. His manner, his dress, countless peculiarities recounted by friends or betrayed by letters, show how much of the romantic survived in him to the last to intensify his disillusion in a materialistic generation from which he drew his analytic temperament. With nature thus at strife within him he took refuge naturally in art, which he paradoxically regarded, not as a means, but as having its reason in itself, with "truths as useful and perhaps more precious for the public than those contained in the subject itself." From this he derived that studious objectivity that makes him see his environments in wonderful detail, but takes something from the life of his characters, whom Bourget does not scruple to dismiss as "walking associations of ideas." And just as he tries to make the myriad little facts of environment support character, so he systematically substitutes sensations for feelings, the material image for the thought, and in thus making environment a link in the chain of association to evoke the past he contributed materially to the art of novelistic development, though his own method first saw its full application in the novels of Daudet.

The importance of Flaubert to the development of fiction for good or ill lies, not in his philosophy, but in his conception of the novel itself as the "synthesis of romanticism and science." To take a plain, straightforward tale of common life such as that of the servant in *A Simple Heart* or of Frédéric or of Emma Bovary or of Bovard and Pécuchet, to put it in an environment that should be minutely accurate, and to treat this "slice of crude life" in the most finished, polished style, a style that might win him the title of "the Beethoven of French prose," that is what Flaubert undertook to do, and it is what the whole naturalistic school have tried to do after him — first, the authors of *Germinie Lacerteux*, with art more meticulous than manful, then Zola, in the grandiose romantic pessimism of *Germinal,* then Daudet with subtle delicacy, and Maupassant, the genial cynic, and Huysmans, and indeed all who follow or have ever followed the banner of naturalism. That he directed the development of the novel for a generation, and that he contributed essentially to maintain its place as a work of art, and keep it from the hands of the philistines of literature, are his titles to lasting remembrance.

CHAPTER XII

AFTER the battle of Waterloo and the collapse of the hopes of revolutionary dominion, republican and imperial, of the two preceding decades, there followed a notable pause in the gestation of literary genius. For five years the only person of literary imagination to be born was the insignificant Paul Féval. But when the romantic movement begins to stir the adult population of educated France, genius comes "not single file but in battalions." Fromentin opens the way in 1820. Champfleury, Feydeau, and Flaubert follow in 1821; the next year Feuillet, Erckmann, Murger, Edmond de Goncourt, Ulbach saw the light, to be followed by Banville in 1823, Dumas the Younger and Énault in 1824, Chatrain in 1826, About in 1828, and as a sort of aftermath Ponson du Terrail and Cherbuliez in 1829, with Jules de Goncourt, Malot, and Fabre to mark the year of *Hernani* and the victory of romanticism. This decade, then, furnishes nineteen more or less distinguished names, while the preceding one counted but six and the succeeding years to the birth of Zola but nine, and all of these distinctly of the second rank, to be succeeded in 1840 by another outburst of genius that gives its character to the generation of Louis Philippe.

Of the novelists born during the Restoration, the most significant in the evolution of fiction is surely Flaubert, whose work and place have just been considered. After him the most important, though far from the most popular, writers are the brothers Edmond and Jules de Goncourt, who show the same delight in minute observation as Flaubert, while they force the elaboration of his style into an artificiality that presages the painful strivings of the symbolists to translate feelings and emotions into words. The Goncourt Brothers have been called the Chopins of literature, as brilliant, as sensitive, and as incorrectly elegant. They had, as all their studies show, an excessively acute perception of the psychic impression conveyed by inanimate objects. They were, as some one has said, "magicians of letters," who gave colour to sound and melody to colour in a "plastic psychology" that made all their contemporaries in fiction in some degree their debtors. They attained this by a thoroughly individual and intensely modern style, often bizarre, sometimes faulty, but always supple and clear and quick. They were artists of such exquisite sensitiveness that their work seems often brought forth in pain and cherished with redoubled love because of long public neglect. Indeed the tardy recognition accorded to their fiction found Jules already dead, and Edmond an invalid broken in health and hope.

Their work was by no means confined to novels. By their discovery for France of the art of Japan and by careful studies of their favourite eighteenth century, whose social life they treated in many volumes, they won the regard of connoisseurs and of a wider public. They essayed the drama also. Indeed their first novel of note, *Charles Demailly*, was elaborated from an unsuccessful play. But their writing began with fiction, and it is by their fiction that they exercised the deepest influence on the literature of the naturalistic generation.

Both the Goncourts were born in Paris. The younger
died just before the outbreak of the Prussian war. The
elder lived till 1895. They were of distinguished family,
and educated in the best Parisian schools. Deep affection
united them from childhood. Their instinctive movements,
sympathies, antipathies were always in accord, their ideas
seemed born in common.

Their mother died in 1848, and the brothers, having a
small competence, resolved to devote their lives wholly to
art and letters. They travelled leisurely in France and
Algeria, in Belgium and Switzerland, and on their return to
Paris in 1850 began to write unactable vaudevilles and a
novel, *In 18–* (En 18–, 1851) which had the ill fate to be
ready for issue on the very day of the *coup d'état.* But
sixty copies of this book were ever sold, and the story,
though since reprinted in Belgium (1884), is interesting
chiefly as an extreme example of the affectations of dying
romanticism. It is unintelligible and uninteresting in matter, and in manner disjointed, rococo, and strange. Edmond himself, writing in 1884, says : " It is an exasperating
search for wit, a dialogue whose spoken language is made
out of bookish phrases," in a style compounded of Gautier
and Janin. Yet the watchful critic may find in it passages
of admirable description, showing the line of future development, so that it is " an interesting embryo of the
later romances," as Edmond remarks, and a curious anticipation of the later modes of thought of the authors, of
their Japanese taste, their determinism and pessimism. It
was a strange presentiment, too, that the heroine of this
tale should be a Prussian spy.

Nine years later, in 1860, the Goncourts returned to fiction and sought in *Charles Demailly* to do for the journal-

ism of 1860 what Balzac had done for that of 1839 in *Lost Illusions*. The book errs from exaggeration and repetition, and still more from indiscretion, a fault of which Edmond was guilty to the last. It cost the authors five hundred francs, and it cost them also many friendships, for most of the literary men of the day figure in it, and if Gautier, Flaubert, and Saint-Victor are treated with kindness, Banville, Champfleury, Houssaye, and Villemessant are handled with scant respect. The morbid, nervous, eloquent, and extreme Demailly is more interesting than any of these, for he is a composite of the authors themselves, a victim of his sensitive nature and of an ill-assorted marriage. The book was, however, quite inferior to their next novel, *Sister Philomene* (Sœur Philomène), by which they first began to influence the thoughtful writers of the new school.

Sister Philomene (1861) is a realistic story of a sister of charity and of hospital life, founded on the experience of a medical friend at Rouen, who had seen a nun reveal in a flash her love for a dead patient, and never again betray any trace of the sorrow that was eating her heart. The youth and gradually maturing vocation of this sister is handled with great psychologic insight. It is delicate and subtle, with greater reserve than the later naturalists are wont to show, and with a little inclination to mysticism. The story is also far better constructed than *Demailly*, but what attracted and held attention was the minute description of hospital and amphitheatre, with their tortured, quivering life, which, however, marked a dangerous step toward that topsy-turvy idealism that was to make the fancy delve where the romanticists had let it soar. The novel becomes painful at times to almost every reader, though it is significant of the tendencies of that day that Flaubert should say that to his taste there

were not in it horrors enough.   This novel was dramatised
with some success in 1887.

Renée Mauperin, of 1864, had for its original title "The
Young Bourgeoisie," and so marked a return to a conventional respectability. Here they say they undertake " to paint
the modern girl as the artistic and boyish education of the
last thirty years have made her," and to show the effect on
young men of the success of the parliamentary régime. We
can trace the beginnings of this social study in the *Journal*
(i. 146) of the brothers as early as 1856. The heroine
and many of the circumstances and minor characters of the
tragic story were real, and in Denoisel we have another
composite of the authors as they conceived themselves.
Renée, after unwittingly causing the death of her brother,
that "perfect model of official banality," is frightened at
herself, lets fall " the ironical mask that covered her virgin
face," and becomes before her death a timid girl again.
This close is of great artistic power, but, as Saint-Victor
said at the time, " the art of the story is effaced beneath the
emotions that it excites, and we are touched before we
admire."   Critics think this the best of the Goncourts'
novels, and Daudet certainly learned from it much of his
art, but it has never won popularity and an attempt to
dramatise it in 1886 was an utter failure.

The Goncourts were now about to produce the most
epoch-making of all their novels, *Germinie Lacerteux*, which
was, as they justly said, " the model of all that has since been
constructed under the name of realism or naturalism," and
so made 1865 a cardinal date in the evolution of French
fiction.   In their Preface they formulated their purpose
and that may speak for them. " We asked ourselves," they
say, " if what are called the lower classes have no right to

novelistic treatment; if this world beneath a world, the people, is to remain under a literary interdict, . . . if there are any classes too unworthy, misfortunes too lowly, dramas too ill-sounding, catastrophes too ignoble in their terror; we were curious to know if, in a country without caste or legal aristocracy, the miseries of the humble and poor would appeal to interest, emotion, and pity as much as the miseries of the great and rich." Now all this was to claim for the novel a new function and a wider scope as a realistic study of contemporary moral psychology and social investigation. The Goncourts were first to make the novel a pulpit for the religion of humanity, an idea eagerly embraced by Zola and his school, so that *Germinie* is historically hardly less significant than *Madame Bovary*. Here first the morbid pathology of one vulgar in her virtues as in her vices is made the subject of minute scientific study, not by way of romantic contrast, as it might have been in Hugo, but as the centre and mainspring of all, as it was to be in *l'Assommoir* and in *Germinal.*

From the Goncourts' *Journal* for July and August, 1862, we learn that persons and events in the novel were almost all within the authors' own immediate experience. Germinie was their own servant; Mlle. de Varandeuil, that curious survival of pre-revolutionary aristocracy, was their relative; Jupillon, the base minister to Germinie's disease, and his mother who ministered to his vice, lived across the street. But though all might be true, all was certainly sordid, and the critics of good society either protested with upturned eyes or shielded themselves in silence. None but Claretie and Zola then recognised the book's significance. For *Germinie Lacerteux* is the real origin of *l'Assommoir*, of *Nana* and of all her swarming progeny. It proclaimed the

divorce between fiction and respectability.   It made the
novel the most effective means of claiming justice for those
outcasts of society who "could find on earth no more place
for their bodies than for their hearts."

Manette Salomon, which followed *Germinie Lacerteux* in
1867, marks the beginning of a further development in
their literary method.   Sure that art could not mend
nature, they sought to approach more nearly to the apparent lack of continuity that the observation of real life presented to them.   Nature for them should be not only
unadorned but unarranged.   They would discard all conventions of structure.   Their book should neither have nor
seek artistic unity.   Its heroine should not appear till the
one hundred seventy-ninth page of what is less a story than
a series of scenes, masterly in their verbal precision, admirable in their picturesque detail of Parisian artist life,
making, as a contemporary critic said, "the work of the
human brain as visible, as palpable, and as real as life."
Coriolis, the painter, is shown us on each step of the
descent into the inferno of union with the reckless and
heartless Manette, "to whom sex was only form," and
who sapped his soul till he sank to imbecility, as Demailly
had been harassed to mania.   For to these hyper-sensitive
brothers woman seemed less an aid than a fetter to genius.
They thought of her as the men of their favourite eighteenth
century thought, not at all with the mind of the generation
nursed on the milk of Rousseau.

Manette Salomon attracted but little attention, for the times
were out of joint and men's minds more set on politics
than on literature.   And this was still more the case with
Madame Gervaisais, the last novel of their fraternal co-
operation, containing some of the greatest feats in all im-

pressionist prose, but adhering so relentlessly to their theory as to "sterilise their human documents," to borrow a phrase from Zola. Daudet, to whom this story served as model for *The Evangelist*, pronounced *Madame Gervaisais* "the most complete, the most incontestably beautiful, but also the most disdainful and haughtily personal of their books." It is, once more, a series of pictures of stages in the corrosion, by morbid mysticism, of a mind burdened with culture, till at last it succumbs wholly to the spell of Roman Catholicism, hypnotised by its pomps, its incense and its chants. Of course, therefore, it called down the interdict of the Church, while the chaste censors of the Empire pronounced it "a dangerous, immoral, and anti-religious book." It is in fact a psychologic study, coldly dispassionate, of the religious spirit, to be enjoyed only by the judicious few.

The coldness of the public to their art might have been anticipated, for it had been invited ; but the brothers felt it keenly, and it seems to have hastened Jules's death, while for a time Edmond was lamed in mind by his disappointment and his loss. It was not till 1877 that he published his next novel, *Eliza* (la Fille Élisa), of which the subject was calculated neither to disarm opposition nor to widen the circle of his readers ; for here he descends beneath the social stratum of Germinie to the brothel and the prison, championing the naturalistic theory of fiction to the utterance and raising a decided storm, which raged long enough to give the author his first commercial success. The double purpose of the book is to study the psychology of prostitution, and to raise an indignant protest against the iniquity of solitary confinement recently introduced in French prisons.

In *The Brothers Zemganno* (les Frères Zemganno, 1879) he continued still on the outskirts of society, giving what many regard as the choicest work of his fancy to a study of fraternal love in two circus acrobats. In a preface he says he chooses such subjects as these because the life of the cultured is more complex. There is in the book, as might be expected, a good deal of psychic autobiography, but it is most remarkable for its vivid descriptions of a tinsel existence and the undulating or darting movements of the life of the hippodrome.

In *La Faustin* Goncourt passes in 1882 from the circus to the stage, and " grazes the boundary of truth in his search for strongly poetic situations " in an endeavour to show, as Bourget puts it, " how an actress's nervous system assimilates its environment." The novel is of peculiar critical interest because it seems to anticipate by several years the next stage in the evolution of fiction, the de-naturalization of the novel by the introduction of the mysterious, the weird, and even the satanic, as we see it now especially in Huysmans. In like manner it might be claimed that *The Brothers Zemganno* had in it the germs of the symbolist movement, and *Madame Gervaisais* of the psychism of Bourget. This is the meaning of Edmond de Goncourt's claim that he was not only the first to state " the complete formula of naturalism " in *Germinie Lacerteux*, but also the first to modify it in anticipation of the later schools of fiction. (*Journal*, viii. 242.)

These studies of low life and of bohemianism had prepared him for *Darling* (Chérie), which he describes as " a psychologic and physiologic study of young girlhood growing up in the hot-house of the capital," " a monograph of the young lady in official circles under the Second Empire."

For this book he sought the co-operation of his feminine readers, begging them to send him anonymously their recollections of youth and first communion, of coming out, of the " perversions of music " and the unveiling of " the delicate emotions and refined modesties " of the first sensations of love. Thus he thought to produce a book that should be almost unique in its refined realism, "an approximation to pure analysis," that " last evolution of fiction," whose realisation he left to his successors.

From his feminine collaborators he seems to have got very little, as was natural, since the French miss hardly understands herself. The *Journal* of Maria Bashkirtseff was a greater stimulus to his divination of the awakening of girlish imagination by the sight of social life, by music and sentimental reading, under the stimulus of Roman Catholicism in catechism and communion, then by dress, and the development of sex, under conditions so artificial as to tend to nervous prostration, that with Chérie terminates in anemia and death. The work is done with acute delicacy, and in a style whose nervous originality is the quintessence of Goncourt's last method.

In *Darling*, as in the two preceding novels, a generalisation is followed by minute psychic descriptions of acts without logical continuity, but all leading to the catastrophe. In *Eliza*, on the other hand, the generalisation follows the acts, and for minor characters Goncourt is content to tell what people do, and leaves readers to determine what they are, in which he follows Taine and points the way to the " scientific sociologic " novel of Zola. His characters are thus less individual than composite, and as he is always intent on rendering action, his style is sensationalist; it seeks to render first impressions in supple, delicate, subtly

suggestive abstractions, bearing us on through novel effects
of syntax, and nervous repetitions, to an acuteness of sense
that responds to the quivering and dazzling of the ultimate
epithet.   It is a style that errs most often by the intoxication of its own virtuosity.

Of course this is morbid, but it has a very delicate poetic
charm.   All the Goncourts' characters are neuropathic, but
they are drawn with great vividness, and endowed with
almost an excess of wit, though the Goncourts can touch,
when they will, chords of the deepest pathos and the most
poignant despair.   They endeavour to be the realistic " historians of the present."   " Write what you see " was their
guiding principle.   To them fiction was " the serious, passionate living form of literary study and social investigation, . . . the history of contemporary morals."   It lay in
their nature that their realism should be external rather
than psychologic, that they should merge individuality in
fatalism, and so be first, here as in so much else, to
mark the weakness of will that characterises modern
French literature ; for their pessimism was less rational
than emotional, more an artistic convention than a living
conviction.

In their style, however, they were idealists, seeking
the prose poem, the cadenced period, the picturesque
image, the rare epithet, even the new word and the solecism, if only they could compel the language to say what
it would not.   They were the dilettantes of emotion, the
artists of realism, or, as they said themselves, " the St. John
Baptists of neurosity," eager to " pin the adjective " to each
significant little fact, having in them, as a French critic has
observed, something of Mlle. de Lespinasse and Diderot,
something too of Poe, of De Quincey, and of Heine.   In-

tensely sensitive, intensely modern, their novels are to fiction what impressionism is to painting, and symbolism to poetry. But all who subordinate substance to form, statement to suggestion, health to morbidity, exception to rule, are in so far romanticists, and so, in a sense, the Goncourts were false to a cause of w. ich they imagined themselves the martyrs, and the study of their disciples will show that this perversion of naturalism may become little else than romanticism in disguise.

Among the writers of their own generation the Goncourts stand apart with Flaubert. Slight though essential contributions to the development of the naturalistic movement were made by Champfleury, by Fromentin, and by Erckmann-Chatrain. Champfleury, the pseudonym of Jules Fleury-Husson, is a novelist whom it is easy to place in the second rank, but difficult to classify there. Most of his work is romantic, some of it bohemian, but his best novel *The Town's-people of Molinchart* (les Bourgeois de Molinchart, 1854), and his essentially realistic *Chien-Caillou* (1847), make a connecting link between Balzac's *Scenes of Provincial Life* and Flaubert's *Madame Bovary*, and so earn him a place among the precursors of the naturalistic school, whom, however, he did not follow in its later development, being a quiet observer of the foibles of mankind rather than a satirist of its vices.

Fromentin wrote but a single novel, *Domenique* (1863), which belongs to no class but that of masterpieces. The author was himself an artist, and analyses with profound feeling and keen perception the state of mind of the artist whose creative powers lag behind his ideals. That self-doubt, disappointment, renunciation, do not involve loss of faith in the ideal is the tonic moral of *Domenique*, but the sternness of its fundamental conception is irradiated by the fresh glow of exquisite description, and by a striking psychic realism.   Fromentin is the last important link in the chain that connects Saint-Pierre with Loti.

More popular but less significant than either of these were Erckmann and Chatrain, who began by being, what at bottom they remained, romantic story-tellers after the manner of Hoffmann, or of Auerbach, but they attained to external realism in their so-called " national novels," dealing with the Revolution and the two Napoleons in the spirit of smug bourgeois egoism that was sure to rouse a wide response in the last decade of the Empire, when men were more willing than since to listen to what Sainte-Beuve called " an Iliad of Fear."   Of their very numerous novels, the best, which will quite dispense one from reading the others, are *Madame Thérèse* (1863), dealing with the national uprising of 1792, and *The Conscript of 1813* (le Conscrit de 1813, 1864).

Some connection with realism may be claimed also for Feuillet, who is, however, like the novelists whom it remains to mention in this chapter, essentially a survival of romanticism, "the family-Musset," as Jules de Goncourt called him, with some affiliations to George Sand, and still more to Madelcine de Scudéry.   Like Flaubert and Maupassant he was a Norman, of talented but nervously organised parentage.   Until 1857 domestic troubles compelled him to live, with brief holidays, in his country home.   It was here that he wrote, besides trifles that it is quite unnecessary to name, *The Little Countess* (la Petite comtesse, 1856) and *The Story of a Poor Young Man* (le Roman d'un jeune homme pauvre, 1858).   Then his father's death released him from this country captivity, and in Paris he developed a second and far stronger manner, that found its best expression in *Monsieur de Camors* (1867), *Julia de Trécœur* (1872), *The Diary of a Lady* (le Journal d'une femme, 1878), and *The Dead Wife* (la Morte, 1886), to be silent of his dramas which do not concern us here.

The most pervading characteristic of all this work is an aristocratic optimism. What heroes and what heroines! All handsome, all witty, all rich, even the " Poor Young Man," all fine riders and endowed with the proper accomplishments of idle wealth, capable of enthusiasms and faith, that contact with practical life has not blunted, and of loves that in the women become the chief excuse for life and occasionally for death, — in short, exactly the fiction to attract the pinchbeck aristocracy of the Empire and of the women who aspired to enter it, especially since Feuillet had the art to season his moralities with suave suggestions of vice, making thus a strange compound, as one of his critics says, of vitriol and opoponax, yet suiting deftly the people of whom he wrote to those by whom he was read. But the evolution of society left him behind, and he could rightly say, as he was nearing his end in 1890 : " I should write no more even were I to live. I should not be understood. Realism cares no longer for my ideal."

But though this was for the moment true, it is not likely to remain so. Bacon assures us that " the mixture of a lie doth always add pleasure," and when the pendulum swings again toward the romantic, Feuillet's novels, or at least four or five of them, will probably survive as the best representatives of that class in our half-century, though it is doubtful if that generation will be such dupes as to select them, with Lemaître, " to cradle young souls and enchant innocent minds," or to think with Brunetière that none since

Prévost, " has made the novel serve more noble ends."
The morality of Feuillet, like that of his characters and
readers, was the thinnest kind of varnish, a sentimental
compound of propriety and impropriety.

As one looks back over his twelve significant novels, one
finds the men shadowy puppets, with the single exception
of Monsieur de Camors, the melodramatic exploiter of
mankind, who is an interesting though painful mixture of a
coxcomb and a prig, till he is made a subject on whom to
demonstrate the superiority of Catholicity to Honour.   It is
impossible to take interest in the others, hard even to
recall their names without a wearied contempt and a wonder how the society they characterised could hold together.
But the women, the martyrs to love and passion, crowd
before the eyes of fancy.   There is the dainty " Little
Countess," who loves, like Chateaubriand's Amélie, a melancholy René, throws herself at this austere Joseph in vain,
and then at another for pique, to die of unrequited passion
at last; there is Marguerite, beloved of the truly " Poor
Young Man," a prudish coquette, compound of Breton and
Creole, and victim of such hypersensitive aristocratic propriety that when she marries the " poor young man " at the
close we feel more pity for him than ever.   Then there is
Sibylle, the child who wanted to ride a swan, and the
young lady who, rather than marry an infidel whom she
loved, preferred to die for his conversion, and so set an
example to her schoolmate, the vulgar vixen Clotilde.
There is the vicious and fascinating Madame de Camp-
vallon, the evil genius of Camors, and the feverishly hysteri-
cal, heroically infamous suicide, Julia de Tréccœur, perhaps
his most pathetic and artistic creation.   There is Madame
de Rias, of *A Marriage in Society* (un Mariage dans le

monde), somewhat exceptionally weak, morbid, and ill-bred, to be sure, but appealing to us as a victim of French education and society rather than as an evil nature, as does Cécile in *The Diary of a Lady*, a rather ineffectual story of a group of rich, frivolous, and lazy liars. A like victim of French marriage customs is the Baroness de Maurescamp, in *The Story of a Parisian Lady*, who, when her husband has killed her lover in a duel, tries to arrange for his death in a similar manner and is respected by him ever after. Then there is the satanic temptress, Marianne, whose just married husband seeks honour in suicide and leaves her " The Widow " (la Veuve) ; and there is the blue-stocking poisoner, Sabine, to point an orthodox moral in a novel (la Morte), that Jules de Goncourt said " was fit to corrupt a monkey ; " and lastly there is Beatrice, who, having wearied of adultery, finally begins to love her husband, when he, in surprised delight, kills himself for fear she would not keep on, and so illustrates " An Artist's Honour " (Honneur d'artiste).

These women are all interesting, though, as a rule, they lack principle and true culture. Most of them are tempters, who make the first advances, sybarites with idle hands and empty hearts ; in short, the typical wife of Feuillet is a type that one hopes is not the wife of anybody else. There is a monotony in these tragic battles of passion in women whom Pellessier has described as ill-balanced, eccentric, bizarre, incoherent, wholly abandoned to instinct, capable of heroism and of crime, restless, agitated, astray, strangely disturbing, and already a prey to that famous neurosity of which Feuillet painted the effects in high society with the perfect propriety of his aristocratic pen, as Zola painted them in the lower classes with the massive power of his brutal genius.   Feuillet's own idea of woman may be seen in these lines on the Parisian Lady : " In this strange hot-house of Paris the child is already a girl, the girl a woman, the woman, a monster.   She behaves, sometimes well, sometimes ill, with no great taste for one or the other, for she dreams of something better than Good and worse than Evil.   This innocence is parted often from debauch by caprice alone, and from crime only by occasion."   " Wo-men are as much at ease in perfidy as a snake in shrubbery, and they wind in it with a supple tranquillity that man-hood never attains."   No doubt this seemed flattery to the ladies of the Empire, but it jars strangely with the conven-tional accompaniment of pseudo-Christian spiritualism, that in such connections seems either ludicrously naïve or hypo-critically repulsive.   There is something snobbish in this perfumed orthodoxy.   But after all reserves have been made, Feuillet remains, not surely a great moralist or a great creator of character, but a very skilful story-teller, with a supple, light, lively style, excellent, especially in dialogue, with sufficient humour and art of sustaining inter-est, who, as the accredited painter of the aristocratic life of neuropathic women unintelligible to themselves or to others, contributed an essential element to the development of realism in fiction.   His successors in this field are Rabus-son and Ohnet, of whom the former serves up aristocracy to itself, while the latter feasts the gaping admiration of the socially ambitious multitude.

Another novelist who stands somewhat aloof from the prevailing current of the fiction of his generation is Cherbu-liez, a born story-teller, whose Genevan origin and wide foreign travel set him somewhat apart from the French ten-dencies of his time.   His novels are usually of cosmopolitan

tourist life, such as Geneva might show. His best characters are foreign, Russians, Poles, English, Germans, or Jews,
as the names of his best novels, *Count Kostia, Ladislas
Bolski, Miss Rovel, Meta Holdenis*, or *Samuel Brohl and
Co.* sufficiently indicate. They are the *condottieri* of modern life, independent and somewhat exaggerated, and the
plots, like the characters, abound in incoherencies and im-
probabilities. As some one has said, they are "novels of
agitation and delirium told by a man of sober sense."
The descriptions are good and varied, but Cherbuliez sees
the world from outside; there is little of poetry or mysticism, the psychology is weak and conventional, and, though
the story is always interesting, the denouements are sometimes infantile, and seem to belong to an earlier age than
our nervous and tense generation. Cherbuliez, then, is the
representative of the old-fashioned story-teller, cheerful,
varied, without a trace of snobbery, but with a sharp and
rather narrow irony. He is a good literary journeyman, with
a felicitous, direct style, and an admirable aptitude for setting his novelistic sails to catch the popular breeze, grazing
burning questions of science or sociology, but always with a
finger on the public pulse.

Among novelists of minor significance we note in passing,
that we may not seem to have forgotten, About, a brilliant,
witty, but very uneven writer, who reflects some of the shal-
lower parts of Voltaire's scepticism. He was wise enough
not to take himself seriously, and ceased writing fiction
with the fall of the Empire, whose frivolity he echoed.

Of the novels of the younger Dumas it is necessary to say
very little. They are the first essays of a man who was to
win laurels in quite another field, coloured almost all by the

sombre reflection of cruel school-days that form the subject
of the best of them, the crude, bold, realistic, epigrammatic
and doctrinaire *Clemenceau Case* (l'Affaire Clemenceau,
1866).   The earlier novels are, by turns, humouristic, medieval, sensational, sentimental, philosophical, fantastic, and
realistically autobiographic.   The last group, *The Lady with
the Camellias* (la Dame aux camélias, 1848), *The Lady of
the Pearls*, (la Dame aux perles, 1853), Diane de lys
(1851), and *Life at Twenty* (la Vie à vingt ans, 1854)
alone have interest to-day.

Another writer who soon abandoned the prose tale for
other fields was the poet Théodore de Banville, whose
style has a mellow warmth and delicate grace, but who is
too apt to deck in fairy gauze the vices of the French capital, so that his stories have an incongruous air and a false
ring.   The same in even greater degree must be said of
Murger's *Life in Bohemia* (Vie de Bohême, 1851), and
other stories that treat of the peculiar society of the student
quarter of Paris in the romantic spirit of Gautier's *Young
France*.   Murger's book, to which we owe the words and the
conception of " Bohemia," and " Latin Quarter," has been
accepted as the best expression of student and grisette life
in the second romantic generation, a sort of classic of literary thriftlessness and dissolute impecuniosity, that has per-
suaded generations of men to look back with dreamy tenderness on the sordid follies of youth, and sigh that Mimi
and Musette and Rose Pompon are no more.   But in truth
they never were.   No vice is ever quite so heartless as the
sentimental.   It is impossible to know Murger's life and to
read his book without impatience, and even nausea, at its
whining sentiment and whimsical hysteria of merriment that

masks so base a reality. The Bohemia of Murger, unlike that of Gautier, lived from day to day with no touch of exalted enthusiasm, of scorn for the commonplace, of the ardour and fervour of renascence. It was not calmly disdainful of politics, but naïvely indifferent. Yet, after all reserves have been made, there is a verve and a touch of nature in some of the scenes of *Life in Bohemia* that will long keep its memory green.

In closing our account of this generation a word must be said of Feydeau, an archeologist of repute, who leaped into novelistic notoriety by *Fanny* (1857), a daringly realistic psychologic study of jealousy, to be associated with Constant's *Adolphe*, while the later novels of Feydeau deserve only to be forgotten. One should note, too, as contributing to emancipate and stimulate imagination in the naturalistic epoch that was to follow, the very talented translation of Poe's *Tales* (1868) by the poet Baudelaire. Meantime the appetite of the *feuilleton*-reading public was being satisfied by the voluminous outpourings of novelists of criminal adventure, such as Belot, by the exotic sugar-and-pomatum sentiment of Énault, by the mild sensationalism of Ulbach, who may serve as types of the novelist *invertebrata*, who produce, like polyps, without travail and without individuality, for a public as amorphous as themselves. But the lowest ebb of the *roman-feuilleton* is attained by Ponson du Terrail, whose fiction flows in a weak, washy, everlasting flood of childish impossibilities, the like of which has not afflicted the world since Cervantes laughed the ghosts of chivalrous romance out of it. The antics in which his hero, Rocambole, who has become a byword of criticism, regaled the readers of the *Petit Journal* shall be nameless here.   Finally, a worthy place apart surely belongs to Jules Verne, who, in tales familiar to every schoolboy, has successfully inoculated science with romanticism, and replaces for us, with tales of submarine ships and flying machines, the interest that our fathers found in the romances of Monte Cristo and of Artagnan.

CHAPTER XIII

ÉMILE ZOLA

PROBABLY no Frenchman of letters has been so promi-
nently before the world during the past quarter-century as Émile Zola. The literature that has gathered about
him is exceeded in mass by that only that has been evoked
by Renan and Hugo, and yet it is doubtful if justice has
been done to the artist, still less to the man, at home or
abroad, until very recent political events revealed to all the
magnanimous character that a too conscientious devotion
to a theory of art had masked from those who saw that the
theory was abused, and did not know that the artist and the
moralist were abused also. That his art was a refraction of
our beautiful, and his morals a deviation from our true,
should not blind us to the greatness of the one or the
sincerity of the other. In art the work suffices to praise
the master, but that we may judge Zola aright there where
he has been most hastily condemned, it is necessary to
know more of his life and methods of literary labour than
has been necessary with his predecessors.

Balzac somewhere says that constant work is a law of
art as it is of life, for art is only creation idealised. No
one since he died has given such an example of earnestness and indefatigable industry as Zola, the most intense
and sombre of those who have set the mirror before the
baser side of modern French life. But to this earnestness

and industry there was added an imagination hyperbolic, idealistic, and essentially romantic. The key to the man and to his work lies in his heredity.

He was born in Paris, but he is in no sense a Parisian. His mother, a beautiful, sweet, simple woman, was from Dourdan in northern France. At nineteen she had married for love the engineer François Zola, whose father had been a Venetian, and his mother a Greek from Corfu. Thus three nations mingled their blood in him, and his birthplace was a matter of chance, for the Zolas, were then living at Aix, the Plassans of his novels. The father was a man of intense energy and vast conceptions, of which the Canal Zola at Aix still bears witness. He was a man of ideals, somewhat visionary, who had left Italy to avoid the Austrians, and had travelled widely in Germany, Holland, and England. He was of romantic disposition and himself something of an author. From him, then, the son might inherit a taste for letters, a tendency to vast conceptions, energy, industry, and idealism. But François Zola was as unpractical as his wife was prudent, and when he died (1846) he left his wife with the boy of six and little else but claims that she could not afford to prosecute.

The child grew up under the influence of his Northern French mother and grandmother, and they with Dame Care tempered the heritage of the father into the iron will of the son. The grandmother, a typical native of Beauce, full of courage and common-sense, witty and canny, quickly assumed the direction of the distracted family affairs. Till her death (1857) they lived at Aix, where the child's health and imagination were fortified by sportive freedom in the verdant wilderness of an abandoned garden, the luxuriant Paradou of *Abbé Mouret's Fault.* At school the boy won some distinction in French and the sciences and showed small taste for the classics, but he had already learned to do the thing he did not like. Even the boy took duty for his watchword.

With the death of the grandmother the family fortunes collapsed, and, after a brief and not very successful experience in a Paris school, the youth of twenty thrown wholly on his own resources obtained a wretched clerkship, and passed two years of shifty and squalid bohemianism, in which it is hard to see how he existed at all. It was then that he learned to know "how good it is and how sad to eat when one is starving," as he makes wretched Gervaise sob, with tears of hungry joy, in the last pages of *l'Assommoir*. At last, in 1862, he entered as bundle-clerk the great publishing house of Hachette, and was presently promoted to the advertising department.

During all these years of squalor the literary instinct had been strong in him always. When he could afford it he bought candles, for light and a pen were more to him than tobacco and wine. Obliged by poverty to live in the lowest company, amid the noise of carousing and debauchery, he passed hours in bed for warmth, writing poetry with chilly fingers, and two prose stories, also *The Fairy in Love* and *The Dancing Card*, now to be read in the *Stories for Ninon* (Contes à Ninon, 1864), both romantic fancies as different as possible from all that we now connect with his name.

Gradually the stress of life brings its lesson, the spirit of the mother asserts itself; he grows more practical, abandons poetry, and by the beginning of 1864 has written a volume of tales, the *Stories for Ninon*, all correct and precise in style and all romantic in sentiment. This volume cost him nothing to publish, but it brought him nothing, and only *My Lady-Love* (Celle qui m'aime) showed anything of his future power. It opened the newspapers to him, however, made him friends in literary circles, and thus he was enabled to move to reputable surroundings from the Bohemia that his sturdy nature despised.

Journalism and his clerkship supplied a scanty livelihood, and he satisfied the demands of his artistic nature by writing a novel, *Claude's Confession* (la Confession de Claude, 1865), a failure that we disturb in its limbo only to recall that it troubled the squeamish censors of the Empire and indirectly caused his withdrawal from the Hachettes in January, 1866.

From this moment he was wholly dependent on his pen. His fiction was still weak; indeed his *Dead Woman's Vow* (le Vœu d'une morte, 1866) was not suffered to run to its journalistic conclusion. But his art criticism gave him great notoriety by its trenchant and unconventional originality. It cost him his post and the favour of the all-powerful editor Villemessant, but from that year he was a personality to be reckoned with in the world of letters and art, a man with the courage of his convictions and with strength to defend them at any cost.

Once more reduced to hack-writing at a penny a line, such as *The Mysteries of Marseilles* (les Mystères de Marseille, 1867), he managed still to steal from his bodily needs time for his art and to produce *Thérèse Raquin*, a novel that all regard among his best, and some as his masterpiece. The hack-work was the better paid and he must eat, but he was as true to his art as necessity would suffer him to be.

Up to this time his fiction had been ultra-romantic, and

the idea of *Thérèse Raquin* was derived from the very romantic *Vénus de Gordes*, a commonplace story of a murder by a wife and lover and their trial for the crime. Zola transformed the situation by a touch of genius. He let the criminals escape all earthly justice, but let them be ever bound yet ever repelled by the haunting memory of their crime ; he let their love turn to hate, and let them perish the moral victims of a divine vengeance. The intensity and minute vision of this terrible analysis of remorse are hardly surpassed in literature, but it is a fierce and sombre art, a morose pessimism that first reveals what Zola means by "naturalism," a word that he first uses in the preface to this remarkable volume, which, however, was long in finding a public to comprehend its excellence.

Madeleine Férat, his next novel (1868), is wholly inferior to *Thérèse Raquin*, but it adds the one element needed to complete his novelistic apprenticeship, the thread that was to bind together his labours for the next twenty-five years, an interest in the mysterious problems of heredity, by which he maintained, nursed, and fortified the fatalistic determinism that pulses through the *Rougon-Macquart*, the most monumental achievement of French fiction since Balzac. It was a daring conception, worthy of François Zola's son. This author of six obscure volumes of fiction, who, in making his mark in criticism had won more enemies than friends, proposed, in twelve volumes linked together by an hypothesis of heredity, to tell "the natural and social history of a family under the Second Empire," and so to be "the secretary of French society" during that epoch as Balzac had undertaken to be for his. The general plan was thought out and a genealogy devised to his purpose in 1869, and it was necessary only to extend and complete this original design when twenty-four years later the twelve volumes, now become twenty, were closed with *Dr. Pascal* (1893). The dates have interest. When the plan was conceived the Empire promised a long life, but before the first volume was published it became necessary to condense into nineteen years what had been devised for many more. Hence insuperable chronological difficulties will beset the too curious reader, though they need not disturb a critical equanimity.

If in this gigantic scheme Zola was the true son of his father, he was also the schoolboy of Aix with the marked predilection for material knowledge, and he was also the grandson of the shrewd lady of Beauce. Having secured a sure market for uncertain production he married on the strength of it, accepted advances from his publisher, and barely escaped being caught in the toils that beset Balzac. For war came, in three years he could issue but two volumes where he had promised six, and it was only after the bankruptcy of his patron and by the far-sighted generosity of Charpentier, his new publisher, that he became once more a free man in 1875, and was able to develop his talent in years before success had brought encouragement or reward.

On the twenty volumes of the *Rougon-Macquart* and the trio of *The Three Cities*, Zola's reputation rests so entirely that we may dismiss very briefly the short stories with which he relieved from time to time the strain of that methodical and exacting labour. All are good and one of them, *The Attack on the Mill* in *The Soirées of Médan*, is a masterpiece, but they are not necessary to Zola's fame or to our critical appreciation of him.

In a preface to the *Rougon-Macquart*, dated July, 1871,

though written in part in 1868, Zola states his purpose. He will show how in a family superficial dissimilarity may mask fundamental similarity, how "heredity has its laws like gravity," how various minglings of blood and environment may reveal the inner workings of humanity, so that, as he said in bringing his work to a close, "It is a world, a society, a civilization. The whole life is there, . . . for our family have spread through all contemporary society, invaded all situations, borne along by overweening appetite, that general modern impulse that snatches at enjoyment and interpenetrates our whole social body."

This is what he attempted, but it is not altogether what he attained, and it as well that it should not be so. It is a theory amalgamated from Flaubert and Taine. Its weak points have been repeatedly and unsparingly exposed, and it has done much to divert appreciation from merits that lie elsewhere. Fiction can perhaps be made to reflect the last light of physio-psychology, but Zola's self-styled "scientific experiments carried on in the free flight of the imagination" do not do it, and his aspiration to be "a new Lucretius" remains a dream. He has indeed always held fast to the idea that "truth alone can instruct and fortify generous souls," and that therefore "to tell the truth is to teach morals, though it be by a *Madame Bovary* or a *Germinie Lacerteux*." But his power and fascination lie in this, that it is given him to see truth with an epic imagination, gloomy and pessimistic perhaps but grand and masterful, in its painting of the animal instincts in human nature, of the *bête humaine* that possesses and tortures him like a nightmare, drags him through vaults of human ordure, and forces him to fix his eyes on the bestial in man till his fancy differentiates it into grandiose hyperbolical types of relentless forces working out the sum of human folly and misery. He wishes to give us slices of crude life, to tell the truth, the whole truth, as he sees it; what he does give is not a photograph of nature, but a poet's vision.

That he might speak of what he knew, he laid the scene of his first novel in Aix, the town of his childhood, which he calls Plassans. Here, as we learn from *The Fortune of the Rougons* (la Fortune des Rougons, 1871), was born in 1787 Pierre Rougon, whose mother, Adélaïde Fouque, after his father's death, had another son, Antoine Macquart, and a daughter, Ursule Macquart, and afterward developed a nervous disease that had been congenital, though dormant, and so appeared in various forms in her descendants in the second and third generation, with whom we have in the main to do. The children of Antoine sink to the proletariat of labour or of vice, showing themselves at their best in the Jean Macquart of *Earth* (la Terre, 1887) and *The Downfall* (la Débâcle, 1892), with a poised sensuality in the Lisa of *Parisian Digestion* (le Ventre de Paris, 1873), and with a resigned courage in her daughter Pauline (*The Joy of Life*, la Joie de vivre, 1884). Meantime the third child of Antoine, Gervaise, has developed the alcoholism of her grandfather and father, and after serving as type of the self-degraded working class of Paris in *l'Assommoir* (1887), bequeaths her tendencies to children who develop them, — Claude into an artist's sterile but ever travailing genius (*The Work*, l'Œuvre, 1886), Étienne into the passionate revolt of a socialistic miner (*Germinal*, 1885), Jacques into the murderous mania of a locomotive engineer (*The Beast in Man*, la Bête humaine, 1890), and *Nana* (1880) into a poison-flower of vice avenging itself on the society that fostered it, a gaudy fly incubated in the heat of a social dunghill, and bearing on its wings a contagion of pestilence. Thus nine novels of the score deal with the lower social classes in the city, the country, and the camp, or with vice. The bourgeoisie is represented by the descendants of Ursule Macquart, in whom Adélaïde's "organic lesion" manifests itself either in a mysticism that evaporates at the touch of earthly love (*The Dream*, le Rêve, 1888), or is intensified to a cataleptic jealousy (*A Page of Love*, une Page d'amour, 1878). The intermarriage of a son of Ursule Macquart with a daughter of Pierre Rougon will furnish us a type of the commercial bourgeoisie, restless and forceful in the Octave Mouret of *Pot-Bouille* and *The Ladies' Delight* (Au bonheur des dames, 1883), while in the celibate priest, Serge Mouret, this restlessness turns to religious mania (*Abbé Mouret's Fault*, la Faute de l'abbé Mouret, 1875). In the Rougons, finally, neurosity takes the form of political ambition (*The Conquest of Plassans*, la Conquête de Plassans, 1874, and *His Excellency*, Son Excellence Eugène Rougon, 1876), or of speculative mania (*Booty*, la Curée, 1871) and the plutocracy (*Money*, l'Argent, 1891), or finally shows itself in the scientific aspirations of *Dr. Pascal* (1893).

As these persons come in touch with all sections of society, they give opportunity for a panoramic picture of the epoch, the gross materialism of the urban multitude whose god is their belly, the sordid monotony of the lives of farmer and fisherman relieved by hours of morose bestiality and dreams of social equality and avenging jealousy, the life of the studio and the workshop, of petty tradesmen and the great stores, of clergy, bankers, demagogues, officers, and aristocrats, of those on whose folly they batten, and of those who batten on their vices.

And as Zola took his scenes from observation, so also he took his characters and many incidents from contemporary history, always striving for truth, though often attaining only a refraction of it. The progress of the work is more interesting to us than a detailed description of the individual narratives. The introductory volume and also *Booty*, were written before the war, though published after it. The latter gave him much trouble. How could he treat realistically the life of wealthy parvenus of which he could learn nothing directly? As a springboard for his imagination he took the house of the chocolate millionaire Ménier in the Parc Monceau, but his hungry fancy could not paint the magnificence of its real interior, as in prosperous days he learned to know it. Carriage builders furnished him details for his equipages, and the vertiginous picture of Renée's conservatory was made from hours spent notebook in hand, in the hot-houses of the public Botanic Garden. His facts and figures he got from real accounts, and also from partisan pamphlets. He worked with methodical seriousness and neither sought nor excited scandal. For strong as is *Booty*, it fell on evil times, and two years later an hundred and sixty dollars sufficed to buy the publisher's rights of a book that has since sold forty thousand copies. Zola's ideas of fiction had not yet made his talent profitable, but with the stubborn confidence of an artist, he persevered in deserving success until he attained it.

Parisian Digestion, his next volume, is perhaps the most extreme expression of his theory, and, therefore, one of the least artistic of his works. It is, as some one has said, "the symphony of eating," the full-fed epic of digestion, an Iliad of the immortal war between fat and lean, where the sleek bourgeois triumphs over the lank bohemian, very typical in treatment of character, and quite too doctrinaire to be enjoyed save in its critical relations. Zola's talent has not yet mastered his theory. He is riding his naturalistic hobby-horse, and Pegasus is waiting. And he will continue to wait while the author returns to Aix and to quasi good society to write of the political *Conquest of Plassans* with as little enthusiasm as success.

Criticism will accord a much higher place to *Abbé Mouret's Fault*, for it will discern, what contemporaries failed to see, the beginning of his literary emancipation from compilation and documents. The Roman ritual, Liguori, and à Kempis gave him much, but only the poet's fancy sporting with childhood's memories could create the swelling life of that wild southern Paradou, whose exuberant and heavy odours give a fit atmosphere to the morbid passion of the tale. He had already written fine studies of intense and morbid character, but in this poet's dream lay the consecration of his genius and it is this that gives to *Abbé Mouret's Fault* its exceptional interest, while its successor, *His Excellency*, owed its immediate success to its supposed picture of Napoleon's prime minister, Rouher, and has interest to-day, not as a story or as a work of art, but for supposed traces of psychic autobiography. For Zola, like his Rougon, loves power because it glorifies the force that is in him and is virtuous for no divine reward, but because virtue is an element of strength.

We are brought thus to the eve of Zola's first great success. He had written twelve volumes of fiction in as many years. No doubt he seemed to others one of those novelists by the dozen who can always sell 2000 copies but never 20,000. Perhaps he seemed so to himself. Daudet, whom he knew well at this time, suggests as much.

He had more reason to be discouraged than ten years before. And he was about to achieve an immediate and immense success by a book constructed like its predecessors from experience, from observation, and from books. What was the spark in *l'Assommoir* that set the literary world afire? It was that he brought the poetic glow of *Abbé Mouret's Fault* from the far-off country presbytery to the heart of Parisian popular life. He had seen these tenements, these festivals and funerals, he knew in his own body that hunger, cold, and squalor, that " slow dying of the poor, empty bellies crying for hunger, the necessities of beasts snuffling with chattering teeth at unclean things in this great Paris so gilded and so gay." He knew these things, as the authors of *Germinie Lacerteux* did not know them, and he treated them with an epic sweep that was his alone. He supplemented his experience by special studies, and threw an atmosphere of sordid reality about the whole by choosing the language of his characters for that of his narration also. Then he took his great mass of linguistic and social notes to the seashore and methodically elaborated this story of pity and of terror with a mathematical precision of which the Italian critic Amicis has given a minute and curious description. The persons were first enumerated and characterised as in a police register, then the action was sketched and each scene, even in its sub-divisions, assigned appropriate space, so that the whole might have an architectural harmony and proportion. It is only after two or three months of this preliminary study, and he made such for all his novels, that he becomes, as he has said, "master of this kind of life, feels it, lives it in imagination, as Balzac used to do, and is sure that he can give to it its special colour and odour and language," aiming at scientific psychology and logical continuity but realising always that the virus of romanticism is strong in him still.

A natural result of this method is that, as his talent develops with success, he comes to describe temperaments rather than characters, types rather than individuals, masses rather than men; and that is why the method of *Abbé Mouret* first realises its possibilities in *l'Assommoir*, to pass from strength to strength through *Germinal* to *The Downfall*. The central figure in *l'Assommoir* is not Gervaise, the wretched washerwoman who gropes her way in sordid misery and wrecks herself on brutal vice, but rather the Dram-Shop, that manufactory of sin and crime, with its panting distillery whose snaky coils ooze their alcoholic sweat like a slow, persistent spring. The whole is an apocalyptic epic of social putrefaction, starvation, delirium, in which all figures are typical of the fearful struggle of the submerged for a life that stifles ideals, inevitably involves its own disappointment, and is not only of the earth earthy, but of the dirt dirty, a grandiose evocation of topsy-turvy idealism.

' This is the fittest place to speak of a quality in Zola's work that more than any other has injured it and its author in the esteem of the literary public at home and abroad. I mean his voluntary crudity of language and persistent mention of the unmentionable. This attained its extreme expression in *Earth*, ten years later. It had found ample expression before, especially in *Booty*, but first in *l'Assommoir* it attracted general notice and very general denunciation.

Base men think, speak, and act basely in life, and they do so in *l'Assommoir*. Many men not base have moments of baseness or of bestiality, and Zola attributes such to men in

whom virtue, or at least respectability, predominates.   If
he did not, he would seem to himself to be writing a lie,
deluding his public into a false social security.   He believes,
for instance, that the social condition of workmen in the
faubourgs of Paris cries out for reform, that it is a pes-
tiferous environment, in which drunkenness and laziness
relax family ties till all honest feeling is submerged in
promiscuity, shamelessness, and death.   What he sees is
indeed not typical or normal, but rather his vision of
whither society is tending.   He thinks it true, however,
and means it so well that he is willing to endure the denunciation that his picture of it invites.   *L'Assommoir,*
he says, " is morality in action, the most chaste of my
books, . . . the first story of the people that has the true
scent of the people."   " I do not defend myself, my
work will defend me.   It is a true book," a story of men
not bad by nature but made bad by an environment of
ignorance, poverty, and toil.

In all this Zola was absolutely sincere, filled with profound sympathy for society's victims and bent on serious
diagnosis of social ills.   He knew that he invited, and
probably expected, misrepresentation.   It is a sad truth
that many men derive an unavowable and morose satisfaction from reading the unutterable and seeing the obscene.
Doubtless this motive impelled some of the eighty thousand who in three years bought *l'Assommoir* after their
attention had been called to it by the efforts of critical
Mrs. Grundys to warn a smug and confiding public to
beware this man of sin.   But Zola is writing for neither
the smug nor the prurient.   He is trying to tell thoughtful
men what bourgeois democracy and the Second Empire
have made of the French people.

Yet in absolving the man we do not acquit the artist. The nastiness, the blasphemy of some melancholy pages in the *Rougon-Marquart* may be true in the sense that each detail is true, but they are not true as a whole and they are not artistic. Zola mars his effects by overloading his colours and falls on the side to which he inclines. Truth is beautiful only when it is normal, natural. The naturalists, so-called, are ever giving us the abnormal, the ideally base. *L'Assommoir, Nana, Earth*, and *The Beast in Man* are to nature what an anatomical museum is to the palestra. Both have their value. But the strength of Zola is not here. We deplore these excesses of a mistaken esthetic, but they must not blind us to his moral sincerity or to his rare artistic power.

Had there been aught of the pander in his nature it would have been easy to follow *l'Assommoir* with another story of the gutter, or to turn from squalid to venal vice. He followed rather his artist's instinct that led him from the Place de la révolution to the Trocadéro, from broad popular frescos to *A Page of Love*, a miniature of a child's morbid jealousy and a mother's passion, worked out in five symmetrical parts, each closing with a picture of Paris in sunshine, darkness, or tempest, that makes the city a material symbol of psychic crisis or calm.

When he had thus satisfied his poetic nature and sought the seclusion of country life at Médan, he turned resolutely to do the thing he did not like, the most difficult and distasteful thing, but the thing that he must do if in his moral and social picture of the Second Empire he would not mask the foreground with a fig-tree. Corrupt and venal women had been among the most prominent figures of that epoch, and Zola has sought to give us epic types of them in his *Nana*.

Himself of eminently correct private life, and having been
in youth an unwilling witness of the baser side only of vice,
he sought help, with a seriousness that is not without its
humour, in the garrulous memory of old beaux and in the
morose fancies of Otway. The result, as a whole, is unpleasant, though not perhaps unedifying ; but the book has
passages of wonderful power, and the close is, as he said,
the most weird and successful thing that he had ever written.   Even now it would be hard to match that death scene
in the upper room of the great hotel, where Nana lies dissolving in small-pox while frantic crowds below are shouting :
" To Berlin ! To Berlin ! "

   As after *l'Assommoir*, so now Zola turned from the Parisian cesspool to a country scene and had begun to write
The Joy of Living (la Joie de vivre) when the death of his
mother, October, 1880, led him to seek relief from the
painful story of Pauline Quenu's unselfish suffering in a
satire of the smugly corrupt Parisian bourgeoisie, that seemed
to his poetic vision a sort of soup-stock kettle, where scraps
and refuse of good food were ever simmering and sending
up their scum.   Therefore he called his story *Pot-bouille*.
He made great efforts to be accurate, even in minute
details, and sought realistic effects in technic by restricting
descriptions, blending several actions, and exhibiting them
in disconnected scenes, as an observer in real life might
see them, — a device that he borrowed from the Goncourts.
But his avowed model was Flaubert's *Sentimental Education*.
He sought to be anti-romantic, clear, condensed, to put, as
he said, a drag on himself and to " finish flatly."   And it is
because *Pot-bouille* aspires to the faults of Flaubert's novel
that it fails to please critics or readers.   Zola's imagination
struggles here with the pettiness of his subject and method,

and creates at last a gloomy, unreal world, where, as some one has said, the porters talk like poets and other people like porters, and where society, like the children, is sick or ill-bred. That his talent was not realistic he had never shown so clearly as here. But the commercial side of his subject attracted him, and he followed *Pot-bouille* with *The Ladies' Delight* (Au bonheur des dames), a study of the great department store, with its socialistic or collectivist tendencies, in all aspects of which he took a very keen interest, striving to enter into the material and mental life of clerks and petty shop-keepers, delving in the mysteries of kleptomania and the temptations of show-windows and bargain-days, and producing an economic study of some interest, but a novel of very little. This was not the field for his triumphs, nor did he find it in his next essay, *The Joy of Living*, a sombre, pathetic study of silent, gentle, magnanimous girlhood falling victim to egoism, like Balzac's *Pierrette*, in her fortune and in her love.

Zola could not have expected commercial success for a story like this. Pathos, to be popular, must be sentimental. His appeal was to the few who see life steadily and whole. His epic breadth finds some scope here in the multitudinous sea, but it was to appeal more effectively both to the judicious and to the multitude when its subject was human nature; and so *Germinal*, that great prose poem of the strike and mine, is a masterpiece in which all his talents find their full development, more even than in *l'Assommoir*. Ideal it was, but real, too, in the higher sense. Every " coron " of miners in France and Belgium has its well-thumbed copy to attest the book's broad truth to nature. It is, as Zola said, a great fresco, so filled with figures that all must be simplified, some only suggested, and the whole composition foreshortened. The treatment is typical. Étienne is any workman into whose brain socialism has percolated and become a fixed idea ; Maheude, any woman whom slow exasperation of suffering goads from resignation to revolt ; Catherine, society's victim, crowded step by step to the last verge of pain and suffering. And so, too, the millionaire Grégoire is but a type of serene egoism, of the incapacity of the rich to understand why workmen should be discontented to labour for their luxury ; and superintendent Jeanlin is typical of the masterful fidelity of an officer in the army of labour. The magnificent descriptive scenes are treated in the same spirit. The strikers as they march past, haggard men and ragged hags, shrieking the Marseillaise and keeping a rude time to it with the clattering of their wooden shoes, brandishing tools for weapons, and shouting the monotonous menace, Bread, Bread, Bread, are a symbol of the revolt of brutalised labour. What if their cry be silenced with bullets? We feel that it has marked another hour in labour's night and brought one step nearer the dawn of a new social day.

Of course the action and reaction of mass and individual demands a magnifying of details, but here, at least, Zola has avoided distortion, for these colliers force themselves on the mind with a vivid, nightmare life that makes their very filthiness and squalor seem as natural to us as their hopeless, socialistic yearnings. And over all there dominates the pumping engine, a symbol of soulless, restless, panting life, vague, yet ever-present, till it is swallowed up at last in the collapsing pit, as though it were incarnate society that had undermined its own base, struggling with futile desperation against an inexorable fate, and leaving behind for our sole consolation an eternal hope in the "germinal" forces of nature, from which a new and better order may arise.

To maintain such a height as this is given to no novelist, and in *The Work* Zola has done little more than expand the idea of Balzac's *Unknown Masterpiece* into a volume. In this "pure psychology of art and passion," where an illusive ideal drives an artist to mania, there are interesting bits of autobiography, but the book is insignificant in comparison either to *Germinal* or to *Earth*, that immediately followed; for this last is a picture of human bestiality that would be unique in literature were it not for the morose fancies of Swift. It is false, but it is grandly false. We cannot but marvel at the atmosphere of fecundity that breathes, pollen-laden, through the whole.

No book of Zola was received with such angry indignation and patriotic protest. But even before its publication he had cleansed his wings for a flight into the blue, and was meditating that precious mystic *Dream*, an exquisite idyl, yet based like all his work on minute and careful studies. But, though he called his book "a scientific experiment carried on in the free flight of imagination," it is but one more evidence of the fundamental romanticism of Zola's genius. And the same romanticism, though topsy-turvy now, riots in *The Beast in Man*, which has homicide for its theme and the locomotive for its symbol; a sad failure as a scientific novel, but very remarkable as a grandiose vision of the Railway. The description, at the close, of the runaway train dashing by, filled with howling soldiers, rushing to disaster and disappearing in a cloud of steam and smoke and fire, is such as no other novelist of our century could have written.

Wealth had thus far had small place in Zola's fiction.

In *Money* we live in a world of speculation and of intangible values, a theme apparently well suited to Zola's talent, so that it is difficult to understand why this novel of the Stock-Exchange is comparatively ineffectual. But it is clear that for one whose greatest triumph had been in *Germinal* there remained, as the subject of all others, War. Here he was sure to be at his best and sure of an audience as wide as the French republic. Zola had not served in the war of 1870, but all confirm the essential faithfulness of *The Downfall.* We need not follow him as, foot by foot, he examines his scene and gathers facts from peasants and citizens. The characters, as in *Germinal,* are types, each representing one of the states of soul that the Empire had tended to produce. But its power and its glory are not in individuals but in masses, in armies concentrating with fatal precision around Sedan, in regiments on the march, or herded in cattle-cars or prison-pens, or surging through bloody Bazeilles or blazing Paris, or lying under fire, or charging to destruction, while the rhythmic recurrence of Napoleon's baggage train punctuates with scathing irony the imperial downfall.

It remained for Zola to sum up for us the lesson of his theory of atavism. He has essayed his vindication and justification in *Dr. Pascal,* a book with some fine passages, others extremely disagreeable, and little interest save as it gathers together the threads of the preceding volumes with the ultimate moral that men should have faith in nature, should stake their hopes on work and on science, and so become at last masters of destiny.

Such is the lesson also of the triad that has followed the *Rougon-Macquart.* The central thought in *Lourdes, Rome,* and *Paris* is, first, that emotional mysticism is a morbid

compound of passion and pettiness, pity and bathos, sure
to be exploited by the spirit of ecclesiastical commercial-
ism. Then when his hero is repelled by the actual church
he takes refuge in the ideal of the neo-Christian socialists;
and when that too fails he "makes haste to bury a dying
religion lest its ruins should infect the nations," and in
Paris proclaims that human happiness "can spring only
from the furnace of the scientist." But throughout the
reader is attracted less by the doctrine than by the art, in
Lourdes by the processions and pilgrimages, in *Rome* by
the contrasts of antique, old, and new, symbolized in the
Palatine, the Vatican, and the Quirinal, in *Paris* by the
long conflict between delusions that flatter and truth that
frees, a struggle to end only with a Twilight of the old
Gods and a full faith in Nature.

This philosophy of life is a revolt against Roman Catholicism as France knows it. It is not necessarily anti-Chris-
tian. Its ultimate base, as we see from *Dr. Pascal*, is
instinct rather than science. He sees that the character of
most men is determined by heredity and circumstance, but
even in the unfree he recognises the potentiality of freedom
as a strict determinist could not do, and so these struggles
between religion and science, between heart and brain, that
from first to last give these twenty-three volumes unity of
aim in their mass of detail, are but one more witness to the
human craving for rest, one more failure to penetrate the
ultimate meaning of life. But where genius is so fertile
and so courageous the effort is its own reward. If he has
pitilessly laid bare the pretentious mockery and hypocritical morality in much of what passes for religion and good-
breeding he has been as merciless to confident materialism
and that hedonistic fatalism that weakens the will by which

alone happiness in self-control is won. His work has grown more virile with the years. It has discarded the excesses of a mistaken esthetic and gained in tonic earnestness. He was always a force to be reckoned with. He has become a force with which we are glad to reckon.

CHAPTER XIV

ALPHONSE DAUDET

THE most graceful of modern French humourists, their most sympathetic satirist, and their most charming, if not their deftest story-teller, is Alphonse Daudet, who was born by a curious coincidence in the year and province of the birth of Zola. Both, then, were natives of Provence, both heirs of its warm sun, that gave to the genius of the one its vertiginous imagination, and ripened in the other a literary wine of most exquisite flavour. Daudet has left us in *Little Thingumy* (le Petit Chose) one of the most delightful bits of child autobiography in literature. Born in a well-to-do manufacturer's family, a reverse of fortune compelled him in youth to seek the wretched post of usher in a school at Alais, after having nursed literary dreams in a novel never published, and now lost beyond hope of recovery. After a year of slavery he left in desperation that " Dotheboys Hall " and joined his almost equally penniless brother Ernest, who has since become a worthy, though mediocre novelist and historian, at Paris in November of 1857.

Here he tried to support himself by literature, at first as a poet, then by prose contributions to the Figaro, which paid better. though ill. " We existed, and that was all," he says. He was too conscientious an artist that his work should be immediately remunerative. No wonder, then, that his verses were sometimes pessimistic, though of sound morale at the core, and always of polished workmanship, for, as his brother says, " his literary conscience awoke in him at the same moment as his literary talent." " It is style that perfumes a book," he wrote, and he would sit for hours sifting, kneading, and molding words to fit his fancy.

His first prose piece, *The Story of Red Ridinghood* (le Roman du Chaperon-Rouge), was characteristic of his whole work before the war of 1870. It personifies the happy insouciance of the artist temperament as a sprite that leads children to truancy, and genius to idleness, and yet, after being devoured at last by the wolf of necessity, is loved by those she injured, and blamed only by the sage Polonius, for whom she had no charm. Like the other prose work of this time, *Red Ridinghood* is essentially poetic, and a poet Daudet remained to the last, seeing, as Zola says, all things in the half-dream of vivid imaginings that magnifies all, and gives it colour and intensity, distilling from nature its elements of pathos, humour, and happiness. Realist as he came to be in after years, he never chose to see the sordid side of naturalism, he instinctively avoided the pettiness that delighted the old Flaubert and the young Huysmans. The romantic fancy of these early tales broods over the later Parisian dramas, and so mingles emotion with exact description that he makes a dainty fancy spring up, rare and delicate, out of reality itself.

Zola describes him during these years as " living on the outskirts of the city with other poets, a whole band of joyous bohemians. He had the delicate nervous beauty of an Arab horse, with flowing hair, silky divided beard, large eyes, narrow nose, an amorous mouth, and over it all a

sort of illumination, a breath of tender light that individualised the whole face with a smile full at once of intellect and of the joy of life. There was something in him
of the French street-urchin, something too of the Oriental
woman." It was then that he made those bohemian ac-
quaintances, the *ratés* of his *Jack*, and it is simply marvellous, as his brother has remarked, that he could have
lived with them without losing aught of his talent, or
leaving behind the bloom of his youth, the freshness of
his mind, and the straightforwardness of his character.
"He shared their miseries often; their disordered instincts never."

Fortune was soon to smile on him, however. There was
a gradually increasing demand for his work in the press,
and in 1861 the Empress Eugénie, fascinated by his poem
on "The Plums," changed his precarious freedom to an
official sinecure, that this rare talent might develop undis-
turbed by daily care. She induced the Duke of Morny,
the Emperor's half-brother and minister of state, to give
the poet a nominal secretaryship, a post that he held till
Morny's death in 1865, and turned to excellent literary
account in *The Nabab* and elsewhere.

Privation had, however, already undermined his health,
and to recover this he was now encouraged by Government
to travel to Algeria, to Corsica, Sardinia, and the south of
France, and thus not only developed his always deficient
sense of colour, but collected the material for the Arab and
Corsican stories in *Letters from my Mill* and *Monday Tales*,
for *The Nabab*, for *Numa Roumestan*, and for the immortal
Tartarin, whose original was for a time his travelling companion. It was now that Daudet made the acquaintance
of Mistral, the Provençal poet, of Gambetta, of Rochefort,

and of Thérion, from all of whom he learned secrets of art
or of character.   From dingy bohemianism he had passed,
he said, to a butterfly life.   From twenty-one he knew only
happiness till shattered nerves brought him their melancholy
reckoning.

He now began to attempt play-writing, but with such
indifferent success that our present purpose invites us to
pass in silence these efforts, continued through many years.
Still, on Morny's death in 1865, Daudet felt sufficient confidence in his talent to resign his post and seek the seclusion of his native Provence, where he wrote a first draft of
Little Thingumy (le Petit Chose), which was not finished,
however, till the autumn of 1867.

This is a very fascinating and yet an unsatisfactory book.
The autobiographical portion is pathetic and charming,
the rest is extravagant and fantastically romantic, though
Little Thingumy is so good-hearted and charming throughout that we pardon his inconsequence and his weakness.
Daudet thought the book written too soon, and wished he
had waited, remarking thoughtfully that " something very
good might have been made of my youth."

It was while writing this book that his second and greatest good fortune came to him, — his marriage with an almost
ideal helpmeet, herself a woman of letters both by birth
and training, whose cool, Northern common-sense supplemented his Southern ardour with a harmony of soul that he
has transposed with infinite art into a discord in his *Numa
Roumestan.*   It is true that for three years he attempted no
great work, surrendering himself to the joy of his new life,
and working up old impressions in the *Letters from my Mill*
(1869), now one of his most popular books, though it met
at first with but small success ; which is the more strange as

it contains that nearly perfect gem of a story, *The Elixir of Father Gaucher*, and other work hardly inferior and most characteristic. But when the Terrible Year came and passed it found him transformed in spirit, fitted for serious work, largely, as it seems, by this most admirable woman, with her well-balanced, healthy mind, though her own fiction, *Children and Mothers* and the *Childhood of a Parisian Girl*, shows touches of the morbid art of Marivaux.

Of their collaboration we have four estimates, his, hers, their son Léon's, and that of their closest friend, Edmond de Goncourt. They talked over all the situations and at every step she revised his work, "scattering over it," he says, "a little of her beautiful azure and gold powder," while she compares their joint work to the decoration of a Japanese fan: "on one side the subject, the characters, and the atmosphere in which they move; on the other, sprays of verdure, petals of flowers, the slender prolongation of a little branch, what remains of colour or of gold-leaf on the painter's brush."

With talent thus aided and supplemented Daudet began in 1868 his *Tartarin of Tarascon* (1872), less a novel than a long satirical tale, a playful bantering of that mirage of gasconade and insincerity that affects the vision of most Southern Frenchmen. The caricature is, perhaps, too subtle for our taste, and indeed it took the French public some years to realise that they were the richer by a masterpiece of most admirable fooling. But once convinced, they have remained faithful, and it is said that the discovery of Tartarin and his exploitation *On the Alps* (1886), and at *Port-Tarascon* (1890), brought to the author of his being $80,000.

Of this profitable hero Daudet says that "judged freely

after many years it seems to me that Tartarin has qualities
of youth, of vitality, of truth, a truth from over-Loire, that
may swell and exaggerate facts, but never lies." As that
other Provençal Zola, says, " it is truth seen from its humourous side." Daudet found vent here for the ardour of
his Southern nature, and thus attained a more sustained
realism in the Parisian dramas that were to follow. No one
has ever caught, with such delicately keen perception and
such sympathy as he, the effervescent imagination of Provence that creates its own environment and yet charms in
spite of persistent self-deception. He has himself described
it in *Numa Roumestan* as " pompous, classical, theatrical ;
loving parade, costume, the platform, banners, flags, trum-
pets ; clannish, traditional, caressing, feline, of an eloquence
brilliant, excited yet colourless, quick to anger, and yet giving anger a sham expression even when it is sincere."
Such was Numa, and such is Tartarin, a cinemetograph of
the Midi.

But between his marriage and the war, and indeed till
1873, Daudet was occupied chiefly with short stories that
were to win him, even before his first true novel was written,
a place among the best of modern raconteurs, and some
claim to be regarded as the inventor of the newspaper story
in France. *The Letters from my Mill* is, perhaps, Daudet's
one book before 1874 that the critic can regard as of primary import, for though the prevailing tone is still romantic, his pathos and humour strike often more realistic notes,
and reveal the student of Balzac. Nowhere was he to render external impressions of Provençal life with such delicate
intimacy as here, where he seems at times, as he said, " hypnotised by reality," whether it be of medieval Avignon, as
in *The Pope's Mule*, of the irony of village pettiness, as in

Old Folks (les Vieux), or of pastoral life in *The Stars*.
There is a medieval verve in *The Elixir* and *The Curate of
Cucignan*, there is a fantasy like that of Hoffmann in *The
Man with the Golden Brain*, the mirage of grotesque exaggeration in *The Beaucaire Stage*, and unsuspected power of
realistic description of nature in *In Camargue*. His gen-
tlest pathos is in *Bixiou's Portfolio*, his deepest in *The Two
Inns*, and there is a hint at least in *Barrack Homesickness* of
the psychological analysis that was to dominate his last years.

Thus in these exquisitely polished cameos of literary art
we have the pledge of all that he was to accomplish, not
only in the *Monday Tales*, the *Letters to an Absentee*, and
Artists' Wives, but in the *Tartarin* books and the novels
also. It was natural that his Southern imagination should
find its first expression in these little jewels, for the faculty
of sustained application came only with the tempering of
war; but there is no need to dwell on them here save to
note the gradual subsidence of romanticism, a growth of the
Parisian element, a stronger and fuller social nature, rarely
with a touch of bitterness, as in *Arthur* or *The Bookkeeper*,
more often with the humour of perennial youth, and the
growth of genial sympathy with human foibles that lends a
grateful aroma to stories that might easily be given a pessimistic turn, such as *Little Stenn, Belisaire's Prussian* and
Mr. Bonnicar's Patties. But most of all one is struck in
the latter tales with the glowing patriotism as it appears in
the superb *Game of Billiards, The Ferry*, the universally
known *Siege of Berlin* and *The Last Class*. It found also
a much more chauvinistic expression in some now omitted
Letters to an Absentee, and in parts of a series of sketches
in war time published in 1874 as *Robert Helmont*, in which
are also preliminary studies for his *Jack* and *The Nabab*.

But while these books were slowly bringing fame they were not bringing fortune. That he was to attain at a stroke by *Fromont Jr. and Risler Sr.*, his first " Parisian Drama," better known to English readers under the name of its feminine incarnation of evil, " Sidonie." It would seem that to achieve popular success it was needful for him to plant the seed of his genius in the muck-beds of Parisian domestic infelicities, but he certainly treated that unfortunate convention of literary taste, or perhaps it were juster to say that inevitable nemesis of French marriage customs, with commendable restraint here and always.

Throughout the " Parisian Dramas " Daudet is a most anxious student of life. Wherever he was he was taking mental notes, and often literal ones. Piles of such memoranda are among his literary remains. All his novels have their roots in things seen, in a love of truth, from which he would at times break away for sudden incursions into the realms of fantasy, never without an artistic purpose, but always with loss of power, that he regained, like Antæus, on touching earth again. So when he plans to write a serious novel of Parisian life he chooses a scene that he could observe from his own windows in the ancient Hôtel Lamoignon in the Marais. A commercial experience of his father furnished the mainspring of the action, " mutual interest coupling together in unremitting labour for years beings different in temperament and in education." His novel is the story of an honest and talented man whose abilities raise him socially into a society against whose corruption he has no hereditary defence, and from which he escapes only by suicide. Beside old Risler, the soul of honour, he places the young and base Fromont, and then he bestows on the base man a noble wife, and on the good man

a base one who shall be jealous of the social position of
Mme. Fromont, as she will be at the seductiveness of the
other. These are the four pillars of the story. Around
them he grouped figures no less real because drawn, they
too, from daily observation. There is the decayed actor
Delobelle, "blooming and sonorous," and his hunchback
daughter Désirée, who seems to have stepped from a novel
of Dickens, and there is Planus with his sturdy Alsacian
honest loyalty. But because these figures are based on
observation, they are portraits rather than characters, and
our interest is more in plot than in evolution of soul. The
principal personages are weak, even Sidonie, that "mush-
room of the Parisian gutter," who, because she has been
humiliated all her childhood with the prospect before her of
becoming a dried up mansard-flower of vanity and envy at
last, finds in prosperity her only joy in malice and in the
humiliation of others. The story toward the last grows
somewhat stagey, and the close seems a regrettable concession to sentimentality, such as was to deface parts of *Jack*
and *The Nabab*, before the romantic virus was finally neu-
tralised, though it was never expelled. Still no one can
read *Fromont Jr. and Risler Sr.* to-day and wonder that
the reader of 1873, nursed perhaps on Feuillet and Cherbuliez, should have hailed it with delight, for as yet there
was none in France who could have been regarded as a
rival, actual or prospective, of its author.

But Daudet was to do better things than this. He had
found himself conscious of a new power and discovered the
joy of sustained creative effort. Even *Jack*, his next novel
(1876), is better, though the critic will hardly accord it the
pre-eminent place that it was said to hold in the mind of
its author. He called it a work of " pity, anger, and irony,"

and here he unconsciously lays his finger on its weakness. It is self-concious and self-revealing, and what it reveals is a hyper-sensitive softness and an abuse of his pathetic power greater than we shall find in his work elsewhere. The central figure is an illegitimate child, by turns petted and neglected by a frivolous and whimsical mother, and forced at last to struggle for existence in a world for which he had been studiously unfitted, to fall the victim of his virtues and of the meanness or thoughtlessness of others. This Jack, wrecked by natural though misdirected affection, was taken from life, and so, alas for human nature, was his mother. Most of the other characters were taken from Daudet's associates, especially those of his bohemian years in the Latin Quarter ; and so frank was the procedure that he did not always trouble himself to change even the names of those failures in literature and art, who formed a sort of mutual-admiration club, envious only of recognised talent. These *ratés* furnish the humour of the story, for here Daudet's good nature is constantly getting the better of his contempt. It is not, however, the part that is most interesting in the evolution of the author's genius or of the fiction of our generation, for here *Jack* holds a very significant place. In bringing his hero into direct touch with the sombre realities of the foundry and the stoke-hole, Daudet was the first in France to make an honest study of the great artisan class, — a very different matter from the study of pathology in low life in *Germinie Lacerteux*. There is a touch of Dutch realism in the wedding-feast at Saint-Mande and in the lives of Dr. Rivals and Belisaire, the peddler. And there is an innovation also in its stylistic technic, for here, in the description of the marine engine at Indre, are the first traces of that personification of material objects that he was to apply so effectively in *The Little Parish* (la Petite paroisse, 1895), and that has become one of the most effective devices of his friendly rival Zola. There is somewhat more development of character here than in *Fromont Jr. and Risler Sr.*, but it is not always consistent, and the plot certainly does not hold the reader and compel attention to the close as did that of the earlier novel.

Better character drawing and better fabulation than in either of the preceding novels distinguish *The Nabab*, whose characters in the main are men who were or had been in the public eye. The central figure, Jansoulet, was obviously François Bravay, who had returned to France from Egypt as the Nabab from Tunis, with wealth acquired even more dubiously, and by lavish use of money had got himself thrice elected to the French parliament from the district of Gard, as the Nabab did once from Corsica, only to find his election thrice annulled, as a useless and inopportune scandal, by the votes of men no whit better than he. This had happened in 1864, and Bravay survived in poverty and contempt the fall of the Empire, whose corruption he had understood without realising its hypocrisy. But this use of a discredited adventurer, in whose fate he discerned one of the most cruel injustices that Paris had ever committed, was not Daudet's most daring blending of history and fiction. The novel owes much of adventitious interest and no small part of its artistic strength to the skill with which he turned to account his years as secretary to Morny in his picture of Mora, whom he has surrounded with a group of easily recognisable adventurers from the strange social scum of the Second Empire. In the main he has been faithful to the spirit of history, though not of course to its letter. In Mora mercy has seasoned what would be justice to the cynical Morny. "I have painted him," said Daudet, "as he loved to show himself, in his Richelieu-Brummel attitude. . . . I have exhibited the man of the world that he was and wished to be; assured that were he living he would not be displeased to be presented thus." And as Mora was in the very letters but a thin disguise for Morny, so the men of 1877 instantly recognised Bois-Landry, Monpavon, Cardailhac, Moessard, Le Merquier, Hemerlingue, and even the servants of the original Nabab, and there were those who said that Felicia Ruys was none other than Sarah Bernhardt. Dr. Jenkins was Dr. Olliffe, though the arsenic pills belonged to another, and the account of the orphanage of Bethlehem, for which the sympathies of the Nabab were so cynically engaged, was copied almost literally from the report of a real institution founded by as philanthropic men with similar purpose and like results.

In contrast to these scenes of high life, of extravagance, frivolity, and luxury, Daudet introduces the family of Père Joyeuse, personifications of idyllic simplicity of heart and mind. But these characters also had a kernel of truth, for Daudet had met Père Joyeuse as a Communist in 1871. These scenes are not without pathos, yet they injure the book as a work of art. The grotesque has been success-fully mingled with the tragic by Shakspere and by Hugo, but sentimental pathos, however skilful, puts the reader out of touch with the impressive dignity of Mora's deathbed and funeral, with the broad fresco-strokes of the Bey's Festival, and the stern satire of Jansoulet's end. This was an artistic device brought over from *Jack*, and Daudet con-tinued to employ it later as a prudent concession, so he told Zola, to popular taste, but his contrasts grew less glaring as he grew surer of his naturalism. Yet perhaps after all *The Nabab*, for its humour and its satire, its idyl and its pathos, its exuberant picturesqueness and tragic power, is the most characteristic, if not the best, of Daudet's work in fiction.

Kings in Exile, of 1879, was a more daring venture, for it was of necessity less a product of personal observation than of current rumour and constructive imagination, such as had guided Zola in *Booty*. Hence he found it, as he says, "that one of my books that gave me most trouble to put together, the one that I carried longest in my mind, after it had appeared to me as a title and dim design one evening on the Place du Carrousel through the tragic rent in the Parisian sky made by the ruins of the Tuileries. It should be a drama of princes exiled to the gay capital by fortune or by choice, a book of modern history from the pulsing heart of life as it is, not from the dust of archives." Again all the characters were patent to every reader. The King of Westphalia was George of Hannover, his daughter was Friederike, the Queen of Asturia was Isabella of Spain, Christian was the ex-King of Naples, Axel the Prince of Orange, and Palma Don Carlos. The minor characters also, Lévis, Séphora, and others, were recognisable; the elder Méraut was Daudet's own father, and Élisée a composite of the author and an old friend. Many of the incidents also had their counterparts in the common gossip of the time, though of course all was treated with the license of poetic idealisation.

Kings in Exile marks a decided advance in the power of developing character. He had never yet shown such clairvoyant vision as in the noble tragedy of Queen Frédérique, and it is surely remarkable that a book dealing with such a subject as the crumbling of an old régime should have had such sympathetic charm as to win the praise alike of royalist and republican. Yet the book was evidently of slow and reluctant production. We feel that this is a realm of thought and interest foreign alike to the author and to us. The fabulation is perhaps closer than in *The Nabab* or *Jack*, but we miss the broad sweep of picturesque description that glorified certain pages of *The Nabab* and make chapters of *Numa Roumestan* quiver beneath the Southern sun. But in Méraut and Frédérique, in subtle psychology and development of motive, where Daudet most needed to grow and where he was still destined to make the greatest progress, this novel shows a distinct advance, that was further accentuated in *Numa Roumestan* two years later (1881).

Daudet regarded *Numa Roumestan* as "the least incomplete of all his works." It is a "Parisian drama," but its central figure is a typical son of Provence, whom men have persisted in identifying with Gambetta, probably because that statesman was as typical of the country of his nativity as Numa himself, in whom there is also a great deal of Daudet's self, though every politician of the south of France might have seen some of his features reflected there. Most of the other characters were, like Numa, "bundles of diverse sticks," the only acknowledged individual portrait being that of the tambourinist Valmajour.

The Provence of this novel contrasts curiously with that of *Tartarin* thirteen years before. It seems to have grown, as Sherard cleverly says, "naturally and morally dusty." Certainly it was not so intelligible, but possibly this was because it was more subtly profound, because he had more completely and successfully fluxed the multitude of observations that crowded his note-books and his mind. In any case the critic perceives immediately that we have no longer here a series of episodes as in *The Nabab* and *Kings in Exile*, but a closely articulated narration, in which the central interest is always the change wrought in character by the clash of Northern and Southern temperaments. From the chime of his own marriage his artist mind seems to have evolved this story of sweet bells jangled out of tune.

Because of this closer articulation there is less breadth in narration, but there is equal humour and closer analysis in the tragedy of an effervescent optimism bruising itself against the realities of life. By his facile promises, by his light-hearted thoughtlessness, Numa wrecks all who trust in him, while he rises buoyant over the sea of troubles that he has caused. It is the tragic counterpart of the comedy of *Tartarin*, and in Henriette we are shown the idyllic side of the same temperament, tragic-comic in Valmajour and wholly comic in Bompard, a figure borrowed from *Tartarin* for the occasion. Opposed to all these is Rosalie, Numa's wife and Daudet's, who sees the world with Parisian clairvoyance, but is not the happier for the vision. In its closely knit structure, in its relentless irony, this book marks the third phase in Daudet's development, from romanticism through external realism to the psychic realism of the interplay of character and environment.

If there were any doubt that this cardinal place belongs to *Numa Roumestan*, *The Evangelist* (1883) would remove it, for here the closer structure and the psychic preoccupation leap to the eye. The general title is now changed. This is no longer a "Parisian drama," it is an "observation;" that is, it purports to be a psychic study, not a novel of action, though indeed the story pulses with vigorous movement, and seems written, as we know that it was written,

under the pressure of indignation and moral revolt, realising
to a wonderful degree the rare combination of " intensity of
feeling and a sage simplicity of execution." Its pathetic
heroine was a teacher of Daudet's son Léon, and in a
letter to the *London Times*, published just after the appearance of the novel (February, 1883), we shall find that his
Éline was not the only victim of the lust for spiritual domi-
nation deliberately exploiting the morbid pathology of
religious enthusiasm. Never has Daudet been so pessimistic as here. No form of Christian idealism escapes his
satire. The love of God becomes in Madame Autheman
the cloak of a domineering ambition, in Mlle. de Beuil it
masks a morose joy in cruelty, in Éline it demands a
deliberate sacrifice of human affections for a morbid ideal,
in Henriette it involves a sapping of character. Force
rules in this spiritual world as relentlessly as in the material
one. Weak and simple natures yield or are crushed. All
who have won sympathy end by claiming pity. There is no
novel of our day in France where cant and hypocrisy have
been so cauterised.

Sapho, which followed *The Evangelist* in 1884, is the last
novel that Daudet wrote before disease laid its racking
hand on him and caused some natural flagging in his intellectual powers. Edmond de Goncourt regarded it as the
author's " most complete, most human and beautiful story,"
and most French critics agree with him that it is at least
the work of greatest power and that most likely to survive.
It certainly has had the largest sale, but, though it is written with great and sustained strength and a realism that is
often almost pathologic, it is not agreeable reading. *Sapho*
is the *femme collante* (Anglo-Saxons will not need the
word while they can avoid the social abuse that it repre-

sents), who clings with the desperation of a last love to the rather weak-willed Gaussin. She loves him after her kind, in an animal way, and he is tortured in spirit by jealousy of her more than dubious past, by the fascination of her presence, and by the impending wreck of his fortunes and his career. " To his sons when they are twenty," Daudet commends this story of facile love that saps the forces of heart and mind. His passion past, Gaussin tolerates Fanny Legrand, then clings to her, then shrinks from her, repudiates her, marries another, yet only to find old custom stronger than new duty. But when he returns to her after this supreme sacrifice the ghastly truth is at last forced on him that for such as she there is no moral obligation but the pursuit of a whimsical fancy, capable only of social disintegration and evil. Critics call this narrative " eternally true." For the sake of French manhood one hopes it is not. In any case Daudet has treated his subject with the relentless seriousness of a demonstrator and has relieved his satirical analysis with no touches of lighter humour, such as sparkled the next year in *Tartarin on the Alps* (1885).

Of the novels of Daudet's decadence from *The Academician* (l'Immortel, 1888) to the posthumous *Head of the Family* (Soutien de famille, 1898), we are content to speak more briefly. The former is primarily a satire on the French Academy and on myopic scholarship, obviously forced but with a lightness of humour and occasional pieces of epic breadth in narration that dispose the reader to condone an action as inexplicable as it is cruel, and a satirical imputation as improbable as it is unjust. *Rose and Ninette* (1891) invites attention to the effects of divorce, especially on parents and children, and *The Little Parish* (la Petite paroisse, 1895) is a study of various phases of jealousy, in which Daudet adopts the symbolic method of Zola and Ibsen, making the rhythmic recurrence of the parish church mark each stage of an action over which it seems to preside, and, what is perhaps more significant, paying his tribute to the evangelical ethics of Tolstoi, before which the stern, pessimistic retribution of the older naturalists degenerates into sentimental pity and pardon, marking thus the anemia of the will that is a characteristic note of the present waning of naturalism, and so seriously marring the psychology of the story.

This was the last novel published during Daudet's life. Since 1885 he had been an intense nervous sufferer and a victim of an insomnia that yielded only to chloral and morphine, so that he often passed months without touching a pen, with alternating periods of mental activity and dead calm, the latter increasing in length till death brought sudden relief at last. This fact will explain the comparatively insignificant production of these later years. He left, however, two posthumous volumes, *La Fédor* and other stories, which, when they are not trivial are saturnine, and *The Head of the Family* (Soutien de famille), decidedly his best story since *The Evangelist*. It is in part, not the best part, the story of a modern Hamlet, whose mind is lamed by responsibilities greater than he feels himself able to bear, and lamed also by the acquiescence of mother and brother in his assumed superiority. In part, and the best part, the book is a bitterly sarcastic picture of French political life, in which characters are taken frankly from reality, even to the President of the Republic, in whom he sees the final flowering of the modern political temperament, an unctuous sentimentality and false fellowship, masking heartless and unscrupulous ambition. This study of "contemporary manners" bears no marks of incompleteness or of failing strength. It is Daudet's literary testament, a Parthian shaft at political hypocrisy, sent true and strong from the grave.

Daudet was a literary artist by instinct rather than by reflection. A beautiful talent, a little superficial in its subtlety, without the forceful virility of Balzac or Flaubert or Zola. He charms, not by ordered masses, but by his variety and suppleness. Even in the novels there is a constant shifting of scene, and the single volume of *Letters from my Mill*, regarded from this point of view, shows an astonishing variety of legend and revery, of symbolism and farce, of sentiment and dramatic intensity. His work proceeds less from thought than from impressions that he received with a definiteness and guarded with a permanence that are alike remarkable. Hence he succeeds best with superficial natures, and where the character cannot be perceived but must be thought out in its complexity, he will exhibit but a single side of it. His Nabab could never make a fortune, his Mora could never govern an empire, nor his Numa a republic. We are more satisfied with Tartarin, Risler, Méraut than with these, and in general more content with the women than with the men. The masculine Mme. Autheman may elude him, but Sidonie and Fanny, Désirée and Aline and many another, even to the posthumous Fédor, are not likely to slip from the memory. Perhaps it is not unjust to say of him, with Doumic, that he lacked wide experience, deep insight or keen interpretation of life, but yet made the best possible use of an acute sensitiveness, of a nervous temperament and delicate imagination, as well as of a very beautiful artistic nature, and so gave of the society in which he lived the broadest, most varied, and most faithful image, while he left behind him the fragrant memory of a noble and sympathetic character.

The young Daudet possessed by nature grace, charm, and pathos, qualities natural to that sunny South around which his humour plays so kindly in Tartarin, so sternly in Numa. The war added seriousness to these qualities and turned playful wit to bitter satire. But he brought to this naturalistic temper the mind of an idyllic poet, so that, as Zola says, " his mind gallops in the midst of the real, and now and again makes sudden leaps into the realm of fancy, for nature put him in that border land where poetry ends and reality begins." On this poet's vision in Daudet it is well to insist, for it gives his work the appearance of a kindly optimism. Even in evil he prefers to see the ridiculous than the base, and hence it is that his profoundly earnest satire still retains much of the irony that characterised his gentler moods. This irony is one of the most evanescent of literary forms, it is hard to define it or its charm, but it is clear that it leads Daudet to greater subjectivity, to more expression of personal sympathy for his characters than strict naturalism admits.

Daudet's style is that of an impressionist. In his earliest work there is conscientious elaboration in structure and phraseology ; later, and in longer works, his care is rather for the single episode than for the whole, and he allows himself liberties in syntax and vocabulary if by these artifices he can fix a passing shade of thought. His work, at least up to *The Academician*, shows increasing limpidity and firmness in diction, and wise restraint in the use of the sources of emotion. While refusing " to consume himself

sterilely for years over one work," like Flaubert, lest by
elaboration he should lose sympathy with his theme and a
straightforward natural diction, yet he was never hasty, but
wrote every manuscript thrice over, and would have written
it as many more had he been able. Thus he attained, at
his best, a style that is at once classic and modern, artistic
without artificiality. His slight, rapid, subtle, lively, suggestive phrases form a curious contrast to the methodical
up-piling of details that marks the vast architecture of
Zola's fiction. He is more spontaneous, delicate, personal,
idyllic ; Zola is a more conscious objective artist, and so
more epic. Both have a vein of romanticism, but in
Daudet the idealisation is toward good, in Zola toward evil.
Both have a noble earnestness, but Zola's indignation has
more tonic virility, Daudet's a more persuasive warmth,
making him, as even captious critics admit, the most lovable writer of his generation.

CHAPTER XV

THE rise and culmination of the romantic movement from 1821 to 1830 had been peculiarly favourable to the birth of literary talent. That of the bourgeois monarchy was much less so, counting no names of the first rank save Daudet and Zola. The romantic movement was gradually spending its force during the thirties, and the novelists born during that time, with the sole exception of Fabre, belong to the class of mildly romantic story-tellers, such as Malot and Theuriet, or of idyllists like Glouvet or sensationalists like Gaboriau. This class is always with us and appears also in the early forties with Claretie and Gréville, to be continued and indeed to reach its typical expression in Ohnet, born at the very close of our period. Meantime, however, with 1840 the new generation who were to take up the work of Flaubert and the Goncourts come on the stage and forerunners of the psychologist school begin to appear, as well as some representatives of Renanism in fiction. We shall do well to consider first the belated offsprings of romanticism, and then to turn to the heralds of change.

Among mere story-tellers a high place belongs to Hector Malot, whose first novel, *Victims of Love* (Victimes d'amour, 1864) promised more strength than his rapid production has since realised, though his *No Relations*

(Sans famille, 1878) has had sufficient force and pathos, joined to a delicate grace of description, to carry this story of Rémi, the foundling and juvenile Gil Blas, into nearly every language of Europe. Malot's central characteristics are his serious probity, his opposition to a false religiosity, and a sympathy with vague humanitarian ideals, all of which endear him to the middle class. He is rude and severe at times, but he is always clean and resolutely optimistic. Typical of his sixty-five volumes are *Romain Kalbris* (1869), *Baccara* (1886), *Conscience* (1888), and *Justice* (1889).

Take the characters of Feuillet without their tragic intensity and treat them with a frivolity akin to their own and the result will be the novels of Gustav Droz, who in his *Papa, Mama, and the Baby* (Monsieur, Madame, et Bébé, 1866) has caught the tone of society in the Second Empire — that society which, as Zola says, played with amiable vices, as the eighteenth century did with pastoral life — perhaps better than any other. His best work is *Around a Spring* (Autour d'une source, 1869), but here, as always, his psychology is weak and his gay irony is stronger than his daintily artificial sentiment.

Closely allied to Droz, at least in his fiction, is Ludovic Halévy, of whom the universally read *Abbé Constantin* (1882) is less characteristic than the three volumes in which he pursues the fortunes of the Cardinal family (Monsieur et Madame Cardinal, 1873, les Petites Cardinal, 1880, la Famille Cardinal, 1883), whose head, that "corrupt puritan Prudhomme of vice," is the incarnation of the dry rot that Sedan revealed. In the early part of *Criquette* (1883), the story of a fair, bright, and impulsive gamine of Belleville, there is an admirable picture of life behind the scenes in a small theatre, but the close of the novel is commonplace and unworthy of the beginning, and the rest of Halévy's fiction does not rise above mediocrity.

The years of the apogee of the romantic drama, 1830–1836, saw also the birth of two men who infused its spirit into the romantic novel long after it had ceased to haunt the stage. Richebourg, who was born in 1833 and died early in 1898, has probably had more readers than any other novelist of France. He was for years the favourite feuilletonist of the penny papers, furnishing by the yard fiction of manifold mediocrity, from the sensationalism of Ponson du Terrail to the sentimentally pathetic narrative whose argument, though it run through four volumes, may be infallibly summed up in the lines, —

> "Marion pleure, Marion crie,
> Marion veut qu'on la marie."

Against this perpetual "weeping of Margery" a stand was made for a time by Émile Gaboriau (1835–1874), whose novels of crime and its detection have given him a European reputation as the reviver, if not the inaugurator, of a widely popular though inferior genre. He has no knowledge of character, no grace of style, and there is spinning of "copy" even in the best of his novels, *The Widow Lerouge* (l'Affaire Lerouge, 1866) or *File* 113 (Dossier 113, 1867) ; but his popularity is perennial, and even the best of his imitators, such as Boisgobey, have quite failed to catch his secret.

Meantime a new note, pleasing and prolonged though never strong, had been struck by André Theuriet, who sings the provincial idyl, usually of the middle class, with a smiling melancholy and dainty naturalism, never intense, but always amiable, amusing, clean, and sweet, with much facile sentiment and an occasional tragic note. Born at Marly (1833) he passed the first thirty-two years of his life in the country. His voluminous work in fiction dates from middle life and 1870. Here he holds a place quite apart, on the frontier of realism and idealism. All that is graceful, gentle, childlike in country life he reproduces admirably, but he ignores the commonplace and shrinks from crass realities and ugliness. Love is his constant theme, the sensuous instinct rather than the tender and artificial passion. It is only gradually that he has brought city and country into effective contrast, as first in *Gèrard's Marriage* (1875), and best in *Autumn Love* (1888) ; and thus by giving humour a place beside poetry he has avoided monotony in his sixty volumes to a degree that could hardly have been hoped.

Throughout, Theuriet shows an emotional temperament. His heroes are phases of himself, his heroines results of his experience. Hence they have psychic reality, though with no minute dissection or motive, just as there is no accurate description of environment. Throughout he writes as much for the ear as for the eye, in a singularly harmonious style that recalls at times Bernardin and even Rousseau, though taken as a whole his work most nearly resembles the third manner of George Sand.

Those rustic novels of the Scheherazade of Nohant were also the inspiration of Jules de Glouvet, and Paul Arène, who do for Maine and Provence what she did for Berry, Theuriet for Lorraine, Balzac for Touraine, Maupassant for Normandy, and Fabre for the Cévennes. There is no reason to dwell on either save to note that their books show a growing interest among the reading public in picturesque moral geography, and that to an increasing number of novelists Paris is no longer France.

With Theuriet one may associate the facile *raconteur* Claretie, whose best novel, *The Assassin*, dates from 1866, while his more recent work has fallen to a dreary monotony of mediocrity. On the borderland of oblivion stand also the swarming multitude of volumes by Henri Gréville, (Mme. Durand), whose sentimental sensationalism has met with much popular success, especially in her novels of Russian life, as for instance *Dosia* (1876). Nor can a materially higher rank be accorded to the fiction of Théodore Bentzon (Madame Blanc), whose interest in America has evoked perhaps an undue interest in her books among us.

A much greater art with the same mild geniality characterises the fiction of François Coppée, who is most felicitous in the half-tones of prose and knows how to be magnanimous with a delightfully naïve suavity. He is at his best in short stories of the lower middle class and of humble Parisian life, as when in *Henriette* (1889) he tells the story of the wreck of a simple heart on the rocks of social convention, or the pathetic suicide of the *Daughter of Sorrow* (Fille dc tristesse), the artist's model, whose social fall had not quenched the pure flame of her love. Occasionally the pathetic sinks to the morbidly sentimental; more often it rises to pessimism or irony. He is excellent in such sketches as *Maman Nunu* or *The Substitute* (le Remplaçant) or in such impressionist descriptions as *The Silver Thimble* (le Dé d'argent) or *Sunset* (le Coucher de soleil) or *The Medal*. He has himself well described his outlook on life as that of " a man of refinement who enjoys simple people, an aristocrat who loves the masses," and so has given a sympathetic and somewhat idealised expression of democratic realism.

In 1848, just at the close of the period we are considering, there was born a novelist whose chief interest to the critic is not in his novels, but in their phenomenal popularity. *The Iron Founder* (le Maître des forges, 1882) has sold in France more than a third of a million copies, and in its translations as many more. Several other novels by the same author, though they lag behind this, surpass all but the most successful efforts of the greatest masters of French fiction. Yet it is obvious that, for men who think, George Ohnet has no claim to be regarded as a thinker, an analyst, an artist, or even as a good story-teller, and for such readers the royal acid of Lemaître's wit long ago dissolved whatever tinsel glamour might have come from a commercial success, which shows at least that the great public knows what it wants, in France as with us, and does not wait to be instructed nor suffer itself to be guided even by a unanimity of criticism. He was created, as Lemaître says, " for the illiterate who aspire to literature." They understand him, as they do not understand in their higher purposes and art, either Daudet or Zola, who are not read by the multitude for the qualities that the critics admire, but often for those which they deplore, while the more delicate artists of fiction are not read by the multitude at all.

Ohnet's method is simple, so simple that any description of it will seem a reflection of Lemaître's masterly essay. He takes a situation consecrated by the approval of generations. He leads bourgeois virtue to a facile triumph, and lets aristocratic barriers sink before the master of modern commerce or industry. His heroes are all self-made men, and proud of their maker. His aristocracy is worm-eaten, but still worthy of the respect and ambition of snobs who are careful to acquire millions before advertising their contempt for sordid wealth in eloquent apostrophes that never materialise otherwise than in the purchase of aristocratic connections.

Those who read without thought desire a conventional story and conventional characters. Ohnet's characters, therefore, are not characters but puppets, and his denouements are of a monotonous optimism. We have the proud, virtuous, unselfish man, usually an engineer, always a romantic hero, a sort of "archangel of democracy." Then there is the heroine, also a straw figure, noble of course, proud, haughty, "incomparably beautiful," who begins by hating and ends by marrying the wealthy and heroic snob. Then of course there is the idle gentleman, seductive and impertinent, and the rich bourgeoise of amiable vulgarity, and by way of spice there is the dime-novel heroine, the gipsy-countess Sarah. The minor characters are equally conventional, and so is the society in which they move. There is no trace of psychological continuity in their outbursts of passion or magnanimity.

Given this vulgarity of situation, of character, and of style, it may be admitted that Ohnet manages his materials with a good deal of melodramatic skill and with an appearance of literary quality that might well have deceived those who were seeking to raise themselves above the level of Richebourg. Of these there are many, and to supply their wants is a legitimate commercial enterprise in which Ohnet has achieved a flattering success. His work has been the pastime of millions, but it has contributed nothing to fiction as a mode of thought or of artistic expression.

This last was the chief care of Flaubert and the Goncourts, with whom in aim, though by no means in method or result, one might class Cladel, whose fiction begins with picturesque sketches of life in Quercy, but who in his later work made himself an eccentric pupil of the eccentric Baudelaire, endeavouring to impose on prose fetters as galling as those that had maimed the classic alexandrine verse, so that his best novel, *My Countrymen* (Mes paysans, 1869–1872), has been described as "a literary jewel, curiously wrought, that one examines with more surprise than interest."

Somewhat similar is the case of Armand Silvestre, in so far as that poetic genius has not sold itself to scatology and pornography. And with him it is natural to associate Catulle Mendès, whose frivolous stories have a curious artifice of style that gives them, as some critic has said, the charm of lace, frail, light, yet exquisite in its delicate puerility. There are moments when he suggests Gautier both in his feeling for art and in his complete lack of any perception of its relation to morals, passing lightly from such toying trifles as *The Nightcap* (le Bonnet de la mariée) to what might be the deepest pathos, as *Old Blas* (le Vieux Blas, 1882), or the bitterest satire, as *The Child-Woman* (la Femme-enfant, 1891), treating all with equal care and equal ethical indifference. .

Among artists, rather than story-tellers, one may class the mobile poet, Richepin, who began his work in fiction with *Strange Deaths* (les Morts bizarres, 1876), fantastic tales in the manner of Poe, and followed these, while still in the fervour of young romanticism, with *Madame André* (1878). Then in the gipsy story *Miarka* (1883) he showed somewhat of the naturalistic influence, as later on, for instance in *The Beloved* (l'Aimé, 1893), he suggests the psychological school. But throughout he is drawn naturally to extreme, bizarre situations, preferring the strange in sentiment and the euphuistic in style, seductive but irritating in its would-be subtlety, most pleasing, perhaps, when the artist in him renders for us the mute poetry of landscape or the picturesque gipsy bands of *Miarka*.

With these artists of fiction Anatole France might claim the highest place, were it not that he seems even more bent on his philosophy than on his art, having in him, as Lemaître observes, something of Racine, of Voltaire, of Flaubert, of Renan, yet always himself, the perfection of grace, the ultimate flowering of the Latin genius. This son of a Jewish bookseller spent his childhood in suburban rambling and among the bookstalls on the Paris quais, and was associated at school with Coppée and Bourget in admiration for Aurevilly. The literary result, in fiction as in poetry and criticism, is a curious combination of folklore, hagiology, and paganism, of spiritism, mysticism, and materialism, of hedonism and kindliness, domesticity and pyrrhonism. He is a satirist and a fantasist. His fiction is only a mode of expressing his doubts or his ideas. The sole exception to this is *The Red Lily* (le Lys rouge, 1894), an imitation of Bourget and his worst and least characteristic production, if we except the youthful *Jocasta and the Gaunt Cat* (Jocaste et le chat maigre, 1879), which, in spite of outcroppings of irony and humour, is feeble, incomplete, and sensational. But already his second novel, *The Crime of Sylvestre Bonnard* (1881), showed a most gentle and large-hearted irony in its story of the rescue of a young girl from abusive guardianship and the hypocrisy of " prunes and prisms "; and the same graceful irony and sympathy with childhood pervades with its dainty moralising *The Book of Friendship* (le Livre de mon ami, 1885), recollections of the author's own youth.

In *Balthasar* (1890) one notes a growing tendency to the medieval and to mysticism, that finds its most striking expression in the prayer of the soulless and immortal Lilith, who desires "death that I may enjoy life, remorse that I may taste pleasure," and this preoccupation with medieval Christian thought finds further expression in *Thaïs* (1890), the story of a hermit of the Thebaïd, an epicurean philosopher, and an Alexandrian courtesan, a sceptical display of Christian scenery, or as it were, a page of the Golden Legend topsy-turvy, "piety of imagination with impiety of thought," a piece of Parisian platonism, truth wrapped in paradox.

The stories collected under the title *The Mother-of-Pearl Casket* (1892), and those in *St. Clara's Well* (1895), call for no special notice, but with *The Cook Shop "Queen Pedauque"* (la Rotisserie de la reine Pedauque, 1893), continued that same year in *The Opinions of Jérôme Coignard*, he makes the novel more than ever a chat, a vehicle for his open or veiled scepticism. An English critic pronounces *The Cook Shop* "a tangled medley of marvels and mysticisms, of religion and obscenity," while the characters are eighteenth-century reproductions of the ascetic, epicurean, and courtesan of *Thaïs*. *Jérôme Coignard* is called by Lemaître "the most radical breviary of scepticism since Montaigne." In the first there is little plot, in the second none at all, but both scintillate with wit and irony that play around every aspect of public and private life in a chain of sparkling epigrams. Very much the same description would apply also

to the last two volumes of this smiling philosopher's fiction :
The Elm on the Mall (l'Orme du Mail, 1896) and *The
Osier Mannikin* (le Mannequin d'osier, 1897), grouped
under the title " contemporary history," that is, a reflection
of the thoughts of typical cultured Frenchmen on matters of
general interest, with an impartial smile of ironical indul-
gence for each, that make these volumes marvels of graceful perversity.

The hedonistic element in Anatole France suggests the
robuster materialism of Juliette Adam, who boasts a paganism that " distinguishes her from other women " and has
made almost her whole work a vigorous plea that, to those
who know how to live, life for its own sake is well worth living.   Each faculty of enjoyment is made the subject of a
" moral tale."   *Païenne* (1883), the most bold, deals with
material love ; *Grecque* (1879) is a materialistic explanation
of patriotism ; *Laide* (1878), also a Greek tale, is a hymn
to physical beauty.   But, to her, Greece and Hellenism are
only a mask for a passionate protest against Christian super-
or anti-naturalism, as she would say, and so, as Lemaître
has observed, it is really a protest of the Aryan against the
Semite, an endeavour to overcome the virus of idealism with
which Christianity has inoculated the Western world.   Thus
her stories form a curious prelude to the anti-Semitic agitation that has recently taken such deep hold on the French
masses, while in literature she has found a most artistic
though dilettant successor in Pierre Louÿs, the author of
Aphrodite (1896) and of *The Songs of Bilitis* (1897).

This anti-spiritualism is on its artistic side intimately connected with the naturalistic movement that we associate with
the name of Zola, and also with the keen, though kindly
criticism of French Catholicism in the novels of Ferdinand

Fabre, which give us the most realistic pictures that we have of peasant life in the Cévennes.

Fabre, who was born in 1830 and died in 1898, studied in his youth for the priesthood, but presently abandoned this vocation for law and letters. He had already published a volume of verse, the usual preliminary libation to the French Muses, when failing health obliged him to leave Paris for the south of France and so turned the current of his whole literary life; for here he began to study with literary intent the clergy among whom he had passed his youth, to such good purpose that at thirty-two he had written *The Courbezons*, a minute analytic study that earned him from Sainte-Beuve the title of "a strong pupil of Balzac." Many novels followed, either rustic sketches, or inspired by close observation of the manners and mind of the clergy. Of these, perhaps the most noteworthy are *Abbé Tigrane* (1873), written on the eve of the death of Pius IX., and *My Uncle Celestine* (Mon oncle Célestin, 1881). The former exhibits the struggle between the secular and regular clergy in a little mountain diocese, the passionate ambition of men whom celibacy has made hard and dry, the apparent entire transformation of character when the ambition is finally crowned or crushed, and the blazing, at the close, of the fire of this same ambition in the aged archbishop at the whispered thought of the papacy. All this is admirably brought out, as well as the way in which the clergy move the laity as pawns in their game. But the full significance of the story appears first at its close, when the Italian Cardinal explains to his young pupil, who had strayed into the paths of rectitude, how though the Church cannot lie, its governors do and ought to do so, and how those traits in the character of Abbé Tigrane that had

seemed to those simple country souls a bar to his elevation
had been discerned by the shrewd men at Rome as so
many reasons for it.

My Uncle Celestine, which in many ways resembles *The
Courbezons*, shows a stronger, but a more sombre art. A
fine effect of irony is secured by putting the story into the
mouth of a boy who narrates with an instinct of good, but
without quite understanding the purport of what he tells.
The scene is once more in southern France, the date 1846,
the central figure a good but simply naïve priest, who dies
in an unsuccessful effort to cope with the soured envy of his
fellows in the minor clergy, with the selfish materialistic
jealousy of the petty bourgeoisie, with the animal brutality
and stupidity of the lower classes, and with the vice of the
parasites of the Church, the Free Brothers, and the ped-
dlers of religious objects. He is too weak to struggle with
this environment, and the few unselfish men about him are
too simple. The work as a whole is depressing, but the
character of Marie Galtier is certainly a very delicate bit of
the psychology of the humble, and some of the country
scenes of fairs and festivals, with their strange mixture of
chaffering, gluttony, and religion, are executed with really
admirable picturesqueness, without minute detail, but with a
free hand and broad effects. But of course the chief interest of the author and his greatest success is in the character
of Celestine, — so good, so unselfish, so unworldly, and
therefore, as the author seems to say, so unfit for the world
he lived in.

Many stories followed, some of them excellent and with
passages of magnificent description, such as The Beggars'
New Year in *Sylviane* (1891), but all directed, in one way
or another, against the pride and self-deception of asceti-

cism, so that the novels named may serve as typical, if not of all, at least of what is best in him.

Fabre's place is quite apart in our generation. His robust, healthy sympathy, his somewhat heavy playfulness, his subjects, and his scenes, are all his own. None has painted the clergy as he. None perhaps could have painted them as he has done, save only the author of *The Curate of Tours*. The priest in France lives a segregated life, he is different from other men, and we feel that it was the thought of an artist to give this foreign life a foreign setting. We move in a new world in his novels, a world of which we tire if we read too many of them together, but which leaves so lasting and clear-cut an impression that one finds it hard to believe that these stories of the clergy are not by a clergyman. Virtues and vices alike of that vocation seem, as it were, revealed to him. As Lemaître well says, The Vicar of Wakefield was a very worthy man ; Abbé Courbezon is a priest and a saint. There is in his imprudent charity a note of Christian sanctity that separates it wholly from philanthropy ; the simplicity of Abbé Celestine is that of the foolish that God has chosen to confound the wise, the direct result of education in a provincial seminary ; and so, too, the pride of Abbé Tigrane is peculiar to those who think they can evoke the real presence of God and turn the keys of heaven. The ambition of the clergy, too, that all-absorbing passion of power, sharpened and intensified by celibacy, is clearly seen by Fabre, though here he yields to the transcendent insight of Balzac ; and, finally, he has succeeded in showing us the result of the normal mind, untransformed by the grace of orders, in *Lucifer* (1884), whose Abbé Jourfier, a Gallican liberal, repeats, or rather anticipates, the experiences of Zola's Abbé Fromont, and

learns at Rome that there is no place for him there, that
there is no possible peace between the lay and the ecclesiastical mind, because religion is not nature and faith is not
reason.   But while Fromont takes to mechanics, Jourfier,
when he sees that the merely human virtues that he possesses are insufficient for his vocation, and that the Church
demands the sacrifice of his whole nature, finds submission
impossible and prefers suicide to revolt.   As some one has
said, " Fabre never showed better what a Catholic priest is
than in this picture of a priest who is not one."   The minor
clerical personages, too, are of great interest.   His peasants
are striking figures, and if they seem exaggerated, it is perhaps because this rude mountainside breeds intense and
violent natures, such as the Rabelaisian hermit Barnabe, or
diaphanous saints like Marie Galtier.

Therefore it is that in his rare attempts at Parisian life,
for instance, in *The Marquis of Pierrerue*, Fabre labours
so ineffectually.   His is a genius that will not bear trans-
planting.   The very style is of the sod.   It labours with
superfluous strength ; it is heavy, but it is full of an earthy
richness and healthy vigour, falling now and then to earth
but rising always from it with renewed force, for he, too,
like Antæus, is a child of nature.

Among the pioneers in this generation of what came to
be known in the next as naturalism, was Duranty, who
abetted in the early fifties the brief efforts of the elder
Champfleury before *Madame Bovary* had given respectability to the movement, and in three novels published
between 1860 and 1862 anticipated by instinct the manner
of 1880, though at the time it might have seemed that his
stories sprang directly from Diderot, as though the romantic
movement had for him no existence.   His novels were

never popular, for the style is bad and there is as little fabulation as in Diderot himself, but, as " slices of commonplace life " coming from the early sixties, they form an anachronism too curious to pass unnoticed.

The other novelists born under the bourgeois king who anticipated the manner of the imperial generation that was to follow are, so far at least as they need concern us here, the Bex brothers, who write under the name of J-H. Rosny, Ricard, Céard, and, far the most important of them all, Karl-Joris Huysmans.

Henri Céard was one of the five who joined with Zola in the naturalistic proclamation of *The Soirées of Médan*, the others being the quite insignificant Hennique and Alexis, with Maupassant and Huysmans, who were of too strong and independent mind to be disciples of any master. Céard is the most scholarly of the naturalists, a man of very refined literary taste, and of a mind too critical to admit of rapid production. His criticism, however, acted both as a spur and a restraint on Daudet and Zola, of whom he was a constant friend, and it is worth while to read his *One Fine Day* (une Belle journée), and Hennique's *Accident of M. Hébert* (1883), if only to see how far the pursuit of " reality in its nauseous platitude " can lead those doctrinaires who are not inoculated, as Zola admits that he was, with the virus of romanticism.

The early novels of Huysmans are also illustrations of the theory that fiction should be a slice of crude life, and yet from the very first the unique quality of his talent set him apart, and through whatever changes he has since passed, his isolation has been more complete than that of any other novelist of his time. His is a restless spirit, of insatiable curiosity and subtle nervous susceptibility, sincere but not always coherent, with artistic melancholy, as though he were homesick for the days of the Latin decadence. His novels picture the evolution of his soul from sensual materialism and aggressive naturalism through spiritism and satanism to a Christian mysticism and spiritualism that has in it still a curious strain of the sensual and material. His novels lose half their significance, or rather they acquire a wholly false significance, if we regard them apart from their sequence.

His work in fiction begins with *Marthe* in 1877, the year of Goncourt's *Eliza* and of Zola's *Assommoir*. His subject is of the same class as Eliza and the treatment as painfully realistic and perhaps even more sordid, so that Zola might justly claim that Huysmans was a pupil of Edmond de Goncourt rather than of himself. In *The Vatard Sisters* (les Sœurs Vatard, 1879) the resemblance to the Goncourts is even more marked in the strained, excessively coloured style, and in a Dutch minuteness and acuteness of vision that suggest the descendant of the seventeenth-century Flemish painter Huysmans de Malines, whose name he bears. He does not see types, but individuals; he does not paint life, but only a corner of it; his bindery girls, the Vatard sisters, are not typical of their class; and what is more they are not agreeable individuals to the reader. Indeed the author seems often a dilettant of moral anguish, sordid wretchedness, and contemptible vice, who sneers with a hollow laugh at his own creations. Or was he a victim of his pessimism, possessed as by a nightmare with the baseness of life?

Such at least might seem to be the state of mind that produced the abdominal preoccupations of *Knapsacks* (Sac au dos, 1880) and *Housekeeping* (En ménage, 1881), a cynical commendation of marriage. So, too, the volume of stories under the title *Down Stream* (À vau l'eau, 1882) has earned an unenviable eminence for the nauseating minuteness of its description of the dishes displayed in the windows of cheap restaurants, side by side with Zola's similar stylistic feat, the "symphony in cheeses" of *Parisian Digestion.*

It is with *Topsy-Turvy* (À rebours, 1884), that Huysmans first turns from description of cross-sections of life under a Dutch microscope to introspection, and awakens in the reader a strong curiosity, if not interested sympathy, in the psychic condition of the author. In this prose poem of neurosity, that has been called a "complete course in intellectual voluptuousness," we see him turning in fierce desperation from materialism to a kind of frenzied spiritism. Goethe shrewdly remarked the inconsistency of real naturalism with pessimism, and this is what Esseintes, who doubtless is Huysmans himself, is here experiencing. His pessimism is driving him, as it did Baudelaire, "to the bottom of the unknown to find the new." He tells us how "all that transfigured or deformed reality enchanted him," how in eager search for unreal pleasures he sought elaborate artificiality of sensations, till he became at the close "an unbeliever who would fain believe," the influences of the Jesuit education of his youth voicing themselves in the sceptic's prayer: "Lord, have pity on the Christian who doubts, on the unbeliever who wills to believe, on the criminal who embarks alone at night under a sky no longer lighted by the consoling torches of the old hope."

Surely here is a most radical and interesting experience in psychical development, and every novel that follows marks a new step in this evolution and adds new interest to our study of Huysmans. It is interesting to note also that *Topsy-Turvy* coincides in date with the first novel of Bourget, so that 1884 may mark for us the advent of the so-called psychologic school, or better, the transformation of an external into a psychic naturalism, though Huysmans is with rather than of this new company. His place is as much apart here as it had been with the followers of Zola.

For a time the effect of the state of soul indicated in *Topsy-Turvy* was to slacken production. *At Anchor* (En rade), that followed in 1887, may well have been written before *Topsy-Turvy*, or in a moment of reaction, for it is nearer his old position. But both this and the short stories collected under the title *A Dilemma* (un Dilemme, 1887) are insignificant, and it is in *Beyond* (Là-bas, 1891) that we first note an obvious advance, though by a spiral that carried him downward; for here a dilettant pessimism has led him through morbid brooding on the diabolical monstrosities of the medieval Gilles de Rais into an endeavour to decide the contest within him between lust and dyspepsia by experiments with astrology and satanism.

Beyond opens with a literary profession of faith. He forswears naturalism in literature and life, for he finds that Zola is incarnate materialism glorifying democracy and having for his followers the bourgeois offspring of Homais (*Madame Bovary*) and Lisa (*Parisian Digestion*). His new hero Durtal is still Huysmans' self, and his point of view is described as "spiritualistic naturalism." "This age of positivists and atheists," he says, "has overturned all except satanism; that it has not forced back a step," for "the greatest power of Satan lies in this, that he gets men to deny him." The book, then, marks a recrudescence of the occult, a reassertion of the extra-natural, a fascinated hovering about a mystic Catholicism, sure to lead to such Christianity as is consistent with a discouraged pessimism in regard to society and the world. The book itself, however, is a distinctly disagreeable medley of medieval and modern nastiness, into which the author has emptied a barrel of notes on Rosicrusianism and demonology, forming a weltering mass fit to be the habitation of "a seraglio of hystero-epileptics and erotomaniacs."

But this book is, as it were, the hell into which Huysmans must needs descend that he might climb the hill of purgatory in *On the Road* (En route, 1896), and enter his paradise in *The Cathedral* (1897). *On the Road* is indeed, as an American critic has said, "one of the most characteristic novels of our quarter-century," and shows how much more ready the France of our decade is than that of the eighties to listen for a voice from the Beyond. It introduces Durtal in the crisis of his conversion, of his struggle of doubt for faith. It is the drama of a soul sick of sense, tired of self, with no wish to pray, yet drawn by the beauty of holiness, by the magnet of Christian art, to the Church, that "only hospital for souls." Constantly falling he stumbles on, admirably directed by Abbé Grevesin, till at last the leaven of pity ferments to a passion of sacrifice, and so brings Durtal to a dawning instinct of divine love.

This plea for the contemplative life will seem morbid and perverse to many who will admire its scholarship and its artistic appreciation. Durtal seems throughout still a fastidious eclectic hedonist, trying to reconcile faith with contempt for the faithful. There is deep converse on the "law of substitution," on sanctity and detachment from the world ; there are striking passages on the emotional effect of plain-song ; yet nowhere do we see clear and full the finger of duty, but only the reaction of an excessive and effeminate culture into a petty artistic mysticism, that last infirmity of esthetic minds who never get beyond those "brightest transports, choicest prayers that bloom an hour and fade."

There is in *On the Road* a great deal of sharp criticism of the Church, old and new, in France, and this often finds expression in words of shocking crudity that we feel to be of deliberate intention. Huysmans did not come into the Church like other men by the common door, but, as a good abbess said, "he entered it through the roof," repelled by a clergy whose ignorant obtuseness took from them "all influence over the patriarchate of souls," but attracted by the symbolic obscurities of medieval art and ritual. Durtal is still a misanthropic impressionist, who loves to despise and to hate. A long retreat among the Trappists does not restore virility to his faith, though it affords Huysmans occasion for a most living picture of a Trappist monastery, of which he had been for some time an inmate, so that it is said that all his monks, even the swineherd saint, Simeon, a modern Junipero, stepping as it were fresh out of the *Little Flowers of St. Francis*, were his friends at Notre-Dame d'Igny. Durtal's struggles here are told in a glowing style, with an almost fierce enthusiasm for the medieval thesis that faith is contagious, and that sensuous natures have the profoundest spiritual potentialities. Yet the lame conclusion of all is that Durtal leaves the Trappists "his mind undone, his heart in shreds . . . too much a man of letters to be a monk, too much a monk to stay among men of letters."

From the purgatory of *On the Road* Durtal is carried to the door of a benedictine paradise in *The Cathedral*. What he found there will form the subject of *The Oblate*, but it is reasonably certain that this "fingering of spiritual muscles to see if they are growing" will not bring a healthy growth, though it may procure a hypnotised peace for those proud and delicate spirits who claim, with Huysmans, to need a refuge in the cloister, for the soul and for art, from the moral and physical hideousness of the world. *The Cathedral* contains descriptions of wonderful beauty; but it is not for this that we dwell upon it here, but because it is a sign of the times, of an age weary of material progress, weary of all except of searching those problems of the soul that defy solution. These last novels of Huysmans are the supreme products of a morbid state of soul, of which the novelists of the next generation will give us many illustrations, as indeed, Huysmans' contemporaries in birth Ricard and "J-H. Rosny" do also, of whom it has been happily said that they throw the dry salts of Stendhal into the juleps of Feuillet, and produce pastilles, half salt, half sugar, the literature of Vichy-water, a morbid and laboured jargon of science and psychology. Of them we need speak no further, but of Huysmans it is only just to say that whatever his faults of taste, and they are many, however recondite his vocabulary, however invertebrate the structure of his narrations, yet no novelist since Bunyan has given us such a study as he, so frank and yet so subtle, of the progress of a pilgrim soul.

CHAPTER XVI

GUY DE MAUPASSANT deserves a place apart, though a minor one, among the novelists of the imperial generation, first, because he was, at least in his earlier years, the most completely naturalistic of modern French writers, in the accurate sense of naturalism, and, secondly, because he is the greatest modern master of a minor genre that is peculiarly French, the short story, which in his hands, as in that of its former masters, is not a condensed novel nor a novelette, but rather the exhibition of character through a single episode, or of the episode itself as a commentary on life.

A third characteristic of Maupassant is his style, and as this remains almost unaltered throughout his work, and is the quality in which his early training is most apparent, it naturally claims first attention. It shows the Norman, born in Lower Seine, educated at Rouen, and for ten years the favourite and almost constant disciple of Flaubert, whose hard mechanical perfection he was to carry to even higher reaches of verbal photography. The man of these early years seemed the counterpart of the style of his first story, *Suet-Ball* (Boule de suif, 1878), robust, sane, material, but with a canny, keen, and vivid vision. Flaubert had given his pupil his exact brevity, his sharp concision, something, too, of his malicious joy in the pettiness of mankind, but he had not transmitted to him anything of his own heritage from romanticism, that "splendid subdued richness and harmonious movement" of which Mr. Symonds speaks. Maupassant's style is a combination of veracity and vigour, of strength and terseness, but it lacks undertones. Whole ranges of emotion are foreign to him. His humour is often boisterous, Rabelaisian, rarely tender, and he never descends with Bourget into the "pottering and peddling of psychology." Indeed, we may go further and say that though his fiction is never without its moral bearing, he begins by looking at life wholly from the animal side, and quite leaves the soul out of his reckoning, being even at his worst less immoral than unmoral, that is, naturalistic. So Zola, speaking at the unveiling of his monument, recognised in him "one of our own, a Latin of good, clear, solid head, a maker of beautiful sentences shining like gold, pure as the diamond, . . . a child of the great writers of France, a ray from the good sun that fecundates our soil, ripens our vines and our corn. He was loved because he was of our family and was not ashamed of it, and because he showed pride in having the good sense, logic, balance, power, and clearness of the old French blood."

Allied to classic tradition in mode of thought, he is so even more in language. His vocabulary is very restricted, and he seems bent rather on making fuller use of old words than on discovering new ones. Yet his words and sentences have not only a lapidarian simplicity and clearness, they carry remarkable effects of colour and plastic in description of city and country, of mountain and sea, and in the shock of simple characters, for he avoids psychic as he does stylistic complexity. Neither is normal, and so neither is naturalistic.

But, while from first to last there is no development in technic in Maupassant, there is change in his ethics, and here first it becomes necessary to consider his work in its chronology. He began, as most French literary men have done, with a volume of verses (Des vers, 1880), printing in the same year his first and one of his best tales, a tragi-comedy in miniature, *Suet-Ball* (Boule de suif) in *The Soirées of Médan* (1880). The poems, while prevailingly sensualistic, suggesting the gambols of a lusty young bull, show here and there a tendency to analysis, and also an inclination to brooding visions of horror, that seemed at the time the sport of a sceptical dilettant of emotion, but came later to have a terrible pathologic significance. In *Suet-Ball* one notes what seems to be a similar moral dilet-tantism, a sympathy with outcasts and scapegoats as such, because they are the victims of a social morality that seems to this pupil of Flaubert purely artificial and adventitious. He is constantly dwelling with pleasure on what he calls "the capacity for sudden innocent delights latent in natures that have lost their innocence."

This story proved him a master-workman, sure of his processes and of his tools, and during the next ten years he produced an average of more than two volumes annually, embracing six novels and some two hundred and twelve short stories of most varied interest and value, though this difference is due more to their subjects than to their art. The moral change to which allusion has been made is more obvious in the novels than in the tales, and to them, there-fore, it is best first to direct attention.

The ethical position of the author of *A Life* (une Vie, 1883) is nihilism. The purpose of this novel, which Tol-stoi thought the best in France since Hugo's *Misérables*, is to bear witness to the purposelessness of suffering. With astonishing power and crudity he paints the hard, naked, sordid reality of shallow joys and bottomless sadness. Nowhere has novelist stripped and scourged so cruelly the bestial lubricity that, according to Gaston Deschamps, " hides itself, cruel and avid, under silk hats and dress-coats." He has here at the outset a disdain of humanity as strong as Flaubert's, a disdain resulting in his generation from the repeated deceptions of 1848, of 1851, and of 1870, and fostered by the scientific habit of thought, the materialistic determinism of Taine. " He came into the world," says a French critic, " just at the time when most of the dreams and mirages were being extinguished that till then had embellished human life ; he underwent the oppression of so many experiments, of so many acquired notions, of such prodigious labour ending in the eclipse of the ideal and a tyrannous nightmare of reality. He felt the mental fatigue that followed so many generous efforts to know the nature of things, and suffered from it, more per-haps than the robust workers of our disillusions."

The futility of a life of sacrifice, as daughter, wife, and mother, of one who tries to be a little noble in an ignoble world, is unable to respect those to whom she is united, father, mother, foster-sister, husband, and son, and finds the pathetic consolation of her old age in the care of an orphan grandchild born to an inheritance of vice, — such is life's mocking irony as Maupassant sees it in *A Life ;* and there is the same moral nihilism in *Bel-Ami* (1885), a novel that recalls Marivaux's *Parvenu Countryman* and the *Perverted Countryman* of La Bretonne. All these are stories of men who use sex as a means of social advance-ment. If *A Life* was the defeat of virtue, this is the triumph of vice, and, since both are fatal products of pre-existing conditions, the author is as morally indifferent to one as to the other. He still paints life as he sees it, with the frank, bustling indelicacy of Smollett, with a robust animalism to which the individual life has no sense apart from the life of the cosmos, the sense of which is so obviously incomprehensible that he makes no effort to comprehend it.

This pessimism, even at the outset, is radically different from Flaubert's sterile contempt or from Zola's tireless social discontent. Maupassant's world-pain is mortal earnest, and during these years of literary triumph he is living as he believes, as though life were a succession of fatalities. It was not enough for him to know that the world was senseless and bad. There was in him, in spite of all and from the very first, a terror of annihilation for which he could find no anodyne. In *Bel-Ami* we have a description of the slow deterioration of a brain by a fixed idea of death. Lemaître tells us that at this time Maupassant would withdraw for months to the solitude of some country retreat or of the sea, that he would desperately attempt a return to a purely physical animal life and then seek escape from self in feverish amusements, orgies of luxury or infantile sports, " but save for the minutes when he was busy in them never did one see such impassivity in mid-festival, nor face more absent."

A Life and *Bel-Ami* were biographies treated with ironic fatalism. *Mont-Oriol* (1887) marks a change from biography to drama. It is not a complete life, but an episode in the life of a Don Juan leading to crises in the lives of two women. There are a number of good minor characters, however, and more action and bustling humour than in *A Life* or *Bel-Ami*. It shows a transition in method, and,

when compared with some short stories of the same year
and with the novel that immediately followed, it suggests
that from now on we have to deal with two Maupassants:
the one a victim of mental disease springing from morbid
speculation on the essential misery of man and nursed by
the scientific investigations by which he assisted in the corrosion of his brain; and then, beside this noble, unstrung
soul, the Maupassant of intervals of lucid calm reaching out
toward a moral ideal that still eludes his comprehension.
So there is in *Mont-Oriol* a beginning of sympathy and
therefore of ethical confusion, and this moral uncertainty is
continued and intensified in *Peter and John* (Pierre et Jean,
1888), which artistically is his best novel and shows an
almost unique power of isolating and projecting a scene,
though that is a quality that belongs rather to the short
story. Here the fixed idea that had been an episode in
Bel-Ami becomes the mainspring of the narrative. John
receives an unexpected inheritance. Peter broods in morbid jealousy till he becomes the inquisitor, the judge, and
tormentor of his mother, whom he forces at last, without a
spoken word, to confess to John the shame of his origin,
and of domestic life built upon a lie. Here more than in
Mont Oriol the author betrays his own emotion, a reaching
out for a moral basis of life. There is here, and in general
in these years, less preoccupation with sex. Love tends to
become less material, and the author's horror of loneliness
gives it sometimes, as between John and his mother, the
form of a league against the evil of life. In her " tender
shop-cashier's soul " he has drawn with sympathetic delicacy the struggle of a great sentiment in a petty nature.
He is still moving here, as in *Mont Oriol*, toward a spiritual
conception of life.

23

In Strong as Death (Fort comme la mort, 1889) and
Our Heart (Notre Cœur, 1890) there is perhaps further
accentuation of this moral unrest, while the dread of the
unknowable beyond broods over both stories and points the
way to haunting hallucination and madness. *Strong as
Death* is a book of great but uncanny power. An artist,
Olivier, has in the flush of young genius loved Countess
Anne. He is now fifty and her daughter has grown to the
age and image of the mother he had once loved. Unconsciously the new illusion of youth replaces the old love.
Countess Anne sees sooner than Olivier what is passing in
his heart, and tries with pathetic desperation to renew her
youth. He, when he perceives his true self, is as tortured
as she. Powerless to aid, they witness one another's torture, till Olivier seeks in death escape from the curse of
age. The novel is highly romantic in subject, intensely
realistic in execution. These are every-day people, who do
what many do, yet perish in despair of life and love. The
book is a power, but for ill, because Maupassant has infused
in it the contagion of his own perturbed spirit. He was
struggling to light but sinking into darkness.

In *Our Heart* the struggle and the submerging is nearly
completed. The mind from which the ideal had been
driven, the swept and garnished house of his nihilism is now
possessed by evil spirits. Nature is herself no longer true.
His hero feels, like the heroine of his *Useless Beauty*
(l'Inutile beauté, 1890), " suddenly by a sort of intuition,
that that being (the lady of his choice) was not merely a
woman destined to perpetuate the race, but the bizarre and
mysterious product of all our complex desires amassed in
us by centuries, turned from their primitive and divine end,
erring toward a beauty half-seen, mystic, and incompre-

hensible." There are in *Our Heart* as beautiful pages of natural description as Maupassant ever wrote, but we feel that, for his sake and ours, it was time that the curtain should fall. This work is no longer un-moral, it is, like Baudelaire's *Flowers of Evil*, immoral, monstrous. He is haunted by evil in all that he tries to depict as good. Uncertain ideals have replaced a solid and sufficing materialism with its confident proclamation of Art for Art, and this cannot but be fatal to any wholeness of literary impression.

That moral disintegration would naturally be much less marked in the short stories, which in the nature of the case may represent only a phase or passing mood of the author's mind. Here we shall find at the outset work that might have been done at the end, and in the last volume tales that would not have surprised in the first, though, if we take the general impression, *Le Horla*, of 1887, and all the collections that follow it, will be found to differ materially from all that precede. Knowing what the novels have taught us, it is possible to corroborate it from the tales, but it is not necessary to do so and more is gained by considering them without regard to their chronology.

It is these short stories that made his fame, and it is they perhaps that will longest preserve it. Men who read *Suet-Ball* in 1880, or *Tellier House* (la Maison Tellier, 1881), or *Miss Fifi* (Mademoiselle Fifi, 1883), and the stories bound with them, felt here in a form thoroughly modern the renascence of a spirit as old as French literature. Maupassant offered, says a French critic, "the singular phenomenon of a sort of primitive classic in a period of aging, decrepit, artificial literature. Ignorant alike of the artistic transpositions of the Goncourts and the nervous trepidation of Daudet, Maupassant gushed out like a spring of

clear, sparkling water." His early training and his theory
of fiction, as developed in a preface to *Peter and John*, predisposed him to this form of composition, which has been
peculiarly French since the days when fabliaus amused the
people, while the nobles nursed their chivalry on the aristocratic epics. From the outset this genre had been
realistic, eminently unspiritual, sometimes coarse, often brutal, and such remain the characteristics of the short story as
we find it in the prose of La Salle, of Des Périers, of Noël
de Fail, and Margaret of Navarre, and in the verses of La
Fontaine, with whom Maupassant has more in common than
with the artificial *raconteurs* of the eighteenth century, or
with any of his immediate predecessors, Daudet, Banville,
Coppée, Halévy, Gyp, and the rest. There is, indeed, more
convention in La Fontaine, both in character and environment, for he has the classic desire to be universal, while
Maupassant wishes to be realistic. The scene of a tale of
La Fontaine might be in France, Italy, or Utopia; with
Maupassant we know always that we are in Normandy, or
in the Riviera, or at Paris, and that, were the scene
changed, the story must change also. And so with the
characters. La Fontaine has hardly more than eight stock
figures : the peasant, the well-to-do middle-class man, merchant or judge, the enterprising youth, the curate and the
monk, the lusty servant girl, the amorous nun, the silly
country lass, the burgher's wife. In Maupassant, on the
other hand, all are individualised. Suet-Ball is herself and
none other. All the sheep of Madame Tellier's flock are
individuals. We should feel a jar at any moment if the
acts of one were attributed to another. But in general the
subjects are the same, and the point of view is the absence
of any moral law whatsoever.

Of course an immediate result of this naturalism is a frankness of speech regarding things that Anglo-Saxons are agreed had better not be mentioned. No doubt, too, there are people who read Maupassant as pigs root for truffles ; and they will find what they look for, though he did not put it there for them, but simply that he might paint a bit of life as he saw it, with a sensuous preoccupation that, as moralists long ago observed, implies always a certain moroseness, which in him finds vent usually in tales of Norman brutality, bestiality, and egoism, while he pours his contempt on the conventional morality of society in tales of Paris, and chooses the war of 1870 to show, not the virtues of racial solidarity, but the unchaining of the beast that seems to him to lurk even in the most peaceful natures. The humour of the stories in lighter vein is dry, ironical, based on a grotesque contrast between human nature and its ideals. Very rarely at the outset we get a breath of airy cheerfulness, as in *Simon's Papa*, and occasionally there is already the note of despair and suicide, as in *Madame Paul.*

Maupassant's first year of publication will thus illustrate all the tendencies that we shall find in his later volumes, except the story of psychological analysis that shows itself first in *Monsieur Parent*, of 1884, and the rare elegiac notes as in *Menuet*, of 1883. Any effort to classify Maupassant's tales is sure to satisfy no one, least of all the classifier. Yet if we bear in mind the dates of the several volumes and classify less by the externals of situation — distinguishing, for instance, tales of Normandy, of Parisian aristocracy or clerks, and of travel — than by the outlook on life that the tales show, we may reach some suggestive results, though within these limits it is possible to allude only to the best.

Of the tales thus classified, the smallest group is that of hearty, bluff, good-humoured cheer. There are not more than a dozen of these in all, none of them written after 1886. Typical of this tone is *Simon's Papa* (le Papa de Simon) or *The Ideas of the Colonel* (les Idées du colonel). The stories of this type are sound and healthy, and nearly as much may be claimed for the more numerous narratives of pathos and elegy, which are rare before 1884 and found chiefly between 1886 and 1889. *Miss Harriet* and *The Baptism* in the same volume (there is another story with a like title) illustrate this division. There is a dainty elegiac note in *Mademoiselle Perle*, an infinite sadness in *Clochette*, and a strange exotic languor in *Châli*. In this direction his first attempts, and indeed the only ones before *Miss Harriet*, were two efforts to catch the tone of eighteenth-century sentiment, *Menuet* and *The Bedstead* (le Lit).

Many times more frequent than either of these modes of feeling is irony, taking on protean forms, among which it is convenient to distinguish the whimsical, the satirical, and the cynical. *The Umbrella* (le Parapluie), or *Denis*, or *André's Illness* (le Mal d'André), will suggest these at their best, but they are capable of descending easily to the vulgarities of the smoking-room through such dubious tales as *Decorated* (Decoré) or *Ça Ira* to the far from dubious *Bolt* (le Verrou). Occasionally, as in *In the Woods* (Aux bois), or *Regrets*, this group verges on the preceding, but there is always here a morbid pessimism, a contempt of human nature, that was absent from the former group. The stories of this type are distributed about equally through the decade of Maupassant's activity, and amount to about a seventh of his entire production.

This irony passes easily into satire, bitter, as in *The Heri-*

tage or *Abandoned* (l'Abandonné), recklessly contemptuous
of social conventions in *Imprudence* or *The Picnic* (la
Partie de campagne), or mocking them with a sardonic
smile in *Suet-Ball* (Boule de suif), *Tellier House* (la
Maison Tellier), and *The Unblessed Feast* (Pain maudit), or
with rollicking humour, as in *The Rondoli Sisters* (which,
by the way, was founded on the personal experience of a
novelist whose work we have still to consider), or with
Rabelaisian gaiety in *Madame Luneau's Lawsuit* (le Cas de
Mme. Luneau), or with what we must call cynical immorality in *Joseph* and *Saved* (Sauvée), or with socialistic sympathies in *The Vagabond*, or with cynical lack of patriotism
in *A Coup d'État*, or with sad discouragement in *Hautôt père
et fils* and in the longest and one of the most exquisite of all
the stories, *Yvette*. This group counts rather more than a
seventh of the whole, with more masterpieces than any
other, and they are distributed quite evenly through the
decade.

We come now to a long series of tales intended to illustrate the almost incredible egoism and miserly meanness of
the French, especially the Norman peasant, or even of the
bourgeoisie. These stories are so painful in their sordidness that it may suffice to name *In the Fields* (Aux champs)
or *At Sea* (En mer), *Reveillon* or *Uncle Julius* to suggest the tone. But this sordidness readily passes into
brutality or wanton cruelty, as in such unforgetable pieces
of detestable art as *The Devil* (le Diable) or *Coco* or
Madame Lefebvre or *The Donkey* (l'Âne). It finds its
most thoughtful and cynical expression in *Père Amable* and
The Little Cask (le Petit fût), its most pathetic in *A
Farmer's Girl* (une Fille de ferme), and its crudest in *The
Sabots* and the Algerian *Mahommed-Fripouille*.

Closely allied to these tales, which count perhaps a fifth of the whole, are the stories of the Prussian war, mainly, as is natural, in the earlier volumes. In *The Prisoners* (les Prisonniers) and *Twelfth-Night* (les Rois) humour tempers horror, but in *Mother Sauvage* (la Mère Sauvage) and *Saint-Antoine* the beast in man seems utterly unchained. There is a mordant irony and scepticism of French patriotism in *Walter Schnaffs*, which is surprising when one considers the really noble note struck in *Two Friends* (Deux amis). But the great story of this group is unquestionably *Mlle. Fifi*, whose heroine, Rachel, the courtesan redeemed by patriotism, is a decidedly agreeable variation on *The Lady with the Camellias*.

We come now to that portion of Maupassant's fiction that is at once most painful and most interesting, the forty or more stories in which pessimism reaches an intensity that was the foreboding of haunting nightmares, by which his mind was gradually shrouded in madness, to find release only in death. Already in *Madame Paul* (la Femme de Paul), in his first volume, he had exhibited sensualism leading to fatalistic despair and self-destruction, and the second volume, *Miss Fifi* contains in *Mad?* (Fou?) distinct premonitions of the author's insanity. There is nothing else of the kind in these books, however, and neither *A Son* (un Fils) nor *Fear* (la Peur) of the next are as morbid. Indeed, save for the Dantesque *Promenade* (*in* la Main gauche, 1884), it is not until we come to his sixth collection of tales (*Monsieur Parent*, 1884) that the fatalistic tone becomes strongly marked, in *The Pin* (l'Épingle) and *Little Soldier* (Petit Soldat), while there is distinct trace of mental alienation in *Solitude* and in *A Maniac* (un Fou). Then with each succeeding volume the number of such tales

increases.   Deepening gloom, preoccupation with death,
satanism, and ghostly hallucination are all to be found in
Yvette and most of them in *Miss Harriet*, and from *The
Rondoli Sisters*, of 1886, nausea at the monotony of life and
haunting terror of death becomes periodic in its recurrence,
so that we pass in chronological ascension from *He* (Lui)
to *Little Roque* (la Petite Roque), then through the terrible
and ghastly *Horla* to the obvious insanity of *Who Knows ?*
(Qui Sait?), both in collections of tales to which they give
the dominant note.

To all these tales Maupassant brings the same careful
elaboration, for in them all he was desperately seeking a
means of emancipation from self, though it is probable that
his writing hastened the progress of the disease to which
he finally succumbed.   A sensuality so profound, so earnest
and complete as that of this pupil of Flaubert implied the
dissolution of moral faith, the paralysis of will.   Many have
written in this spirit, but few have also lived in it.   None
may deny the ideal with impunity.   Others have toyed
with pessimism, Maupassant was its victim.

CHAPTER XVII

IT is curious to note that of the writers whom we may classify as belonging by birth to the Second Empire, the two most distinguished, Maupassant and Loti, were born, as were Gyp and Rabusson, before the *coup d'état* and Bourget very shortly after, while the remaining eighteen years of the empire count but seven names worthy of mention as novelists, and of these none of primary importance, unless perhaps we accept for performance the promise of Margueritte.

Of all these, Maupassant is far the greatest genius, but Pierre Loti has qualities of his own that place him much above the commonplace, though aside from the main line of novelistic development. This recently retired naval lieutenant, whose real name is Pierre Viaud, was born in the seaport of Rochelle, of Huguenot ancestry, entered the marine service in 1867 when but seventeen, and in twelve years' cruising had absorbed into his receptive nature so much of the inner spirit of exotic life that he was able with his very first venture to strike a chord that charmed the cultured public and gave him a place unchallenged and apart in his generation. The two elements of this unique chord were his power of description and his vague melancholy. Both were of peculiar quality. He had an exquisitely keen observation, but it is no photographic

description of strange horizons that gives charm to the
Constantinople of his *Aziyadé* (1879), the Tahiti of his
Marriage of Loti (1880), the Senegal of his *Spahi's Romance* (1881), the Brittany and the ocean of *My Brother
Ives* (1883), the fishing smacks and northern seas of *The
Iceland Fisherman* (1886), the Algeria of *The Kasbah*
(1884), the Japan of *Madame Chrysanthème* (1887), or
to the later impressions of *Morocco* (1890), the Syrian
Desert (1894), and *Galilee* (1895), or to the Basque
country of *Ramuntcho* (1897). The unique touch lies in
this, that to every landscape he gives an individuality and
as it were a soul. Environment seems not only to explain
but to condition character. It casts its spell around us
and gives in each case its own refraction to our ethics of
civilisation. And this fascination is increased and per-
petuated by the witchery of his vague melancholy, suggesting Chateaubriand and his René, but more sincere, more
frank and honest in its self-revelation. There are times
when, as in *The Story of a Child* (le Roman d'un enfant,
1890), he seems almost eager to show us all the steps by
which his soul was brought out of the Protestant severity
of his infancy, through the beauty of Catholic ritual and
the soothing of Catholic dogma, to the cold heights of
pessimistic doubt, to "the horrible consciousness of the
vanity of vanities and the dust of dusts." So his stories
tend more and more to become "log-books of sentiments
and feelings" interpenetrated with a hate of hyper-culture
and a longing for simplicity. "Who will save us," he somewhere exclaims, "from modern sham, false luxury, uni-
formity, and imbeciles?"

Thus it happens that he is drawn naturally to the primitive races. He is not cosmopolitan, but exotic. The

interaction of races would but tend, he thinks, to recipro-
cal deformation. He is a decadent yet a primitive, and as
the natural element of primitive natures is the picturesque,
he is far more artist than psychologist, drawn to the primitive not alone in landscape but in character, either to
the stubborn, resisting African nature and barbarism or to
the immobilized Far-East, whose wars remind him of the
days of Jengiz and Attila.

In his earlier books it is primitive types of love that
interest him : Aziyadé, in the tragic fatality of her devour-
ing passion ; Rarahu, that sweetest of moral infants cradled
in a sensuous Eden ; or the fierce sensualist Fatou-gaye ;
or the enigmatic and naïvely immoral Madame Chrysanthème ; or Gaud, the pathetic betrothed of the Iceland fisherman. Gradually, however, love yields in his mind the
first place to death. A shrinking from the thought of annihilation had possessed him from childhood, as we may see
from *The Story of a Child.* The more he loves, the more
he dreads in his discouraged pessimism ; in the *Book of
Pity and Death* (1891) his feelings escape in a cry of intense
though subdued sadness, and at last in *Faces and Things
that Pass* (Figures et choses qui passent, 1897) he has
reached the point where " the need of struggling against
death is the only immaterial reason that one has for
writing," and love is banished not only from his Annam,
but from his whole mental horizon. Resignation, pity,
intensity of feeling and of sympathy are the permanent
moral characteristics of his work.

All this work bears in it an element of morbidity, of
hyperesthesia, that makes every sensation a pain, vague
and far off perhaps, yet never absent. There is perversity even in his exotic affections, never a union of hearts,

as how should there be? For Loti has brought with him from our Western world not only the burden but the dignity of a life of struggle with nature and her forces. There can be for him no peace in Fatou-gaye's bestiality, in Madame Chrysanthème's toying with existence, nor even in the dreamful ease of Rarahu. It is as though life and nature brought to him only suggestions of sadness, as though a rational, normal happiness were contrary to some law of his nature, which in *An Old Man* (un Vieux, 1893) and *Sailor* (Matelot, 1893) utters itself in tones as plaintive and penetrating as the sighing notes of a violin.

For the instrument on which he plays contributes essentially to the charm of his art. He has made prose the vehicle of sensations that one might have thought belonged solely to music, surpassing in this the efforts of Flaubert and the Goncourts. He has, in Brunetière's words, "a singular faculty of impregnating the senses with the form, colour, even the very odour of things," and thus gives to his descriptions a vivid intensity attained by none other in modern France. And he attains this by marvellously simple means, by a direct style and a small vocabulary with never a sense of effort or of strain. Language to him is an instrument on which he plays at will. He can make it convey the most precise impression beneath which shall play the most dimly delicate suggestion, attained perhaps by some unfamiliar combination of the familiar. His is an impressionism whose virtuosity lies in its simplicity; it produces on the reader a sort of hallucination, less of a land than of a life, a mode of thought and sensation unlike any we have known. We do not so much see the Tahiti of the *Marriage of Loti* as feel its languor of gratified desires and the beneficence of its exuberant nature, "where the abundance

and continuity of agreeable sensations cradles you in an
endless dream." We carry away no defined pictures, yet
we have a very intense impression. And so to the last in
Ramuntcho and in *Faces and Things that Pass* we feel,
much more than we see, the smugglers' perils and the convent's peace and the corpse-strewn fields of Annam. The
critic who would define or describe Loti's qualities or his
charm is sure to find himself at last, like Lemaître, so much
the more incapable of rising beyond the sphere of feeling,
as he yields himself willing captive to the charm of this
mind, perhaps the most delicate sensation-machine that we
shall ever meet. He gives us a pleasure too great and
too acute, too penetrating that we should judge him, or
say too confidently that his charm is that of decadence, or
that there is in him, as he himself has said, citing lines
from Hugo's *Ondines*, something both of —

> " The sky that paints the scarcely creeping seas,
>   And bottom ooze, in dark, dull, dread repose."

Loti had no immediate literary ancestor, indeed except
in a very superficial way he has no literary ancestor at all
in France, and his art has found no imitators or pupils
worthy of the name. To return to the normal categories
of fiction, we shall find the feuilletonists best represented,
perhaps, by Maizeroy, but tending to degenerate into witty
and frivolous *conteurs*, of whom Gyp is surely queen, and
Lavedan perhaps her prime minister. His short stories, for
instance *The Upper Ten* (la Haute), have a remarkable self-
restraint of style that exactly befits his cynical morgue and
this phosphorescent reflection of aristocratic degeneracy.
They sparkle with dry wit, with a delicate yet mordant
irony. There is a savour of the old Gallic salt in Lavedan's

humour, but in the main he typifies those disintegrating forces in literature and society that found their philosophic expression in the aristocratic pessimism of Renan.

Gyp is, perhaps, even more characteristic of this deliquescent " end-of-the-century " society. Herself an aristocrat and great-grandniece of the revolutionary Mirabeau, her books are the faithful mirror of the society in which she moves, the society of Feuillet's novels a generation further advanced in light-hearted insouciance, malicious idleness, and that cynical irreverence that the French call *blague*, and that seems quite without ethical or artistic sincerity. It is literary absinthe, a charming poison, a " flower of evil," fit emblem of a social order that has outlived its usefulness, whose luxury is ever merging in corruption. Characteristic of her very numerous volumes are *Petit Bob* (1882), *Marriage* (Autour du Mariage, 1883), and *Mlle. Loulou* (1888). She published forty others in the space of thirteen years.

Dealing by preference with the same class and at first in a spirit hardly more noble, is Paul Bourget, the son of a professor, who began life as a journalist and in 1883 won notice by a volume of critical essays in which he seemed to take himself so seriously that he induced others to take him so. He is the self-proclaimed herald of a new school in fiction, the psychologists, who undertook to analyse the complicated sensations of those who could afford to have them, and so delighted both them and those who aspired to be received in their charmed circle. " You cannot make psychology easy reading," said Cardinal Newman, and the masquerade of science, falsely so called, that Bourget obtrudes in his narratives is tedious reading for healthy minds. It has been happily described as " a seductive if somewhat sickly product of the hot-house of an outworn civilisation," for it is in no sense a plant that has its roots deep in the national soil, while in the author himself there has still remained a little of what Augier called " the melancholy pig."

He brought to his fiction a studious mind, an analytic disposition, reflective rather than creative, supple rather than strong, subtle rather than profound, and somewhat morbidly interested in the mysteries of moral life.   His style was like his mind, suave, graceful, elegant, but extremely uneven, now simple as Mérimée, now mannered as Marivaux, careless to the verge of a dandified solecism, but capable of rising on due occasion to a terse and nervous concision.   He describes himself as a moralist of the decadence, a moralist not a reformer.   The world to him was out of joint, introspective, analytic, lustful, faithless, shallow, and dilettant.   It was as though his intellect and moral fibre had been blighted by the upas shadow of Renan's scepticism.   His diagnosis of moral anemia might be brilliant, but he had no tonic remedy.   Such was the Bourget of the *Essays*, in which he had sought to gather materials for the historian of the moral life of contemporary France, of which the dominant note seemed to him " the pessimism in the soul of contemporary youth."

Thus disposed and thus qualified, Bourget published in 1884 *The Irreparable*, possibly the most pretentiously analytic and perversely morbid of his works, whose hero is a nasty Valmont, borrowed from Laclos, and the heroine a person incapable of either enjoying or bestowing happiness, who shoots herself at the close, as she sensibly remarks, " for nothing."   The psychology of the tale is as unnatural as it is laboured, and its chief merit is its brevity.

It came, however, at an opportune moment, just as the class to which he appealed were beginning to turn from naturalism and to seek a new shibboleth. The people that he painted here, and to whom he continued to appeal for the next ten years, are not typically French at all, but a narrow segment of society that by inoculation with Jewish and cosmopolitan ideals has become denationalised. His scene shifts easily from Paris to England or to Italy, and indeed his characters are so utterly preoccupied with themselves that they seem as much at home in one country as another.

The morbid futility of *The Irreparable* pervades *A Cruel Enigma* (Cruelle énigme, 1885). The " enigma," is the perplexity of Herbert, whose love could not redeem a vicious mistress, on the discovery of which he " made an irremediable shipwreck of his soul," being a victim of idealistic anxiety, after the Ibsen-Tolstoi manner, for whom one feels more contempt than sympathy.

A Lover's Crime (Crime d'amour, 1886), which a French critic says should be named " Died for Nothing," takes us into a hot-house atmosphere of sensual jealousy and topsy-turvy sentiment about the " supreme beneficence of pity " and " the religion of human suffering," whose god is the familiar unholy trinity. In its morbid kind, however, this study of " states of soul " is stronger than anything Bourget had yet done, and decidedly superior to the diagnosis of a similar case in *Second Love* (Deuxième amour, 1884). *André Cornelis* followed in 1887 and closes the first period of Bourget's development. Up to this point he subordinated inner nature to environment, let his personages express their natures by their tastes rather than by their feelings, and left us exasperated by their apparent inconsistency,

24

while wearying us with details of luxury of upholstery and
bric-a-brac, of silk stockings wonderful in their variety of
weave and shade, and of spherical geometry applied to a
corsage.   He has never since repeated his former errors in
this regard, and he more than once allows his spokesman,
Claude Larcher, to mock his earlier self in *The Psychology
of Modern Love*.

With *Lies* (Mensonges, 1889) Bourget seems to attain a
clearer vision and stronger grasp of character, yet here, too,
there is far too much patho-psycho-physiology, and we
feel some debt of gratitude to the faithless Collette that she
brought the putative author of *The Psychology of Modern
Love* to an early grave.   But while in this novel the men
are little more than playthings, the women have a strong
though disagreeable individuality.   Collette is less frank, less
good-humoured than Zola's Nana, her social sister.   "There
was a cruelty in her greenish eyes, in the curl of her lip,
and a sort of hatred. . . . She loved even while she deceived, tortured, and humiliated."   Yet she is as gracious
as she is malicious and perverse.   Higher in the mental,
lower in the moral scale than Nana, she drags her lover
relentlessly down, and in *The Psychology of Modern Love*
you may see him sink out of sight if you will.   And beside
her is Mme. Moraines, the society lady, with a Madonna
face and a coquettish rosary of lies always at command ; as
perfectly corrupted as she could be, but quite unconscious
of the utter baseness into which she had insensibly drifted.
"A complicated sort of animal," says Larcher, to whom
Abbé Taconet, the still small voice of common-sense in this
psychological wilderness, replies : "Complicated !   She is
just a wretch who lives at the mercy of her sensations.   All
that — it 's just dirt."   We breathe freer for the word, but

the moral triumph of the book is with cynical selfishness. There is here something of the Mephistophelian spirit, a false note of flippant cynicism which is absent from the later novels.

With *The Disciple*, also of 1889, Bourget joins to his reaction from naturalism in fiction a reaction from materialism in morals, allying himself to some extent with the neo-Catholic movement, and in a preface making a formal attack on the scientific spirit and the philosophy of Taine, which he thinks, or affects to think, dangerous to the youth of France, whom he exhorts to be neither brutal pessimists nor disdainful sophists, nor yet cynics, who in pride of life juggle with ideas. What they are to be instead he does not yet say, and his novel, though founded on fact, is indeed a minute and accurate analysis, but a morbid and uninteresting story, too dull to be unhealthy, disarmed by its own tediousness. And the same may be said of the ten *Portraits of Women*, written at intervals since 1884 and collected this same year. They demand great effort to follow an analysis of little interest. This is true also of *Woman's Heart* (Cœur de femme, 1890), which is simply an experiment in dual affection of a lady whose affinity was "a Casal with the heart of a Poyanne," and who sought refuge from her self-tormenting folly in a convent, which to this dilettant neo-Catholic represents "the alcohol of romantic femininity."

Ten Portraits of Men (Nouveaux pastels, 1891) has for its chief contents *A Saint*, a most genuine and wholly charming story of an old monk whose other-worldliness is set off by the ferocity of a young man's precocious ambition. Bourget's touch has never been so exquisite as here, certainly not in *Cosmopolis* (1892), that "romance of inter-

national life," in which he proclaims his adhesion to a
kind of Catholicism that is more curious than Christian,
and savours of the sensuous mysticism of Huysmans. Yet
Cosmopolis is the best told of all Bourget's novels. It is
less morbidly analytic, a study of races rather than of individuals, of French, English, American, Polish, Italian, and
Creole-plus-negro traits, which in Bourget's theory persist in
spite of environment, and are certainly drawn with great
cleverness and insight, and share in an action of unusual
interest and life.

It is strange that while able to do this work Bourget
should have been willing to write *The Promised Land*
(Terre promise, 1892), a dreary piece of psychic vivi-
section and self-torture that could interest only an alienist,
and comes to a most lame conclusion. Yet in this painful
narrative are imbedded some admirable descriptions of
scenes on the Riviera, and some traits of child life that
are really charming. The novel marks, however, the
beginning of Bourget's decline. He has never since
attained the level of *Lies*, *A Saint*, and *Cosmopolis*. *A
Scruple* is an artistic study of a subject quite unworthy of
art, and the coarse *Tragic Idyll*, with its moral inanity and
complacent pretence at religion, shows a still further descent toward moral nullity and senile cynicism, from which
New Beginnings (Recommencements, 1897) and *Lady
Travellers* (Voyageuses, 1897) show no disposition to
rise, — and here therefore we will leave him.

The transitory vogue and talented snobbery of Bourget
naturally suggested imitation. Older men, such as Ricard
and " J-H. Rosny," set their sails to the new breeze, and
among the younger devotees of literary dandyism Rabusson
has at least a curious interest for the diligence with which

he treats the subjects of Feuillet with the methods of Bourget, and spices the ragout with Crébillon *fils*. He has published more than a score of novels, of which perhaps the best is *The Adventure of Mlle. de Saint-Alais* (1885). His most recent work, notably the *Chimeras of Mark Lepraistre* (1898), is beneath serious criticism. And one is tempted to say the same for the entire work of Paul Hervieu, who satirizes society in a dozen novels with what a decadent critic calls "happy cruelty," that is, with perverse keenness and fundamental untruthfulness, of which *The Armature* (1897), is a recent and sufficient example.

A more subtly delicate genius is that of the Swiss Rod, a critic of much sanity, whose fiction up to 1890 is distinctly naturalistic in tone, but passes in *The Sacrifice* (1892) under the influence of Russian mysticism, and maintains a strain of exquisite melancholy in *Michel Tessier* (1894), and *The White Cliffs* (les Rochers blancs, 1895), all studies of misunderstood feminine virtue struggling against narrow or brutal virility, and attaining the misery that, according to Rod, is the normal reward of virtue on earth. Very recently he seems to have shaken off this nightmare, and in *Above* (Là-haut, 1897) has given us a fine picture of Alpine life, and an effective contrast of petty interests and vast environment. He will always be analytic, but it is as though the Alpine air were clearing his brain from the taint of Bourget's dilettantism.

A greater critic, but a much less successful novelist than Rod, is Jules Lemaître, of whose *Sérénus* (1886) it has been said that the hero is a saint whose tombstone is his greatest virtue. His *Ten Tales* (1889) are projections of the critic's spirit into the realm of imagination, and *The Kings* (les Rois, 1893) is a modernized *Kings in Exile* freshened up with dashes of recent scandal, and spiced with Luise Michel and Prince Krapotkine.

Another novelist, to be named less for performance than for hereditary claim to genius, is Léon Daudet, son of the great novelist, and himself author of several novels remarkable for vigour and action, but bizarre in conception and uncertain in ethics. The most striking of them is probably *The Ghouls* (les Morticoles, 1894), an attack on experimental medicine with which his father, to judge from his posthumous *At the Salpetrière,* would have sympathised. Thinking with Rabelais that science without conscience is the ruin of the soul, he abhors Renan and all his works. Curious, too, is the extreme individualism and the utopian or rather anarchistic politics of *The Black Star* (l'Astre noir, 1893).

This plea for egoism leads us naturally to the self-proclaimed apostle of that creed, Maurice Barrès, whose first book appeared under the sponsorship of Bourget, on whom he has bestowed all flattery but that of imitation. For the early volumes of Barrès, *Under the Eye of the Barbarians* (Sous l'œil des barbares, 1888), *Bérénice's Garden* (le Jardin de Bérénice, 1891), and *A Free Man* (un Homme libre, 1889), were so uneven in style and so obscure in substance that he affixed to the last of them an essay of fifty-six pages to explain his explanation of egoism as a working rule of life. And yet the observer of the signs of the times in letters will note in Barrès one of the first conscious efforts in the generation that felt most strongly the influence of Renan to throw off that moral lethargy without returning to the outworn determinism of Taine or to the naturalism of Zola.

For if Barrès is to be taken at all he must be taken seriously. The nickname Mademoiselle Renan given him by a Parisian jester is both shallow and false. Nor need we follow the critics in setting persistently the mark of irony on all his doings, literary or political. Perverse and over-subtle in his idealism he has ever been, but there is no fear that we shall be our own dupes if we hold him serious and earnest always. His early novels are hard reading. They have never been widely read, but they render better than anything else the state of soul of a large class of over-civilised French youth, repelled alike by the altruism of the neo-Catholics and by what they are pleased to call the bankruptcy of science, that can but grope where they would have it leap like Euphorion to meet Euphorion's fate.

Barrès's first three books are metaphysical autobiography. He compares them himself to Goethe's *Truth and Fiction*. "All in them is true, nothing exact;" "They are not psychology, but spiritual memoirs," he explains. Their purpose is to define the ego, to justify its cult, to show how it must be daily recreated and directed in harmony with the universe. Not as though this cult were a finality; "Negation has not yet finished its task," but it is "the best waiting-ground." "Why should not a generation disgusted with much, perhaps with everything except playing with ideas, try metaphysical romance?" So in his first volume he describes "the awakening of a youth to conscious life, first among books, then among urban brutalities." The second recounts the experiments of the hero Philippe, who by striving always to be ardent yet clear-sighted grows to be "a free man," and so first becomes ready for action. "It is we who create the universe. This is the truth that impregnates each page of this little work. . . . Let each develop his own ego, and humanity will be a beautiful forest, beautiful in this, that all, trees, plants, and animals, develop freely there, grow according to their nature." Thus in Barrès fiction becomes the handmaid of psychology, with whom in Bourget she had claimed a nominal equality. It is a curious witness to the disorientation of an old civilisation, in which cynical democracy mocks the sensitive delicacy of the over-refined, that a considerable number of young talents befuddle their brains for a time with such social metaphysics before clarifying them by work, which is the ultimate though somewhat ironical teaching of these volumes. For the *Spiritual Exercises* of Loyola and retirement in a Lorraine hermitage lead to the conclusion that the pursuit of wealth is "the asylum where spirits careful for the inner life can best await" some organisation to combat the suppression of the ego; and so Barrès's hero applies for a license to open a suburban hippodrome.

No doubt much in these volumes is due to a morbid desire of singularity and French love of system. When he escaped from these bonds, Barrès showed even in these early novels remarkable power of irony, directed especially against Renan, exquisite feeling and sympathy in the pages devoted to Hypatia, and beautiful descriptions of Lorraine landscape. We are constrained often, as we read, to exclaim with his Seneca, "Qualis artifex pereo!" What an artist, and yet how sure of perishing. For it is the spirit, not the art, that quickens, and selfish negation, if it endure for its beauty, endures only as a warning that the old culture is out of touch with the new environment. Democracy is beginning to realise itself in the life of the people, to change the popular character. In such transformations those who cannot go with the current find consolation in a perverse Pyrrhonism. This is still the position of *The Enemy of Law* (l'Ennemi des lois, 1892), but in *The Uprooted* (les Déracinés, 1897) the genius of Barrès has worked itself out of this aristocratic dilettantism to the point where he is ready to write "the romance of national energy," preaching the gospel of brotherhood as earnestly as he had done that of egoism, seeing at last that in abstraction and logical ideals there is only waste, disillusion, and disappointment; that a nation is made by its traditions, and that all growth is development. Thus Barrès offers in his way as interesting a case of physic development as Huysmans, and as significant.

In the generation of the sixties there are many men of promise whose general characteristic is eccentricity. It is still too early to characterise the talent of Ligaux, of Estaunié, of Brada, or of many others who may achieve distinction. Two only have done so, and this volume may close with an appreciation of the work of Prévost and of Margueritte.

The former is two years the younger, and now but thirty-six. His first novel, published at twenty-five, *The Scorpion* (1887), is an attempt at hereditary psychology, an analysis of the fusion in a child of a woman's religious monomania with the sensualism of a commercial traveller. The life in a Jesuit school, from which the book gets its name, is exceedingly well done and shows the influence of Zola. The close is sensational, but few novelists have entered the lists with a work of such power and promise.

In a preface to his next novel, *Chonchette* (1888), shrewdly seeking between the naturalists and the psychologists a name that should antagonise neither, Prévost posed as the originator of a romantic naturalism, with which he sought to attract those weary of aristocratic "states of

soul" and plebeian states of life. In *Chonchette* there is
less crudity, more of the idyllic, elegant, mannered, and
even sentimental, and the same might be said of *Mademoiselle Jaufre*, though there is here a luxuriant freshness of
style that reminds one of George Sand rather than of
Marivaux. The purpose of the book, like that of Feuillet's
The Dead Wife is to show that young ladies should not
have a scientific education. But in the next year, in a
preface to *Cousin Laura* (1890), he ceased to pose as a
moralist and claimed for the moment no higher aim than to
amuse the public. He avowed himself here, what he had
always been at heart, a keen mocker of society, an amateur
collector of the distortions of love ; and he illustrated this
position excellently by his next story *The Lover's Confession* (1891), a piece of sentimental romanticism in which
the hero's ideals of womanhood contradict nature so radically that the tortures of his soul, which occupy the larger
part of the book, can but lead to an impotent conclusion.

This book was followed by the very popular *Letters of
Women* (1892), which with the *New Letters of Women*
(1894), and the *Last Letters of Women* (1897), are supposed to be written by ladies and to deal with one phase
or another of love.   These tales are as graceful and ingenious as those of Maupassant, as ironically witty, and very
much more indecent. The society for and of which they
are written appears to consist solely of idle, inconsequent,
lustful, and wealthy vagrants, with the instincts and preoccupations of a cage of monkeys. Occasionally there is another strain, but the dominant note is of a sensual or
cynical perversity, illustrating most painfully the hardness
that underlies the superficial sentiment of French culture.

A Woman's Autumn (l'Automne d'une femme, 1893)

has a nobler tone. It is a story suggesting Maupassant's *Strong as Death*, of love rising imperious in a woman who can no longer inspire a corresponding passion, and is fain at last to give to fresher beauty the man she loves, who is himself a sentimental sensualist, so that the situation suggests also George Sand's *Lucrezia Floriani*.

Prévost's most sensational success was attained by *The Demi-Vierges*, of 1894, a study of maids who have lost their bloom by a social freedom alleged to be imported from England and America, and who in Prévost's opinion tend thus to become morally impure in spite of physical purity. The novel is a sensational appeal to a narrow provincial nationalism, and is neither creditable nor characteristic. It is hard to see how any training could produce a more rotten femininity than that illustrated by the aristocratic writers of his *Letters of Women*, and the picturesque interest of the story does not mask the careless laxity of its psychology.

In his interest in feminine vice or folly Prévost does not forget the men of France. The peculiarly discreditable bestiality of the hero of *The Nazareth Mill* (le Moulin de Nazareth, 1894) makes him as revolting as the fate of his victim is pitiful. We can but trust that the Frenchmen who spy through keyholes servants at their toilet are no more characteristic of their country than " naptha queens " from Boston who send their immensely wealthy husbands to German universities and find delight in the society of such disgusting little beasts as Jacques Ebel. Prévost should let America alone. He returns to more familiar ground in the short stories of *Our Country* (Notre campagne), which are never vulgar, always clever, and sometimes pure.

With *The Hidden Garden* (le Jardin secret, 1897),

Prévost takes us, almost for the first time, to the middle class, and with the moral of Goethe's *Fellow-Sinners* tells the strongest and noblest story that he has yet written. A woman discovers that she has linked her life to an epileptic adulterer, lapses from despair to rage and desire for vengeance, but shrinks from divorce, and, gradually recalling the secrets of her own life, sees that her faults balance her husband's, and so is brought to a tolerant charity. But the interest here lies less in the story than in the light it casts on the nature of conventional marriage, both on its physical and psychic side, and on the explanation that this affords of the prominence in French fiction of extra-marital love and its seemingly irresistible crises.

Regarding Prévost's work as a whole, he will be found most nearly allied to Maupassant, less profound, less pessimistic, less cynical, and far less powerful in his conceptions, but almost as deft, lucid, compact, swift, and unerring in attaining the lesser effects that he essays.

A more virile spirit than any whom we have considered in this chapter, one in whom is a healthier view of life, a new, profounder, and purified realism, and the best promise of the immediate future, is Paul Margueritte, whose development from *All Four* ('Tous quatre, 1884) to *The Disaster* (le Désastre, 1897) is as interesting as that of Huysmans during the same period, and far more inspiring and reassuring. Margueritte was always serious and never base, but his early work was extremely, almost defiantly, naturalistic, though it was rather the naturalism of the Goncourts than of Zola, both in conception, structure, and style. In *All Four* he seems restless, unquiet, working by short, sharp strokes, as nervously anxious as the Goncourts to " pin the adjective " and to startle by a crudity of expression at which you feel the author himself shrinks, for all his determination to look life steadily in the face, even in its most repulsive details. Yet here at the outset there is a questioning conscience and a moral purpose, obscured and perverted as it may seem. He feels that to strip vice is to shame hypocrisy, and the hypocrisy that most irritates him is that of the philistine bourgeois and the intriguing man of letters. There is in *All Four* a morbid tendency to introspective revery and to pessimistic fatalism, which may be traced in all his work for the next six years; but even in his next novel, *The Posthumous Confession* (la Confession posthume, 1886) his hero feels that "he has failed in action in leaving a great responsibility to chance," and recognises that his misfortunes "have come from his lack of will," — words that probe the ulcer of the neuropathic culture of his generation.

From *Pascal Gafosse* (1887) onward, action becomes more and more the motive power of Margueritte's fiction. He says here that naturalism, as he had at first conceived it, is "a form of decadence, base and vulgar." There is still over much revery and crudity, too, but the tonic moral of this book is Work. And in *Days of Trial* (Jours d'épreuve, 1889, written in 1886) there is the same fortifying lesson, a lesson that none in France to-day teaches with such power except Zola, and none with such confidence. This study of the humbler aspects of bourgeois life, of "lowly happiness, narrow, resigned, but sure," breathes a spirit of deep compassion and yet of valorous hope. It is not only a good book, but in spite of all its crudities, it is a *good* book, a tonic to the will that sets the nerves vibrating with the need of action.

The doctrine of *The Force of Environment* (la Force

des choses, 1891) is at first not quite so clear, but as we look more nearly we see that here it is our will-not-to-do that is forced by life into action, that it is not well that love should clasp grief forever, or that sin should demand a long repentance, that humanity claims us from ourselves for its good and ours; and so this book is neither fatalistic nor pessimistic, but the trumpet of the triumph of life, of the germinal forces in our human nature.

In this direction *Over the Crest* (Sur le retour, 1892) marks no advance. But the hero is still the human will, this time in a man passed middle age conquering a late-born love with a chaste and vigorous reason. The book shows less crudity of expression than any that had pre-ceded. It is clean, but it is sombre and ill constructed. Nor is there reason to dwell at length on the novels of the next four years, — *The Whirlwind* (la Tourmente), *Ma Grande, Save Honour* (Fors l'honneur), and *The Flight* (l'Essor), — except to note that there is growing delicacy and tenderness, and the same grave, strong, simple sincerity. Nor is it necessary to speak of the short stories of these years gathered in *Lovers* and in *The White Cuirassier,* for all his art and all his moral power is concentrated in *The Disaster* (le Désastre, 1897), written in collaboration with his brother Victor, a story of the fall of Metz in that war with Prussia in which their father met a glorious death. Zola's *Downfall* alone in France can compare with this picture of war. His is the more artistic book, but it is also the more gloomy. Both are patriotic, but this is the more tonic and inspiring, tempering the mind to hardness in that military school of whose " servitude and grandeur " Vigny had written so nobly. There is here a virile grappling with the problems of duty, a power of moral self-control and abnegation, that the authors inherited from General Margueritte as the most precious of his legacies. It means that there is iron yet in the culture, as there has ever been in the heart of France, that in literature also there is a saving remnant to whom war has taught endurance, solidarity, heroism, in whom the example of the dead has strengthened the living. The book is a noble tribute of a son to a father and of a patriot to his country. Among the dilettants of Christianity and Symbolism and Psychology and the cultus of the Ego and of Decadence, of mysticism and paganism and pessimism, it is refreshing to come upon a man at last on whom may fall the mantle of Zola, with as noble a purpose and a clearer moral vision.

Index

Containing authors and titles of French fiction in the nineteenth century only. Names are alphabetised after omission of *de*. Titles are entered without their initial articles, and in their French form only. Each title is followed by the author's name in parentheses.

25

www.ingramcontent.com/pod-product-compliance
Lightning Source LLC
Chambersburg PA
CBHW072336090426
42741CB00012B/2813